CHILD BEHAVIOR PROBLEMS

AN EMPIRICAL APPROACH TO MANAGEMENT

Roger McAuley

Patricia McAuley

 THE FREE PRESS
A Division of Macmillan Publishing Co., Inc.
New York

The Free Press
A Division of Macmillan Publishing Co., Inc.
866 Third Avenue, New York, N.Y. 10022

First American Edition 1978

Library of Congress Catalog Card Number: 77-94495

Printed in the United States of America

printing number
1   2   3   4   5   6   7   8   9   10

Contents

Foreword

Efforts to help psychologically troubled children have changed drastically over the past 20 years. The prevailing tendency to bring these children into direct contact with highly trained professionals has shifted to an alternative focus on the children's natural caretakers. In this latter strategy the caretakers are viewed as therapists, rather than having this role fulfilled by professionals. The professional's role has changed from therapist to consultant—one who 're-educates' the parents and schoolteachers of troubled children. This re-education notion is based on the assumption that caretaker and child are locked into problem relationships with one another. By teaching the caretakers some new ways of responding to their children, it is reasonable to expect that the children's deviant behaviours should change. In essence, the problem relationships should disappear; both caretaker and child should develop mutually supporting therapeutic behaviours.

This new trend in child therapy has been given the popular label *applied behaviour analysis* (ABA). The ABA strategy argues that deviant behaviour is developed and maintained by its short term stimulus associations. The discovery of these associations, usually dispensed by parents and teachers of the troubled child, should permit a systematic shifting in how the stimuli operate. Given that the caretakers can be convinced to alter their stimulus output for the child, it should be possible to develop new and desirable child behaviours.

Like any therapeutic strategy, ABA has a theoretical model connected with its application. Most ABA consultants rely on reinforcement theory to guide their assessment and intervention work. 'Learning' in an operant sense makes up the bulwark of the ABA consultant's view of how stimulus contingencies produce and maintain a child's problem behaviour. The theory also guides the consultant's teaching efforts to modify these contingencies.

The happy marriage between applied behaviour analysis and reinforcement theory has prospered, but there have also been recent episodes of domestic strife. Therapeutic changes in child behaviour have not always been sustained: the application of reinforcement prescribed treatment techniques does not always work; there is increasing evidence that successful intervention may be accompanied by side effects not understood on the basis of reinforcement principles. The overall implications of these difficulties must be considered by any proponent of applied behaviour analysis.

The McAuleys present a text responsive to these new developments in applied behaviour analysis. While prior texts have given readers a standard, rather simplistic view of the ABA helping process, these authors give us an updated version of complexities inherent in this strategy. Their version of how one intervenes with the troubled child is by no means a panacea for the field. They present the problems of assessment and treatment honestly, and they outline a most reasonable way of dealing with these constraints.

ROBERT G. WAHLER

University of Tennessee, Knoxville, October 1976

Acknowledgements

Many people contributed in one way or another to this book. The authors wish to thank John Barcroft and Bob Wahler who read preliminary versions of the manuscript and made valuable suggestions. We are further indebted to Bob Wahler for writing the Foreword. We are grateful to Jerry Harbison for comments on selected chapters and to Jim Quinn who first encouraged our interest in behaviour modification.

The Royal Victoria Hospital, Belfast and the Eastern Area Health and Social Services Board assisted the first author in that the former awarded him a research fellowship, during which time much of the clinical work described was completed and ideas formulated, and the latter seconded him to the USA, where he was able to consolidate his knowledge and conduct useful discussions with friends such as Bob Nay and Denis Moore.

Colleagues in the Department of Child Psychiatry, Royal Belfast Hospital for Sick Children, also deserve special thanks: William Nelson for providing cases; Kathy McKeown, Anna Fyfe, Bruce Stewart and Anne Hutton who were the principal therapists in some of the case studies presented in the text; and the staff at Lissue Hospital who nursed the in-patients.

Geraldine Duffy and Gertrude Heron typed preliminary versions of the manuscript and Twy Miller typed a remarkably rapid final draft. We would also like to thank John Morrow for arranging photocopying facilities for the reproduction of the final draft.

The main contributors to the book are, however, the parents and children. We have preserved their anonymity by altering names and other details of identification.

Although this book is a collaborative effort, the contribution of each author was clearly defined. The first author contributed his clinical experience in child psychiatry and a thorough working knowledge of the practice of behaviour modification with children, and its associated literature. The second author helped in the formulation and writing of the text, and viewed the venture as a professional helper who had hitherto been uninitiated in the mysteries of behaviour modification.

Introduction

Behaviour modification as a clinical strategy has gained in popularity over the past 15 years, especially in the USA. During the past 4 years we have exclusively used behavioural techniques in our clinical work. We have necessarily had to learn many of the practical skills, through a process of trial and error, using American texts to provide the basic knowledge. This text summarises the skills which we have thus acquired, and is written in an attempt to relieve others from a similarly protracted method of learning. The behavioural techniques described are within the capacity of all those who work with children, whether they are teachers, doctors, nurses, social workers or psychologists.

In introducing the text we have used the following case history in an attempt to answer briefly some of the questions which are often posed about behaviour therapy.

Recently we were asked by a paediatrician to see James, an 18-month-old child who presented with a history of vomiting. At the time of referral this symptom had been present for approximately 7 months. Although James ate all meals without difficulty, vomiting frequently occurred each day after meals. At home the vomiting was so persistent that James lost weight and became dehydrated. His parents felt helpless and eventually he was admitted to hospital, where he had to be tube fed at night. Extensive investigations failed to reveal any significant physical cause. Since James almost always vomited when adults were absent, the staff hypothesised that the behaviour was used to gain adult attention. Briefly, a history from the parents indicated the following points: James was the second and youngest child. His parents reported that he had always been difficult. He cried persistently and his parents were frequently up at night nursing him. They had never left him with baby-sitters because of the problem. They felt that nursing James seemed to help. The vomiting began following a cold. Although they did not report a pattern to the vomiting, the parents stated that James never vomited while in their arms. Frequently they had observed him with his fingers deep in his mouth. They felt that on occasions the vomiting was self-induced.

Presented with this information most therapists, whatever their orientation, would carry out further investigations, draw up initial intervention plans and then commence therapy. Peculiar to behaviour therapy, the investigation (or assessment) involves obtaining a clear description of the events which precede and follow the behaviours of interest (which in James's case would be his vomiting). Such a description can most clearly and reliably be obtained by observing the behaviour (that is, the vomiting) as it occurs.

Early behaviourists hypothesised that behaviour is logical and subject to laws. They concluded that an understanding of the development and complexities of social behaviour would be accelerated by the application of scientific and objective measurement. Of course, measurement can only be reliably applied to events which we can observe as they occur. We can easily count how many times James vomits when adults are absent, but we cannot easily measure what he thinks or feels at such times. Whilst not denying the importance of cognition and emotion, behaviourists have concentrated on building a theory solely from their observations of overt and easily measurable behaviour. Such work avoids assumptions and hypotheses which are not readily testable. This is in contrast to other theories (for example, Freudian theory), which attempt to explain the development of behaviour on the basis of hypothetical and assumed, innate or original instincts. Assumptions of this nature are and will be extremely difficult to prove or disprove.

In clinical practice it is impossible to be experimentally precise; however, by observing the antecedents and consequences of James's vomiting we can ascertain whether his behaviour follows a pattern. If we alter the consequences of his behaviour we are not only providing treatment but also testing our hypothesis about his behaviour (that is, that it was used to gain adult attention).

We initially arranged to conduct three 1-hour observational sessions in which James was observed in the ward setting. In order to ensure that records were as objective as possible, the observer did not interact with James or respond to his approaches. After approximately 10 minutes in the first session James ignored the observer. Selected observational records demonstrate the problem:

Wednesday 20 July, 1976. 12.00 Midday. Ward Observation.
J.=James. N.=nurse.

12.00 N. has just finished feeding J. Tidies up and leaves J. sitting in cot playing with rattle and plastic car. Cries for approximately 1 min. when N. leaves room. Sits and looks out of window. Not playing. Glances to corridor.

12.05 Vomits small quantity (seemingly effortlessly). Eats vomit. Sits, stares, eats vomit. Vomits small quantity again. Eats vomit. Sits and stares out of window.

12.10 N. comes in. 'J., you're a bad boy', crossly. J. holds out arms and babbles. N. does not speak but changes him. He smiles frequently.

12.15 N. puts J. on floor, hands him some toys, plays with him for approximately 2 min. Talks to him approximately every half-minute (now pleasantly). Changes J.'s bed.

12.20 N. plays with J. on floor for few minutes. Lifts him up and takes him to window. Talks to him about people passing; about colours of cars.

12.25 Plays with J. on floor for 2 min., then leaves. J. cries and goes to door (glass door). Cries. Stops in approximately 1 min. J. sits down on floor. Sits, looks at floor. Lifts piece of thread. Chews it.

12.30 Vomits small quantity. Eats it. Messes it on floor. Vomits again 3 min. later. Eats it. Rubs it on floor. N. enters. 'J., stop that.' J. puts arms out. N. says 'No', and lifts him away.

12.35 N. cleans floor. J. plays with toys. N. changes J., plays with him. This sequence repeated itself once more in this observational session.

The other two observational sessions demonstrated a repetition of what was seen in the session outlined above. On the basis of the observations it seemed reasonable to assume that, in this case, vomiting resulted in staff attention. Certainly the staff recognised that attending to the child reduced the frequency of vomiting. Clearly the symptom was maladaptive and dangerous (because of the possibility of dehydration), and it had to be eliminated. When planning the treatment we presented the case to a small group of nursing students, who had had only two lectures in behaviour therapy. The therapeutic plan which that group devised is the plan which is described below.

In this text we have placed considerable emphasis on the planning of therapy. It has been our clinical experience that this stage of therapy is neglected too often. Frequently plans are vague, the techniques to be used are not clearly specified and the objectives in mind are difficult to visualise. Goldberg (1976) has discussed the importance of planning and goal-setting in some detail. We suggest that planning must involve at least four components:

(1) Specification of behavioural goals. In James's case this was to reduce vomiting without seriously reducing adult attention (which he

3

requires for continued social and emotional development).

(2) We must decide which methods or techniques we will use to reach the objectives. The student nurses decided that the technique which they would adopt in James's case would be differential attention (see chapter 9). To eliminate the vomiting the ward staff would not interact with James following each such episode. Staff members would clean away the vomit without talking to James and then quickly leave the room. In order to intensify the effect the curtain over the door of James's room was then to be drawn for approximately 2 minutes. During these 2 minutes James would have no direct visual or interactional contact with any adult. Since adult attention is important for the child's social progress the plan aimed not at reducing the total amount of attention, but ensuring that it followed more appropriate behaviour. It was therefore decided that adult attention (in the form of talking to, nursing, playing with, etc.) should only be given to James following episodes when he had not vomited. In the initial stages James was to be checked every 10 minutes. If he had not vomited during that time a staff member would interact with him for a period of at least 2−3 minutes.

During the discussion with the student nurses it was pointed out that, since vomiting would no longer gain adult attention, James might increase the frequency of vomiting in an attempt to re-establish the old attentional pattern. As James was still in hospital it was possible to arrange that he could continue to be tube fed at night (under sedation if necessary), until such time as the vomiting disappeared or it became evident that the therapy was unsuccessful.

(3) During planning a provisional assessment should be made of the duration and intensity of therapy required. The programme outlined for James would involve a large amount of staff time. However, James had already been in hospital for 6 months and had taken up a vast quantity of staff time. Once such a programme has been instituted it is our experience that if it does not begin to have some effect within approximately 7 days it will probably not succeed, either because it is not being properly administered or because our initial understanding of the case was at fault.

(4) Methods for assessing progress should be built into the plans. In James's case simple records were kept which recorded each episode of vomiting and each episode of staff attention for non-vomiting behaviour (figure 1.1). Record-keeping forms an integral part of any behavioural treatment as it helps to remind the therapist of what he has to do and

BEHAVIOUR RECORD SHEET

NAME..James..................DATE...19/7/76........ BEHAVIOUR Vomiting

ASSESSMENT DAY ..../TREATMENT DAY ...3.... SETTING Inpatient unit

PROCEDURE Record time of each episode of vomiting. Enter amount of vomit (xxx = large amount, xx = medium amount, x = small amount). Record antecedents and consequences.

TIME	AMOUNT	ANTECEDENTS	CONSEQUENCES
3.30pm	x	In dayroom with 4 other children who were playing. I had left him just 5 minutes before, after giving him orange juice.	Cleaned vomit. Did not talk to him or play with him. Placed him in his cot behind screen for 2 minutes. A.F.
3.32	x x	Occurred in cot during 2 minutes' isolation.	Cleaned him. Did not talk to him. Left him for further 2 minutes. A.F.
7.00	x x	Had just been put down for the night. I had changed him and played with him for approx. 20 mins. before putting him to bed.	Cleaned and changed him. Did not play or talk to him. Put him back in his cot. E.G.
7.15	x x	Noticed him sitting up in his cot eating vomitus. This episode followed directly from the one noted above.	Repeated procedure as above. He was asleep in approx. 10 mins. E.G.

Figure 1.1 Sample recording sheet of the antecedents and consequences of James's vomiting, taken on treatment day 3

5

also informs him as to whether the treatment is succeeding. Records provide us with behavioural measurements and facilitate us in reaching decisions about altering or discontinuing therapy.

The above programme was put into effect 10 days after James was first seen. The vomiting reduced rapidly over a 2-day period. With its reduction there was a marked rise in the frequency of tantrums. An analysis of the records revealed that these were occurring in situations similar to the vomiting. The attentional strategies used to cope with the vomiting were extended to include tantrums. After 5 days of treatment both behaviours were occurring infrequently. The reduction in vomiting and tantrums is depicted graphically in figure 1.2. The staff involved found this immediate improvement very rewarding. It is

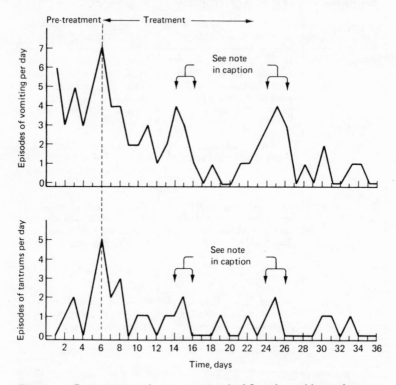

Figure 1.2 Pretreatment and treatment record of James's vomiting and tantrum frequency per day. (*Note*: the increase in vomiting on both these occasions coincided with the absence of James's nurse therapist)

6

almost certain that this had the effect of motivating their continued consistent handling of the treatment.

Although the major part of treatment was conducted by a psychologist and two trained nurses, it was student nurses (relatively inexperienced in the use of behavioural techniques) who were responsible for its design. Had they still been available they certainly would have been quite capable of managing the treatment. This illustrates clearly one of the major advantages of behaviour therapy, which is that enormous sophistication is not required prior to the use of behavioural techniques. Wahler and Erikson (1969) demonstrated that voluntary workers with little knowledge of psychology or psychiatry, and with only a few hours' supervision, operated as effective behaviour therapists to families with problem children. This study, which was conducted in a small understaffed welfare clinic, resulted in a threefold client turnover rate, without any apparent reduction in effectiveness.

The procedure of giving and removing attention which was employed with James does not require very detailed instructions as it is reasonably simple. The most important factor in the treatment was the scheduling. We had to ensure that James was regularly checked each 10 minutes and attended to when appropriate, and that he was not left isolated in his room for longer than the designated 2 minutes after an episode of vomiting. One major strategy was used to ensure close procedural adherence. For 1 hour during each treatment day the therapy was conducted in a two-way screen room by two of the staff members involved in the management. One of the staff observed while the other carried out the treatment. During and after the session the procedural adherence (such as timing) was discussed by both persons and corrected where necessary.

Since this is an introduction we will not dwell on the variety of behavioural techniques which can be employed in therapy. The most common techniques are described in the text and they all deal with the learning or relearning of parental or child skills. The therapist requires practice to become confident in their application. In dealing with very simple problems (as in the case of James) this presents no difficulties. However, in other more complex cases (for example instructing a client in child playing skills) some practice in the use of role-playing is useful if not essential. The therapist's confidence in the use of such techniques will often be important in the outcome of treatment. We suggest that it is important for interested professionals quickly to begin to gain practical experience in the use of the methods rather than devoting

7

considerable time to understanding the theory. Work by Gardner (1972) tends to suggest that behaviour therapy knowledge and skills are most effectively learned when they are taught in the practical situation. A knowledge of chapters 2, 4, 5, 7 and 9 should be a sufficient starting point for the therapist dealing with most simple behaviour problems (disobedience, tantrums, crying at bedtime, etc.).

Behaviour therapy has been demonstrated as an effective strategy for managing a wide range of childhood problems. These include problems such as disobedience, tantrums, destructiveness, aggression, stealing, truanting, enuresis, encopresis, stuttering, food fads, school-refusal and other phobias or fears, and problems occurring in subnormal or autistic children. This text focuses on problems which are most commonly presented at the child psychiatric clinic where the first author is employed. We have not included techniques useful in the management of childhood autism or severely subnormal children. We see few children in these categories and therefore our experience with such problems is limited. Therapy with these children often involves a considerable element of basic social skills training, for example the teaching of dressing, eating and toileting skills. Watson (1973) has written a text which should be found useful in the training of such skills.

It is difficult to estimate the amount of treatment success which can be expected. The literature reporting on the effectiveness of a wide variety of therapeutic approaches (including analytical and behavioural approaches) is somewhat confusing. Widely varying ranges of success have been reported. This confusion has occurred mainly because different studies have used different criteria in determining success. For example, in treating enuresis one study may consider success has occurred after two complete weeks of dry nights, whereas another study may only report success after two months of dry nights. Chapter 14 further discusses the ways in which therapists have reported on outcome, and examines some theoretical concepts which relate to failure in behaviour modification.

From our own reading and clinical experience we would suggest that the following six variables should give a rough guideline as to the level of success which might be expected in the individual case. These factors, which are discussed in greater detail in the text, would usually be considered by any therapist whatever his orientation.

(1) The type and number of presenting problems. A child who presents with many problems (for example disobedience, lying, stealing, truanting and poor peer relationships) will generally be more

difficult to treat. Serious antisocial problems which occur outside the home (for example stealing and breaking and entering) are difficult to treat, partly because they are beyond the jurisdiction of involved adults.

(2) The duration of the problem. Behaviours which have been present for several years will be more difficult to reverse than those of shorter duration.

(3) The degree of family pathology. If the parents are psychiatrically ill or have marital and other social difficulties it is unlikely that therapy will be effective unless it is extensive. Parental motivation and ability will probably be reflected in the extent to which they are prepared to work in the therapy—in terms of completing assignment tasks, turning up for treatment, etc.

(4) The amount and intensity of therapy which can be made available. The value of long term therapy seems to be in doubt (Shepherd, Oppenheim and Mitchell, 1971). In our application of behaviour therapy we have tended to implement a short term intensive approach. It is our impression that if progress is not being made after approximately six sessions then the situation should be carefully reassessed. This quick feedback of therapeutic effectiveness (usually within 10 days of commencing treatment) is another major advantage of behaviour therapy.

(5) The effect of previous unsuccessful therapeutic efforts is an important variable which is not often recognised. Clients who have failed in several past treatments probably expect to fail in future therapy. There are, of course, clients whose problems are so extensive that they are almost untreatable.

(6) Therapist variables, such as ability to relate well and confidence in his method, are of obvious importance.

This text provides a complete description of our experience with behaviour modification techniques commonly used in managing child problems. We have attempted to discuss the practical problems which may occur in therapy. Problems of this nature are not often discussed in behavioural textbooks. Theory has been minimised and readers interested in gaining further theoretical knowledge should refer to texts such as those by Bandura (1969), Kanfer and Phillips (1970) and Rimm and Masters (1974). Further reduction of theoretical material would have adversely affected the completeness of this text. Much of the technical language of behaviour modification has been included. This language has a precise and specific meaning and without its use the text would have become unduly vague and verbose. Definitions of the terminology are provided in the glossary. The case examples in the text are selective in that they tend to illustrate our successes. However (while they may be less severe), they are representative of the type of problem which we most commonly encounter in routine clinical practice—that is, the problem of oppositional behaviours. We recommend that readers new to this form of therapy should read through some of the case examples before embarking on a systematic study of the text. In this way their introduction to the subject may be made less arduous.

PART I

ASSESSMENT

2

The Case History

George, a 7-year-old boy, was referred to our clinic with a wide range of behaviour problems. These included disobedience, physical and verbal aggression and tantrums. His mother complained that he was very destructive in the home, that he frequently refused to go to bed, or else got up during the night and woke the family. His toileting behaviour was also a problem as he would smear faeces around the walls. Meal times were difficult because George ate with his fingers and often threw food around the room.

How do we even begin to deal with these problems? First, more information is required; therefore, both parents are interviewed with the object of obtaining a case history. An initial interview with the child is also necessary.

This text aims at describing specific and empirical methods of managing child behaviour problems. The information which is required before intervention is detailed and several therapeutic techniques are described explicitly. In so doing we have minimised nonspecific factors such as therapist empathy, warmth and acceptance. This does not mean that assessment and intervention should be carried out by the therapist in a cold or objective fashion. In fact it seems that therapist variables such as empathy, experience and skill are important determinants of outcome (Luborsky *et al.*, 1971). Experience suggests that intervention will not succeed if the client perceives the therapist as cold and disinterested. A therapist who is warm and concerned about the client's well-being will facilitate a relationship with the client which aids therapy from the stage of information gathering and observation, through to intervention and eventual termination of the case. Therapists should be an important source of reinforcement for progress in treatment; in fact the use of continued therapy made conditional on client improvement may be an effective technique.

Within this chapter we specify the information which should be gathered from the parents, using the interview (rather than observation or psychometrics) as the means of investigation. The layout of the case history below is designed to facilitate the reader's understanding of the information which he should be seeking. It is not intended to be used mechanically by the therapist as a semi-structured interview. The pace, order and extent of information gathered will depend on the circumstances and character of each interview. Studies which have attempted to standardise therapist behaviour have found that major differences in gross variables (such as degree of therapist objectiveness, positiveness and specificity) remained (Carter and Levy, 1972; Jayaratne, Stuart and Tripodi, 1974). Fortunately the 'standardised therapist' does not exist.

Below are specified those areas in which the therapist will require detailed information if he is to instigate a behavioural programme; however, we have assumed that readers of this text already possess basic interviewing skills such as listening, questioning, clarification of feeling, restatement of content, acceptance and encouragement.

Our treatment is more likely to succeed if the information is reliable. When a mother says her child has been anxious, can we report this as reliable information or should we ask her to define what she means by anxious? This mother may use the word 'anxious' to explain certain aspects of her child's behaviour; for example, it may mean that he is not going to sleep until 11 p.m.; that he is not eating his food; or that he is rarely going out to play with children of his own age.

Look through some old case notes and count the number of inferential words such as 'anxious', 'aggressive' or 'depressed'. Ask your colleagues to define these words and compare the differing interpretations of so-called reliable information. Similarly, parents' descriptions of actual behaviour can be misleading. To one parent a tantrum may mean lying on the floor and screaming, whereas to another it may mean stamping and shouting. Information relating to the past may also be unreliable. Parents often retrospectively connect the emergence of behaviour problems with significant past events. In many cases this connection may be erroneous and misleading. Can we be sure that the laboratory explosion was causally linked to the school phobia or did it merely exacerbate an already existent problem? Parents may only become aware of problems long after their inception.

The format of our case history falls under the following headings: the problem behaviours; the child's behavioural style; parental use of reward and punishment; genetic factors and developmental history; family history; present family environment.

The Problem Behaviours

We shall outline specific guidelines useful in obtaining non-inferential material about the problem behaviours.

DESCRIPTIVE EXAMPLE

The parent is asked to give descriptive examples of the problem. If it is a state behaviour, such as anxious, tense, nervous, he is asked to describe the observed behaviours which led him to suppose that the child is anxious. Having done so, he can then give a verbatim account of the last two or three occurrences of such behaviour. Similarly with situational behaviours, such as tantrums or disobedience, the parent is asked to describe the most recent occurrences of the behaviour. These accounts should contain information about what preceded the behaviour, what happened and what followed; that is, the stimulus, response and consequence.

Below are two examples of a parent description of an incident involving disobedience and a tantrum. One of these descriptions is inadequate as it contains inferential material.

(1) 'John was watching television but father asked him to get ready for bed. John looked annoyed and refused to go. Father switched off the television and there was a row. In the end, John had a tantrum and became very angry with father.'

(2) 'John was watching television. Father said it was eight o'clock and time to get ready for bed. John said that he wanted to watch the programme for 10 more minutes. Father asked John once more to get ready for bed. John said "No" and then father switched off the television. John hit the television screen with his slipper and father slapped John on the arm. John lay on the floor and kicked at father's legs; he shouted, "I hate you".'

FREQUENCY

The frequency of the problem should be assessed in quantifiable terms. This should include not only the overall rate, that is, how often does it occur (daily or weekly), but also indicate any tendency of the problem to occur in episodes or at particular times. If we find that there is a clustering, this would be an area for further investigation.

At first glance it may seem impossible to quantify the occurrence of behaviour states, such as depression. However, as indicated in the previous section, we have already asked parents to describe this state in overt behavioural terms and they can therefore recount the frequency of these observed behaviours.

For example, Mrs Brown told us that her husband usually came home drunk, that he was often violent and that he never gave her any money. We discovered that he did not drink on the first five nights of the week but was always drunk on Friday and Saturday nights. He had physically assaulted her on two occasions in the previous month. She had been given half her housekeeping allowance on the previous four Thursdays but had not been able to get money from her husband on other days. In taking a case history we should always obtain a definition of the client's use of words such as 'often', 'occasionally', 'frequent', 'rare'.

INTENSITY

This is an attempt to measure the severity of the problem. It can be approached by asking two questions: how long does the behaviour last and how extreme is it? An intense behaviour problem usually suggests that the child has initially succeeded with this behaviour and that the parents are still making ineffective attempts to gain control of the situation. The interaction of these two elements may make it more difficult to eliminate the problem behaviour. This is because the child has learned that by increasing the intensity of the behaviour he can eventually force the parents to comply with it—he has coerced them into acceptance.

For example, on the first day Kate goes to the shop with her mother and asks for sweets mother says 'No', so Kate screams, and because mother feels embarrassed, she buys the sweets. For the next few days the same pattern is repeated. Eventually mother is able to tolerate a certain amount of screaming without embarrassment and she therefore attempts to regain control of the situation. Kate, however, has already discovered that she can control her mother's behaviour by screaming, and she therefore intensifies her tantrum behaviour. This again reaches a level at which mother feels embarrassed and so she buys the sweets. In this way the problem escalates. Even if mother only submits occasionally, Kate recognises this and deviates more on each occasion.

She is no longer discouraged when mother refuses to buy the sweets because she has learned that sometimes she will get her own way.

SITUATIONAL FACTORS

It is important to discover the situation in which the behaviour occurs, principally because the effects of treatment may not generalise from one situation to another (Wahler, 1969). We may need to devise treatment plans for each situation. In examining situational factors we are interested in three variables.

First, the physical characteristics of the situation. Does the behaviour occur in the home, in the school or in other areas such as shops or friends' houses? If we discover there are problems in the school, we apply the same method of history-taking for each problem behaviour as we have already described. Ideally we should visit the school rather than request a written report, as such reports tend to be short and phrased in general terms.

Secondly, the people who are present in or notably absent from the situation. Does the behaviour occur only in the presence of certain people, combinations of people or all people? Are there some people with whom the behaviour never, or rarely, occurs?

Thirdly, the time at which the behaviour occurs. Perhaps the behaviour occurs in the evening when mother is tired, or in the morning when she is too busy doing housework to be diverted by the child.

For example, John is disobedient and verbally abusive to his mother but not to his father. This happens at home and also when they are out visiting. John's schoolteacher complains of similar behaviours. In this case we ideally need to consider three treatment strategies: procedures to help the mother deal with the problem (a) when at home and (b) when she is out visiting, and (c) a procedure for the teacher to use in school.

PRECIPITATING AND AMELIORATING FACTORS

Parents who present with problem children are often aware only of the child's disruptive behaviour and are unable to report on the situations or events which precipitate or ameliorate any chain of deviant behaviour.

For example, Bill's parents complain that he screams regularly for several hours each evening when put to bed. They do not realise that their constant attention to his behaviour (by talking to or lifting him) could be teaching Bill that screaming earns him parent attention.

Often parents are so involved in the situation that they fail to see their own behaviour as either precipitating or prolonging deviant child behaviour. Specific descriptive examples, combined with later observations, should in most cases clarify both the precipitants and the ameliorators of the deviant behaviour. Parental inability to perceive the relationship between their own behaviour and their child's behaviour may be a major cause in the development of deviant behaviour. One of the primary aims of any treatment programme would be to teach parents how to track behaviour, that is, how to observe any behavioural sequence from inception to solution.

Behavioural Style

Having obtained specific information about the problem behaviour we also require a more detailed description of the individual child's behavioural style. We should obtain information on the areas described below.

OTHER PROBLEM BEHAVIOURS

It is necessary to seek information about the whole range of behavioural problems which present at the child guidance clinic. Often parents only talk spontaneously about problems which are more intense, more recent, which cause more annoyance or which are either more or less socially acceptable. The therapist who is unaware of other problem behaviours which the child also presents can run into difficulties. For example, one child whom we recently treated was encopretic (faecal soiler). Failing to make a full assessment we hastily set up a therapeutic programme designed to deal with this problem. The plan did not succeed and on reassessment we realised that there was a more general problem of disobedience. The parents had been unable to operate the plan because the child was unmanageable, but after being helped with the management problem the child began to toilet normally.

When taking a case history it is helpful to look at the following checklist of problems. Ask the parents if these are occurring now or if they have occurred in the past. Obtain a descriptive example. Also acquire some information about frequency, intensity, etc.

(*i*) Habit behaviours:
sleeping (any difficulties going to bed or during the night)
eating and appetite

‹ nocturnal or diurnal enuresis
encopresis (faecal soiling)
. speech (any stuttering or abnormalities of speech)
mannerisms or tics.
(*ii*) Aggressive, antisocial and delinquent behaviours:
disobedience
tantrums/whining/crying
verbal abusiveness (for example swearing, backchat)
· physical aggression (towards siblings, peers or parents)
. destructiveness
lying
stealing
breaking and entering
fire-setting
truancy
running away
in trouble with authorities (for example police, expulsion from
school, etc).
(*iii*) State or mood:
anxiety
depression.
If the parents think the child is depressed or anxious then the
interviewer should ask: 'What is it about his behaviour which makes
you think that he is depressed or anxious?'
Often it will be found that parents describe the mood on the basis of
the child exhibiting behaviours already mentioned in the checklist. For
example, they may state that he is 'highly strung' and by this mean that
he has tantrums and cries frequently.
(*iv*) Phobias or special fears:
separation fear
school fear
object/situational fears (for example of animals, people or
places).
(*v*) Physical complaints thought to have a partially psychological
origin:
nausea and vomiting
headaches
asthma
stomach-ache
other physical complaints.

The assumption that such complaints have a psychological element can only be made once physical abnormalities have been excluded and other precipitating factors have been found. For example, a child may present regularly with stomach-ache each morning before going to school. This example demonstrates a pattern. It is important to establish if any such pattern exists when physical complaints are mentioned.

BASIC SKILLS AND CAPABILITIES

Parents come to a clinic expecting to discuss the negative aspects of their child's behaviour. There are some therapeutic advantages in asking them to look at areas in which his behaviour is socially appropriate. This may increase their own self-esteem as parents and also help them to establish a more balanced view of the child's behaviour. If parents focus their attention more on the positive behaviours, such as helping in the home or doing shopping, then these behaviours will increase and therefore leave less time for the occurrence of antisocial behaviour.

Assessing the child's prosocial behaviour also enables us to gauge the level at which we have to set our programme. We must decide whether a child has the basic social skills to carry out a programme. For example, does a young child who is disruptive at the dinner table have the skills to use his knife and fork properly? If not, then as part of treatment we must ensure that he learns these skills.

The following checklist of basic skills and capabilities may be found useful. Careful use of this list will obviously be more appropriate when dealing with the younger or retarded child.

(*i*) Eating behaviours (for example, has he learned to use a knife and fork?).

(*ii*) Dressing (can he dress himself; can he tie his laces?).

(*iii*) Toileting (can he wash and bath himself and use the toilet appropriately?).

(*iv*) Verbal skills (can he ask appropriately for things, introduce himself, initiate conversation, etc?).

(*v*) Management of money.

(*vi*) Simple chores and messages.

(*vii*) Self-occupation (can he read and play on his own?).

INTERACTIONAL SKILLS

By the time this stage in the history-taking process has been reached you will probably have a reasonable idea of how the child interacts with his parents. Peer and sibling relationships may not yet have been touched upon. These are important since their disturbance is very common in children who attend child guidance or child psychiatric clinics. The anxious child will often tend to be inhibited, shy and fearful with his peers, whereas in similar situations the disruptive child may tend to demand, fight and bully. We often find that parents are unable to provide a clear picture of peer relationships. In these instances information from the child's teacher should be helpful. Below we provide a checklist to cover interactional areas.

(*i*) Interaction with parents. Is he co-operative? How much time do you spend together? Do you talk and play together? Is there any difference in how he relates to each parent?

(*ii*) Interaction with other adults. Is he shy? Is he over-familiar? Does he behave appropriately with other adults?

(*iii*) Interaction with sibs and peers. Is he co-operative? Does he lead or is he led? Does he have regular friends? Are his friends of his own age? (We often find that retarded children favour friends of a younger age.) Is he bullied or teased? Does he belong to any clubs?

Parental Use of Rewards and Punishments

Careful questioning about the use of rewards and punishments (that is, the positive and negative consequences for behaviour) may help us to some degree in understanding the child's problem. Usually this information is of greater value if it can be supported and extended by observation of the parents and child interacting together (see chapter 5). In planning our eventual treatment we usually require a list of effective rewards (for increasing the frequency of appropriate behaviours) and punishments (for suppressing disruptive behaviours). This should include rewards used both frequently and infrequently. We often find that parents are convinced that the rewards and punishments which they commonly employ are ineffective. In these instances treatment may be facilitated by adopting positive and negative consequences which have been infrequently used in the past.

REWARDS
When enquiring about the parents' use of rewards we are interested in the relationship of the rewards to the child's behaviour. Is their reward dependent (or contingent) on his behaving in a certain way (for

example being quiet when there are visitors in, or putting his bike away)? Alternatively do they use their rewards indiscriminately? Is there consistency in their pattern of rewarding? Does mother immediately show the child that she is pleased with his behaviour or does she wait until the evening and tell father, 'John was a good boy today—he dressed himself all on his own'? Whilst some time lapse is feasible with an older child who can see the link between behaviour and reward, it is not feasible with a younger child who needs relatively more immediate reward to maintain his behaviour.

We then ask the parents what rewards they use and which rewards they believe to be most effective. Usually they are only able to give a few examples, probably because their recent thinking about the child has been negative, and thus frequently a checklist is useful. When going through this list it is helpful to assess the relative values of possessions, events or privileges which are thought to be rewarding.

(i) Social rewards:
   verbal praise
   physical approval (for example a hug or kiss).

(ii) Material rewards:
   pocket money
   sweets/other foods
   comics/books
   small presents
   specially prized toy.

(iii) Rewarding or enjoyed activities:
   watching television (special programme)
   staying up later
   bedtime stories
   attending clubs (for example cub scouts)
   going to pictures
   activities enjoyed in the company of the parents (for example
     going shopping, playing games, special trips)
   having peers in to play
   is there anything which the child anticipates he might like in the
     future, for example a bicycle, record player, football, books,
     etc. (under a treatment programme, special items might be
     obtained by continuing to exhibit appropriate behaviours
     which earn points, which in turn can be saved towards a
     requisite number—see chapter 10)?

We ask the parents why, when and how they punish their child. Does the punishment depend upon and follow the child's behaviour; is it immediate or delayed; what is seen as punishing? Do parents increase the punishment with the degree of deviant behaviour? These questions are important since the timing, intensity and consistency will significantly determine the effectiveness of punishment. For example, White, Nielson and Johnson (1972) demonstrated that deviant behaviours in delinquent adolescents were well suppressed when they were each immediately punished with a 30-minute period of isolation. Later the isolation time was reduced to 15 minutes. Following these less intense punishments the deviant behaviours returned almost to their initial level. This experiment demonstrates the importance of consistent punishment intensity. For a full discussion on the many variables important in punishment see chapter 8 and Parke (1972).

Genetic Factors and Developmental History

Genetic or congenital factors may limit the individual or predispose him to certain behavioural styles, but they do not cause specific behaviours. For example the 'brain damaged' child may suffer from prescribed difficulties such as short attention span and restlessness. These difficulties, *per se*, are not sufficient to cause behaviour problems— rather it is their interaction with the environment which causes the problems. Too often case histories rationalise behaviour problems in terms of genetic or congenital factors. Nevertheless these factors are important and we would require the usual information about the pregnancy, delivery and genetically carried family illnesses. The developmental history can be divided into three areas:

(1) Physical. This includes information usually elicited in case histories about developmental milestones such as feeding pattern, toileting behaviour, talking and walking ages, physical illnesses and hospitalisation.

(2) Intellectual. This involves an assessment of the child's current intellectual ability and academic attainments. Psychometric testing may be required. As stated previously contact should be made with the school. If the child has a history of attending a number of different schools we should ascertain why this is so.

(3) Significant events. Information is required about incidents

which may have been traumatic to the child, for example separations or bereavements. As already suggested parents tend retrospectively to connect the emergence of a child's behaviour problems with past traumatic incidents. We should carefully enquire into the child's behaviours before, during and after such events in an attempt to clarify their significance.

Family History

In this chapter we have concentrated on those parts of the case history which are particularly relevant to behaviour therapy with the child. However, we also require the usual details about the family history and circumstances which would be obtained in any clinical setting. These would include information on the following:

THE PARENTS

Personal details about the parents will help us in understanding the problem and in planning intervention. As the parents will be implementing the therapy, we require some indication of their capability to do so. In reaching this assessment we would particularly consider their educational, employment, physical and psychiatric history.

A brief description of their family and childhood is valuable because their childhood experiences may be reflected in their current handling capabilities. For example, the battering mother may herself have been battered as a child.

OTHER SIBLINGS

This information includes a list of the names and dates of birth of other children in the family. It would give an account of their developmental, educational, social and work history as well as details of critical events in their past. It may be helpful to use our checklist of problem behaviours with each child, as often the child presented at the clinic is not the only one with problems. Parents may not present another sibling at the clinic because they are unaware of his deviance or because his behaviour, although a problem, is not so antisocial. It is also important to consider other siblings when looking at the situational variables of the problem behaviour. We may discover that the presence of a certain sibling has an effect on the behaviour of the deviant child.

Present Family Environment

In taking our case history we shall ultimately require information about the parents' life-style and their marriage. This information may be difficult to obtain at first because the parents expect us to focus attention on their child. However, we require the information for two main reasons. First, it may be that the parents have a marital problem which will require attention before we plan therapy for the child. Secondly, we must assess the parents' life-style in order to ensure that the treatment which we design is both socially appropriate to them and also within their capabilities. If the father's role in the child rearing has always been minimal, it may be more realistic for us to accept this fact and concentrate our programme on the mother. Had we not assessed family roles we may have wasted time in assuming that father was capable of implementing a treatment which was completely foreign to his whole way of life.

Once more it is helpful to use a checklist as a cue in examining different areas of the family's life. Within each of these areas we would look at role differentiation, mechanisms for decision-making and for communication.

(*i*) The parents:

management—how much does each partner contribute to and what part do they play in child management, home management, financial management; is there parental agreement on how each of these areas is managed?

leisure time and activities—how is leisure time spent; how much is spent together; what interests does each have; how many interests are shared?

sexual—what is the frequency; is there mutual satisfaction?

disharmony—are there rows; have there been separations; are there problem behaviours in the spouse (for example gambling, drinking, extramarital affairs, etc.)?

(*ii*) The extended family. Other adults who are frequently present or involved in the family life (for example, grandmothers) need to be carefully considered. We should ascertain how much they contribute to the child and family management. For example, do they have any say in how the child is disciplined? If such persons are involved then we will have to decide what part they are to play in the treatment.

(*iii*) The community:

neighbours—the extent and quality of the family's interaction with their immediate neighbours may help us to assess the family's interactional skills: problem families often have poor relationships with their neighbours and live in relative social isolation; these families also present the most intractable problems to the therapist.

In eliciting this information useful probes are: do you visit neighbours; do they visit you; how much time do you spend with your neighbours (for example, nights out together); is there any co-operation with shopping, baby-sitting, etc?

(*iv*) Community services. It is important to know if any other helping agencies are involved with the family, since co-operation or role clarification will need to be established prior to intervention. This is especially important with the problem family, as generally they tend to be involved with a wide range of helping agencies.

Preliminary Interview with the Child

On the initial assessment day we do not attempt any prolonged or in-depth interviewing with the child. There are two main reasons for this:

(1) When interviewing the child we will usually attempt to gather information about how he feels, his level of disturbance and how he views his own behaviour. For this information to be of value we should have some idea of the reliability of the components of the interview. Rutter and Graham (1968) have demonstrated that global assessments of whether or not the child is psychiatrically disturbed are quite reliable. Unfortunately this information is of little value in providing treatment guidelines. We are unaware of any studies which have examined the reliability of the child's own reports about his past behaviour. We would suggest that reliability in this context is quite low. In a recent follow up of 50 enuretic children we noticed that the children gave markedly lower estimates of their bedwetting than did their parents. In this study the parents had been keeping continuous behavioural records. It must be remembered that children are brought to clinics ostensibly because of their behaviour and therefore they are often reluctant to discuss this behaviour.

(2) Much of our assessment of the child and his problem behaviours is based on observations where possible. These observations are conducted by the therapist or the parent, but the child will also keep records which will later be used in planning intervention.

Nevertheless, the initial interview with the child has some important functions. First, it affords us the opportunity of assessing the child's physical state, especially if there is any suspicion of a physical disorder, such as delayed growth, neurological impairment, etc. If battering is suspected then a physical examination of the child may reveal signs such as bruising, abrasions, bone deformation, etc. Developmental problems in the child may also be detected at this stage. For example, delays in speech development or social development may alert us to problems such as retardation or autism. Secondly, older children (those approximately over 7 years of age) are generally involved in planning and implementing the intervention programme. For example, they may be involved in behavioural record-keeping and in establishing bargains or contracts about their behaviour. Thus the main value of the preliminary interview with older children is that it provides us with the opportunity of beginning to establish a working relationship with the child.

We began this chapter by describing some of the problems presented by a child named George. In the second detailed case example in chapter 9 we continue with the story of George by describing the observations, planning and therapy employed in his case.

Key Ideas

The standardised therapist does not exist. Therapist attitudes to the client will affect treatment outcome.

In this chapter we have set out guidelines for acquiring non-inferential material about problem behaviours. This is important because intervention is more likely to succeed if the information obtained is reliable. For each problem behaviour we obtain: a descriptive example; information about the frequency and intensity of the behaviour; and some indication of the situational, precipitating and ameliorating factors which effect the behaviour.

If a parent states that his child is anxious, he is asked to describe the observed behaviours which led him to make this inference.

A reliable estimate of the child's prosocial skills is just as important as an assessment of his problem behaviours.

3

Introduction to Observation

Traditionally, behaviour modification has laid great emphasis on the assessment of behaviour by direct observation. This involves looking at and describing the behaviour as it occurs in its natural setting. This chapter will examine the rationale of observation and subsequent chapters will outline the methodology.

Observation affords us the opportunity of making a detailed and accurate examination of the problem behaviour, its antecedents and consequences. Had we alternative means of access to this material, observation would not be necessary. The other main source of information is the case history. Although valuable it is often biased by factors which influence the ways in which parents report on their child's behaviour. For example, if a child has presented many behavioural difficulties on the day before he arrives at the clinic, then the parent may report the child's general behaviour as being worse than is actually the case. Alternatively parents may fail to report stealing because they feel embarrassed about such socially undesirable behaviour. Attitudes which bias (in this case parental) reporting in this manner can be referred to as response-sets. It is useful to examine some of these response-sets and consider how they can be circumvented through observation.

(1) Parents may feel the need to justify their attendance at the clinic and therefore report the problem in exaggerated terms. When intervention has been completed the same parents may falsely report the problem as ameliorated. They respond in this way because they view it as a socially desirable response. This phenomenon has been described as the 'hello – goodbye' effect (Hathaway, 1965).

(2) Parents often tend initially to focus on deviant behaviour and to overlook, or fail to recognise, prosocial skills. These would probably be uncovered through observation.

(3) Certain parents may not recognise the extent of the problem and complain only of an isolated behaviour. In these cases we may observe a more generalised problem which on the basis of social norms would be viewed as deviant, but which is accepted as normal by the parents. Often low rate (that is, infrequently occurring) behaviours such as stealing, are presented by the parents as isolated problems. However observation in the home may reveal high rate (that is, frequently occurring) deviant behaviours such as disobedience. It may be that the parents have become immune to this high rate behaviour or they may tolerate behaviour which can be contained within the home and only seek help when the deviance results in outside social consequences. Parental child management skills and their expectations of their child's behaviour are partly based on their own childhood experiences. The child's deviant behaviour may reflect these experiences. For example, the parent who comes from a family broken by marital strife and psychiatric illness may not have any knowledge about the importance of consistent disciplining. In such instances the parents may not report home behavioural difficulties because they do not regard their child's disobedience as abnormal. A history which suggests that the parental childhood has been of the kind mentioned above will alert us to the possibility of deficient child management skills. Observation of parent – child interaction should reveal whether or not this is the case.

(4) Parents may choose to focus on one child because his behaviour is very difficult. However, observation may demonstrate deviance of significant degree in other siblings. Patterson, Cobb and Ray (1973) have found that it is common for siblings to be deviant, although usually to a lesser degree.

(5) Parents cannot usually provide us with detailed and accurate information about deviant behavioural sequences, in terms of antecedents, responses and consequences. Often, for example, parents at the clinic will complain that their child rarely complies with commands. On observation we may discover that the parents often do not follow up (consequate) a command. We have counted, in some instances, up to 40 specific and non-consequated commands per hour. Usually these parents have been unaware of their high commanding rates.

Observation supplements the information given in the case history and because it is conducted in the natural setting and does not rely on verbal report alone it circumvents many of the difficulties described above. Other techniques can also be used to supplement the material given in the case history. It may be helpful to assess briefly the clinical value of these techniques.

INTELLIGENCE TESTS

In situations in which there may be doubt about a child's intellectual ability (for example, in the child who refuses to go to school) intelligence tests can aid us in setting realistic goals (for example, the child may require some form of remedial education). Before interpreting intelligence quotients we should be aware of their limitations. Three general factors contribute to a test result and a brief examination of these reveals some of the limitations of the intelligence test. Although we realise that these factors all affect the ultimate score it is difficult to assess with each individual child which factor is most relevant. We cannot, therefore, always be certain as to what we are measuring. Factors contributing to the test result are:

(1) Genetic or innate endowment.

(2) Environmental, social and interactional factors such as educational, social or emotional deprivation will contribute towards a lower intellectual score. Physical factors also affect the score adversely, for example malnutrition or brain damage resulting from trauma or infection. Tests depend on the child being able to communicate verbally, and as younger children have fewer verbal skills the test result is less reliable.

(3) Factors in the assessment situation, for example intense anxiety, may retard the child's performance. Recent exposure to the test may result in a better score on the second testing, due to practice. Low motivation to do well may result in a low score. Ayllon and Kelly (1972) demonstrated that intelligence quotients could be raised by a significant amount in a group of children when the test administrator simply rewarded the act of responding (regardless of whether the response was correct or incorrect).

Intelligence tests provide general guidelines as to the child's ability but they do not give detailed information about specific attainments, for example his reading ability. In making educational plans it is therefore advisable to employ attainment tests in addition to the intelligence test. Decisions about the child's educational future should not be based entirely on the intellectual assessment but should include an assessment of his peer and teacher relationships and of his ability to concentrate and persevere. For instance, a dull child with a high level of persistence

30

and good relationships may be able to continue in a normal school with remedial help.

PERSONALITY TESTS

The value of standard personality tests in routine assessment is doubted by the authors. Many of these tests attempt to measure personal characteristics or traits such as anxiety, neuroticism, hostility, etc. From intelligence or attainments tests we can derive some idea of behavioural capabilities, for instance verbal ability, whereas the personality test does not provide us with any such comparable correlates. For example, we may know that Jack has a high anxiety or neuroticism score, but this tells us nothing about how he might behave when in school, at home or playing with his peers. Further it will not tell us whether he is highly neurotic in all areas of his life. An added difficulty is that tests of this nature are difficult to standardise in children, since stable traits are only in the process of development throughout childhood. In general, our case history and observations of the child should reveal any such traits (through his recorded and observed behavioural pattern) without the necessity of personality tests.

ATTITUDINAL MEASURES

In addition to successfully managing the child problems we hope that negative attitudes (parent to child, or child to parent) would change in a positive direction. There may be some time lag between child behaviour change and parent attitudinal change, but we often observe that parent consequating behaviour improves considerably when the parents are able to feel and talk about the child in positive terms. Attitudinal ratings can also help us to identify behaviours or areas which seem to be correlated with most negative parent feeling. For instance, following each observation or at the end of each day we could ask the parent to rate the child on a simple rating scale such as this: Good 1 2 3 4 5 6 7 Poor. Over a baseline period we could then examine the observational records and the ratings. High rates of certain child behaviours may be associated with poorer parent attitudinal ratings. Perhaps we should focus on these behaviours first when we plan intervention.

It is partly for these reasons that researchers such as Wahler, Berland and Leske, (1976) and Patterson, Cobb and Ray (1973) have begun to use attitudinal measurement in addition to observational measures of behaviour. However, we must remember that attitudes are global summaries of the parents' feelings towards the child and do not afford specific information about the child's behaviour. For example, parents may say that their child makes them feel angry—this might be because he has tantrums, is emotionally undemonstrative or frequently sulks. Generally, we can assume that parent–child attitudes are largely a result of interaction between their own and the child's behaviour. When this is not so, we must consider other areas which contribute to attitude formation. Unfortunately the attitudinal measure does not supply information about these other areas which influence the rating. For example, in one case a residential house-mother felt that one of the children under her care had 'bad genes' and that he was doomed to delinquency. In this case the house-mother had access to information on the child's background. The child's natural parents had both been involved in frequent criminal offences. After completing an intervention programme she was able to successfully manage the other children in her care but she was unsuccessful with this particular child. Without positive attitudinal change we can predict that any improvement in a child's behaviour will not be maintained.

DIAGNOSIS

Many behaviour modifiers, such as Ullman and Krasner (1969), question the use of current diagnostic practice and its value in dealing with psychological problems. This is understandable as psychological diagnosis at its present level tends mainly to relate to symptom complexes. Ideally a diagnosis should extract the peculiar elements of aetiology, treatment and prognosis. However, these elements are only meaningful within a theoretical framework and if this is unspecified then we remain uncertain as to the implications of the diagnosis. For instance, Quay (1972) discusses the definition of the anxious personality which was reached by the Group for Advancement of Psychiatry in 1966, and demonstrates that this was derived from several different and perhaps incompatible theories. A set of diagnositc criteria based on a unitary theoretical framework could be more meaningful. For example, Wahler (1976) has described four main types of child deviance. He labels these according to the major behavioural problems exhibited. The categories are: oppositional behaviours; behaviour deficits; age-inappropriate behaviours; and cross gender behaviours. The behavioural aetiology, social impact, treatment and prognosis—both short and long term—are discussed for each category. The major advantage of this particular work is that the problems are described in terms of behavioural learning theory, and thus the validity of the categorisation is scientifically testable.

Observation has often been presented as the most important assessment strategy. However, with the time restrictions operating in routine day-to-day clinical practice, we must rely heavily on the case history and the other techniques discussed above. Nevertheless we recognise the limitations of all these methods and regard even a minimum amount of observation as essential. Apart from supplementing our other assessment procedures, observation has some particular advantages.

(1) Observation can be used to trace the effectiveness of the treatment programme. If the feedback is negative the therapist quickly realises the necessity for a re-evaluation of his assessment and treatment strategies. If the feedback is positive it is reinforcing both to the therapist and the client. Wahler and Leske (1973) demonstrated that trained observers can detect minimal behavioural changes very early in an intervention programme. They trained one set of teachers in observing deviant behaviour and paired them with an untrained group of teachers. They then asked both groups to rate the behaviour of a child on film. This film demonstrated a gradual improvement in the child's deviant behaviour. The trained group immediately responded to early, finer behavioural changes, whereas the untrained group continued to rate the child as deviant until the change was very marked. Thus, untrained observers may continue to harbour the attitude that the child is deviant, despite the fact that demonstrable behavioural improvement is occurring.

Parents and therapists who have been trained in observational methods show early awareness of change and, when this change is positive, hopefully it motivates the parent who gains confidence in himself and in the treatment. He becomes more willing and able to carry out the therapist instructions and this, combined with a regeneration of positive feelings towards the child, may have a cumulative effect in treatment.

(2) Often at a clinical level we tend to focus exclusively on the presenting problem and neglect other behaviours. Observation affords us a broader spectrum of behaviours.

(3) Observation is not only an assessment strategy, it is also an intrinsic part of intervention. Parents who learn the technique of observing or tracking behaviour have acquired a skill which they can use and develop after the treatment programme has ended. In some

33

cases simply training parents to observe may result in an amelioration of the presenting problems. For example one mother, whose 9-year-old child was encopretic, started recording his toileting behaviour and checking his pants three times per day. The boy reported to the mother when he was going to use the toilet and she checked that he did so. In this case, parent attention and approval at tracking times was sufficient to effect a positive change. After 7 days the boy was clean and remained so at a 9-month follow up.

Key Ideas

Observation is a skill which is useful to both parents and therapist. It is conducted, where possible, in the natural setting and does not rely on verbal report. It affords us accurate information about a broad spectrum of behaviours and detailed information about the problem behaviour, its antecedents and consequences.

4

Methods of Recording Behaviour

In learning to record we use the same approach as stressed in the history-taking. We are interested in a clear, specific non-inferential account of interaction. Learning to do this efficiently usually necessitates some formal training plus a large measure of practical application. The Wahler and Leske study, which we quoted in the previous chapter, demonstrates the need for observational training. In this study the trained observers were able to specify and track the components of behaviour and therefore they observed behaviour more accurately. However, the process of describing interaction in non-inferential terms is difficult and usually cannot be learned from the formal instruction alone.

Several methods of training have been employed. Major workers, such as Patterson, Cobb and Ray (1973) and Wahler, House and Stambaugh (1976), have used a three-tier system. First, verbal instruction in their observational method, then training observers with video tapes which demonstrate deviant interaction and, finally, active field training. This extensive training is designed for research purposes and the authors have found that, for routine clinical practice, verbal instruction and field training are sufficient. This chapter presents an outline of observational procedures which should be of value to the reader provided he consolidates it with practical experience.

Observational strategies commonly employed by behaviour therapists are as follows:

SPECIMEN OR DESCRIPTIVE RECORDING
This is a description of all interactions which have occurred during the observational period. It can be recorded in personalised shorthand or spoken quietly into a cassette recorder. The advantage of the cassette

recorder is that in addition to our commentary we can (with the client's permission) record samples of their interaction.

Specimen recording is the most important form of therapist recording. It is initially used to obtain a broad perspective, rather than focusing prematurely on target or problem behaviours. It is therefore the precursor to other forms of recording. In clinical practice we may not have time to proceed to other more sophisticated techniques. We may only take a few specimen recordings, later followed by some simple frequency counts of the behaviours in which we are interested.

The detailed example below is an outline of a specimen recording sheet within which two accounts of interactional sequences are included. One of these accounts is unsatisfactory because it does not clearly specify observable events.

Example of specimen recording

Subject:	John (J.)	Who present:	Mother (M.) and John (J.)
Place:	Home	Instructions:	No television, confine acti-
Date:	3/4/74		vities to living room and kit-
Time:	3.15–4.30		chen.

Sample (1)
M. sewing at table, J. walks to M., J. 'I want a biscuit.' M. 'No.' J. repeats request. M. 'No, not now.' J. (shouts) 'I want one.' M. (loudly) 'Stop shouting; you know that annoys me.' J. cries, stamps and shouts continuously 'I want one.' M. (shouts) 'Stop it or I'll smack you.' J. continues. M. smacks J. on legs 3 or 4 times. J. cries and screams louder. M. (shouts) 'All right, I'll give you one if you will be quiet.' J. cries but stops screaming. M. gets him a biscuit.

Sample (2)
M. sewing at table. J. approaches and requests a biscuit. M. refuses. J. requests again. M. refuses. J. demands one. M. shouts at J. to stop. J. has a tantrum. M. punishes angrily. J.'s temper becomes worse. M. gives in and J. quietens.

EVENT AND FREQUENCY RECORDS

The case history and the initial specimen recordings will have indicated target behaviours which warrant further observation. We can focus more on these behaviours by describing them as they occur or by taking frequency counts of their occurrence. In keeping records of low rate behaviours (for example stealing), we usually ask parents to write a descriptive account of each incident. Often the therapist is unable to view these behaviours because of their infrequency and we rely on the parents to keep a clear record of the incident and their own consequating action.

36

Taking a simple frequency count of a behaviour as it occurs is one of the least time-consuming methods of observation and is appropriate for use with high rate behaviours. For example, if parents are recording a child's swearing, then each time this occurs they simply enter a check mark on to the recording sheet. These frequency records are useful during intervention as they provide numerical feedback as to whether the deviant behaviours are increasing or decreasing.

Before deciding either to describe specific events or to record their frequency we must first define what constitutes an occurrence of the behaviour. For instance, before observing disobedience we could assume that it begins if the child has not responded 15–20 seconds after a parent command which requests an immediate behaviour. We could assume that disobedience ends when the child responds appropriately or when the parent changes the subject, or no longer tries to enforce obedience. When parents are recording it is important that we clarify this definition with them, otherwise they will run into difficulties with their observations. For instance, they might say that they were unsure about when disobedience began or ended. They may only record the child as disobedient when he has failed to respond to three or four commands to carry out a task. When we are keeping frequency counts of events the definition should impart enough information to enable two recorders to reach exact agreement. The definition of parent commands might run as follows: a verbal statement made by the parent to the child which clearly and directly requests some immediate behaviour on the part of the child. Commands which do not imply immediate obedience are not recorded. For example, 'This evening you will go to bed at eight o'clock.' Commands which are verbally indirect, for example, 'I think those toys should be cleared away', or commands which suggest a response choice, for example, 'Don't you think we should tidy up your toys?', are not recorded.

One major disadvantage of event recording is that it does not give any account of the situation prior to or following the recorded behaviours. The behaviours are examined in isolation. This is important as the interaction between the child and the environment may have contributed significantly to his behaviour. For example, if the parents have been ignoring the child or if he has been teased by his siblings he may exhibit a higher rate of deviant behaviours. By adding a time dimension to our event records we may ascertain times when deviance is higher. This is discussed below.

As we have noted, behaviour may have important temporal aspects. In making event records it is often important to know when the events take place. At the simplest level we can record, or ask parents to record, the time at which the events occur. Parent records should then be carefully reviewed and discussed if they show clustering of deviant behaviours. For further assessment we should, if possible, carry out therapist observations at times when clustering has been demonstrated by the parents. A more complex method of examining the temporal aspects of behaviour is to carry out time-sampling. In the method discussed above we record only when specific events occur. In time-sampling, however, we record only at specific times, no matter what the behaviour of the child. We take a sample of the child's behaviour over a period of time; for example, we might ask a parent to observe for the presence or absence of deviant behaviours for the first 5 minutes in every 15-minute period during certain parts of the day. If the behaviours tend to be

BEHAVIOUR AND TIME RECORD SHEET

NAME ....Bob............... DATE ..23/5/75.... OBSERVER ..Mother..........

PRETREATMENT/TREATMENT/POST-TREATMENT   SETTING ..Home.......

SITUATIONS .Tea-time, 6.15 p.m. – Bob's bedtime at 7.45p.m.

WHO PRESENT ..All family

BEHAVIOURS TO BE OBSERVED

(1) Swearing – record ✓ for each swear word

(2) Tantrum – record ✓ for each episode of screaming

(3) Non-Compliance – record ✓ for each command non-complied

(4) .....✓

BEHAVIOURS	6.00-6.05	6.15-6.20	6.30-6.35	6.45-6.50	7.00-7.05	7.15-7.20	7.30-7.35	7.45-7.50	8.00-8.05	✓
Swearing			✓✓ ✓			✓				
Tantrum			✓					✓		
Non-compliance			✓✓ ✓✓					✓✓ ✓		
✓										

Figure 4.1   Simple time-sampling sheet used by a parent

worse during the latter half of the day then we may ask them to carry out this procedure between the hours of 6 and 8 p.m. (figure 4.1). Records taken during specified time intervals have a number of uses:

(1) We have already mentioned that observation of the child over a period of time may reveal clustering of his deviant behaviours. The early detection of deviant clusters is important because decisive action in the initial stages may prevent their escalation. By delaying, we frequently have the added problem that both the parent and the child are angry and upset. Under these circumstances decisive and confident action is difficult. A careful analysis of the events preceding these clusters is of obvious value in our management planning.

(2) We may be interested in the non-occurrence of deviant behaviour. Knowledge of the setting during non-occurrence of deviant behaviour may further help us to understand the problem. This approach is particularly relevant if we are considering sustained activities such as homework. For example, during homework time we may ask parents to record once in every 5 minutes whether or not the child is working. Analysis of the records may reveal factors conducive to successful study. For example, 10-year-old John was doing his homework when other siblings were also doing theirs and when there was no background noise such as the radio. In this way we can identify and foster the stimuli which are associated with on-task behaviour.

(3) With larger families, or in classrooms, it is important to ascertain the possible deviance of children other than the referred child. As we have already stated it is common to find significant levels of deviance in the siblings. The simplest method of taking this measurement is to observe each child for rotating intervals of equal length. For example, during 1 hour we may observe each of 5 children for periods of 2 minutes. In this way each child's behaviour would be sampled 6 times. While this method yields a broad picture of the setting, it does not reveal much about the quality or flow of an individual child's behaviour. To acquire such information we would need a more continuous record. Observers who have a limited amount of time may use scanning as a form of time-sampling. For example, the working mother may be too busy when she returns home in the evening to take event records of a high rate behaviour such as disobedience. In this case we could ask her to set aside 1 hour. During this time she would record disobedient behaviour for 5−10 seconds every 15 minutes. In a classroom setting, the teacher might be asked to observe the occurrence of target behaviours 3 times every half-hour—aided by a cueing device such as

an egg-timer or stopwatch. Scanning takes little time and has shown itself to be reliable in detecting deviant behaviour (Johnson and Bolstad, 1973); it is a device which parents can easily use after intervention to ensure that there is no unobserved deterioration in behaviour (figure 4.2).

BEHAVIOUR SCAN SHEET

NAME Jack   DATE 20/4/75   OBSERVER Teacher

PRETREATMENT/~~TREATMENT/POST-TREATMENT~~   SETTING Classroom

SITUATIONS 9.30-10.00 teaching class. 10.00-10.30 class doing arithmetic / English assignment

BEHAVIOURS TO BE SCANNED

(1) Off task - not attending to teacher or work = x

(2) Out of seat - out of seat without permission = 0

(3) Disruption - interacting with others without permission = +

(4) On task - attending to teacher or work = ✓

TIME	MON Scan		TUES Scan		WED Scan		THURS Scan		FRI Scan	
9.30 to 10.00	1	x o +	1	✓	1	x o +	1	✓	1	x o +
	2	✓	2	✓	2	x o +	2	✓	2	x
	3	x	3	x, o, +	3	x o +	3	x o +	3	x o
10.0 to 10.30	1	x o	1	x	1	✓	1	x	1	x o
	2	x o	2	✓	2	x	2	x o +	2	x o
	3	x +	3	x	3	x o	3	✓	3	x o

Figure 4.2 Simple scan sheet used in the classroom by a teacher. She was instructed to observe Jack three times each half-hour between 9.30 and 10.30 and to record behaviours observed, using predetermined symbols

(4) Time-sampling can be used to check the reliability of recordings. We might carry out a simultaneous recording with parents in which we both record the occurrence of target behaviours over predetermined time intervals. In this way we can check whether they are accurately recording behaviours as they occur. This method is commonly used in training clinicians to observe.

(5) Time-sampling is frequently used by behavioural researchers. In studies where a large number of behaviours are under observation it is usual to incorporate a short recording interval between observations.

For example, Wahler's observational system examines 25 different behaviours with 10-second intervals for observation followed by 5-second intervals for recording (Wahler, House and Stambaugh, 1976). This strategy is not often used in clinical practice. Interested readers should refer to Wright (1960).

Graphical Recording

Traditionally, behaviour therapists have presented observational data in graphical form. An obvious advantage of such a presentation is that it affords us a visual perspective of the situation. By using graphs we quickly become aware of trends in the observed behaviour. Major fluctuations indicate that we should carefully examine the behavioural antecedents. For example, deviant behaviour might be reduced prior to valued events such as boy-scouts night. The parents may be more successfully controlling behaviour at this time by the threat of privilege removal.

During intervention we would expect the graph to demonstrate a decrease in deviant behaviours. This concrete and visual display of change provides motivation for both clients and therapist. It is recommended that graphical recording of parent observations be continued for some time after the behaviour has stabilised—in this way we quickly detect any deterioration in behaviour (see, for example, figure 1.2).

Reliability

In some situations it is desirable to estimate the reliability of observational data. It is insufficient to train parents or other professional workers how to observe, without ensuring that their observations are reliable. However, this is an ideal which cannot always be put into practice in routine clinical work. There are a number of methods of computing reliability but only the most commonly used form is presented here: two observers, one of whom is trained, are asked to simultaneously record the same behaviours. Reliability for event recording can be computed using the formula below:

$$\frac{\text{Number of agreed events}}{\text{Number of agreed events} + \text{number of disagreed events}} \times 100 = \% \text{ agreement}$$

Unfortunately, in computing this reliability we cannot be sure that the observers are actually recording the same events. They may agree that a child was disobedient 42 times and yet each be referring to different behavioural events. Time-sampling can be used to provide a more stringent computation of reliability since agreement may be assessed interval by interval. The formula for time-sampling is:

$$\frac{\text{Number of agreements interval by interval}}{\text{Number of agreements interval by interval} + \text{number of disagreements interval by interval}} \times 100 = \% \text{ agreement}$$

Acceptable levels of observer agreement depend on a number of factors.

(1) The method used to compute reliability. We would expect reliability to be high for event recording when we are computing reliability only on the summed total of events scored by each observer. (We can still compute reliability in this way even if time-sampling has been the observational method employed.) However, if we check reliability interval by interval we generally find that it is lower.

(2) The number of behaviours being observed. When a large number of high frequency behaviours are under observation we would expect a lower percentage agreement.

(3) The nature of the behaviour being recorded. We expect a high agreement for easily definable behaviours such as tantrums. It is unlikely that agreement will be as high if the behaviour under observation is difficult to define. For example, negative adult verbal attention may be difficult to define since components such as tone may also be of importance.

For data analysis of event records the minimal acceptable level of observer agreement is usually 80 per cent; interval-by-interval agreement is usually at least 65 per cent. The methodology of reliability has expanded and developed rapidly over the past 10 years and further information may be obtained from Johnson and Bolstad (1973).

Key Ideas

Specimen recording is the most important form of therapist recording. It is used to obtain a broad perspective rather than focusing prematurely on target behaviours. It is therefore usually a precursor to other forms of recording.

Nevertheless, event records and time sampling (with subsequent graphical presentation) are also useful—they provide us with substantial information during assessment, with feedback during intervention and with a system for monitoring behaviour, after intervention. They are economic in their use of time and can be employed to record the behaviour of a number of children. To be of value these records must be reliable. Before deciding to record a target behaviour we must ensure that the observers have defined and understood what constitutes an occurrence of that behaviour.

5

The Therapist as Observer

Normally in the home setting younger children, that is those below approximately 8 years of age, quickly adjust to the presence of an observer. Thus both their deviant and prosocial behaviours may rapidly and readily be observed by the therapist. Children in the older range usually take much longer to accommodate to the observer's presence, for example 6 or 7 sessions. Generally in the observational situation they will tend to exhibit less deviant behaviour. However, with these restrictions in mind and the usual circumstances that therapist time is limited, some observation of the older child can be valuable since it may yield useful information about the maturity of his prosocial and interactional skills (for example, how he responds when his parent makes a request or engages him in a conversation). In addition we will occasionally observe the full range of deviant behaviours and interaction in the older child—commonly we find this to be the case when the behaviours have been reported by the parents as occurring extremely frequently, for example verbally abusive behaviours occurring 15−20 times per day. On many occasions when older children are involved we must rely heavily on parent observations (see chapter 6).

Observation requires the therapist to consider a wide number of factors which we have grouped under three headings: choice of setting; preparation of clients; and selection of behaviours to be observed.

Choice of Setting

Having decided to observe the child we must select the setting in which to make the observations. We have the basic choice of whether to observe him in the clinic or a natural setting (in home, school or at

44

play). Clinical observation saves the therapist valuable time which he would have to use travelling to the natural setting, but it is associated with disadvantages. First, it has been shown by Lobitz and Johnson (1974) that deviant children's behaviour seems to vary critically according to the observational setting. In this study a sample of normal and a sample of deviant children were observed interacting with their parents in both home and clinic. In the clinic the behaviours of the two groups of children were not significantly different, whilst in the home setting the deviant children exhibited significantly more high intensity deviant behaviour. However, in contrast it was still possible to identify the deviant children in the clinic by the behaviour of their parents. In both settings these parents gave significantly more commands and negative responses than did the normal parents. More seriously, it has been noted by Sajwaj (1973) that treatment conducted successfully in the clinic may fail to carry over (or generalise) to the home. The 4 children reported in this study, who were 'cured' in the clinic, later required additional therapy in the home. Secondly, we would suggest that parents feel relatively more anxious when they are observed with their children in the clinic. The situation is unfamiliar and puts them 'on trial'. In their own home they can occupy themselves with tasks if they are initially anxious.

In view of the above findings we advocate that both observation and treatment are conducted in the home. In those cases where this is prevented by the time factor, we strongly recommend post-therapy assessment in the home to ensure that generalisation to the home has occurred.

A decision to make observations in the school would be based on findings in the history. If the problem occurs in the home and the school then ideally we should observe in both settings. If we are specifically interested in the child's peer interactional skills then the school provides a more appropriate observational setting. Generally accommodation to observer presence is less of a problem in the school than in the home (see beginning of this chapter). In this larger and more structured setting, child reactivity to the observer is less.

Preparation of Clients

This is of critical importance as therapist observation is one of the most antisocial procedures used in behaviour modification. The aim of observation is to obtain 'naturalistic' recordings and therefore the observer tries to be completely unobtrusive. In one recent instance, parents were not adequately prepared for the observer's non-interaction with the family and they became hostile and annoyed. We must therefore explain the reasons for observation clearly to the parents. This means ensuring that they understand the rules which are necessary for observation. These rules are usually of three types:

(1) Personal. This rule states that the observer will not interact with the family during the observation period. Any approaches made to the observer are most easily terminated by a monosyllabic response. The authors have found this to be more successful than observer non-response. Apart from directly approaching the observer, children will often test him out initially by exhibiting high rates of deviance. For example, on a very hot day one 6-year-old child turned on all the heating and throughout the session checked that the observer had not turned it down. In later sessions the child did not persist in such attention-seeking behaviours and we hypothesised that this was due to his initial failure to seduce the observer from his non-interaction role.

Whilst non-interaction is a commonly used strategy we are not certain that this approach is always the most appropriate. In recent discussion with a group of parents whose families had been observed, it became evident that some parents may feel more relaxed if the observer integrates with the family. We do not know of any research which has examined different observer behaviours and related these to parental attitudes towards observation. However, we still believe that observer non-interaction is usually the most practical method. First, because it could take several weeks for an observer to become integrated with the family and, secondly, data may be less accurate when the observer is interacting with the family.

(2) Physical. This rule implies that during the observation period the parents and child stay within two adjacent rooms. The parents are asked to continue with normal household activities but any distractions, such as television, visitors or lengthy telephone conversations, are prohibited. These restrictions intensify interaction and help us to make the best use of our time. The observer selects an unobtrusive position on the edge of the main thoroughfare of interaction.

(3) Temporal. The parents are told exactly when the observation periods will occur. We select this time on the basis of two sets of criteria. First, we should observe at a time when the child's behaviour is reported to be most deviant. Secondly, we should try to observe when most

members of the family are present. Success in treatment correlates positively with involvement of both parents and so we should, where possible, schedule their presence into the observational timetable. We would also plan to observe the other siblings' interaction with the parents and the deviant child.

The parents are instructed to prepare the child for observation—this includes explaining the rules. We leave this to the parents because it is they who will implement the treatment programme under our supervision. As therapist observation is only used with younger children it is not necessary for the parents to give them a detailed explanation of the observer's presence and purpose.

The group discussion with parents mentioned above revealed that they were unanimously against lengthy observations. On balance, while they habituated somewhat to the observer's presence they continued to find the observation stressful. In addition they felt that much of their private family time was encroached upon. Obviously the restrictions we impose put strain on the clients and therefore we suggest that an observation period should not last longer than approximately $1\frac{1}{2}$ hours. It should be carefully explained to parents that treatment will not begin until the observational phase has been completed. As observers we must remember that we are only collecting data and that lengthy and frequent observations may affect our image with the parents when it is time to actively intervene. It is therefore important to limit the number of observations as far as possible. An examination of our own records shows that on the average we take about $3-4$ hours of observation during baseline (pretreatment) recordings. Clearly defined observational goals should be described initially to the parents so that they have an idea of the amount of time and effort which will be required. This information will enable them to reassess their own commitment to the programme. The plans may be somewhat modified to suit the parents; for example we could arrange to implement the programme during father's holidays. The majority of parents are initially upset by the observational situation. However, there are some strategies which we can employ in order to alleviate their anxieties. Obviously it is very important to interact positively with parents after the observation and to reassure them that the data collected are valuable. Initially, with parents who are over-anxious we may bend the rules and give them some verbal reassurance during observation. Another technique which we may use with over-anxious parents is task-setting. Normally, parents are asked to continue with their usual household activities during observation, but some parents may find the situation easier if they are told exactly what to do. For example, we could ask a mother to play with her child for 15 minutes (using a familiar game), then to do housework for 15 minutes and finally to organise the child in a task such as sorting out his toys. In most cases we wish to examine the behavioural interaction between parents and child, but stressing this to the parents may elicit extreme anxiety which could be counterproductive. Parents are generally more relaxed if they understand initially that the main emphasis of observation is on the child's behaviour.

Selection of Behaviours to be Observed

In the initial observational sessions we do not focus on one deviant behaviour, but take specimen (descriptive) recordings in an attempt to gain a wide picture of parent–child interaction. After this general assessment we are able to select target behaviours for more detailed observation. In the specimen recordings we examine a whole range of behaviours and then decide which would be the most appropriate for further observations.

Learning theory provides us with a model by which to assess the significant factors in any behavioural sequence. Every behaviour can be viewed as a response which has antecedents and consequences. In observing the child we look at the antecedents, content and consequences of his deviant and prosocial responses. In observing the parents we look at the antecedents, content and consequences of their rewarding and punishing and also at their verbal and non-verbal styles.

CHILD DEVIANT BEHAVIOURS

(1) Antecedents. We observe temporal factors, such as the time at which the deviant behaviour occurs, and contrast this with behaviour at other times. If the behaviour has a strong temporal element we may also observe variation in the parents' consequating behaviour. For example, by dinnertime mother may be tired and so she is inconsistent or more easily coerced by the child. Situational factors are also important. It may be that the child's behaviour is better in father's presence, or worse when all the children are at home and mother has less time to deal with deviant behaviour. In our observations we often discover that parents have failed to perceive the situational antecedents. For example, they

48

may not have noticed that the child's disobedient behaviour was partly maintained by the amusement of another sibling.

Parents frequently fail to track or follow escalating episodes of deviant behaviour. This means that a sequence may be well under way before they make any attempt to gain control. Typically with these families, we sit through periods of observation during which no deviant behaviour is exhibited. However, then we find that one deviant act triggers off a whole run of child problem behaviours. In other words, deviant behaviour often occurs in clusters. As therapists, we are most interested in ascertaining this sequence at the beginning, since at this stage behaviour is more easily changed. Later in the sequence both the child and the parent are highly aroused (that is, anxious or angry). By this time the parent is less capable of appropriately asserting himself and the child is less likely to comply. Examples of typical antecedents which often initiate a deviant run are as follows: John approaches father and asks, 'Please may I go out to play?'; father ignores this. John repeats his request in a louder tone; father frowns but continues reading the paper; John says, 'I want to go out to play', and he starts to cry; father says, 'Why are you always whining? Just go out and give me peace'.

In fact, deviant runs may sometimes stem from parents ignoring appropriate behaviour on the part of the child, and only acknowledging him when he produces deviant behaviour. In this way parents shape up coercive behaviour in the child. Apart from the parent finally submitting to the coercive behaviour and saying, 'Just go out...', further interaction between parent and child often focuses not on the original and appropriate request ('Please may I go out to play?') but on the child's later deviance ('Why are you always whining?').

Another example ran as follows: Phil's dirty pants are lying on the outhouse roof; mother says, 'Did you throw your pants there?'. (She knows this to be a fact.) Phil says, 'What underpants?' Mother says, 'You know what I'm talking about.' Phil says, 'They're not mine.' Mother, raising her voice, 'Who else would throw underpants there?' Phil says, 'Maybe it was somebody from next door....' This sequence eventually escalated and the mother became very angry and Phil was increasingly rude and verbally abusive.

This is a common pattern in episodes of what is sometimes referred to as escalating aggression. The mother's intention (to have the child remove the underpants) was not made clear initially and the argument developed because of her failure to clearly specify actions and consequences. Often parents become embroiled in arguments as to whether the deviant behaviour has occurred, rather than asserting that it has occurred and what the consequences will be. Typically, these situations are started by the parent asking the child, 'What did you say?' or 'Did you do that?' One can hypothesise a number of reasons for this style of interaction—the parent is anxious and wishes to avoid a confrontation; he lacks assertive skills; his idea of a punishment sequence is that the child must first admit that he is in the wrong even when this is obvious.

We have given two examples of parental behaviour which contributed to an escalating sequence but clearly there are many other causes. Thus when we observe episodes or clusters of deviant behaviour, particular attention to detail is important since we may find many factors which maintain the deviant behaviour.

(2) The response. Usually the response (that is, the deviant behaviour) has been accurately described in the case history. However, it is still useful to take frequency counts. These help us to focus more clearly on deviant clusters and they may also be used as a baseline against which we can measure intervention. Occasionally the frequency and intensity of the response has been exaggerated by the parents. If we find the presenting problem to be less deviant than anticipated, we may need to examine parental expectations of the child, as in the following example. The mother of 4-year-old Gary was watching television, while Gary played quietly with a toy car ramp. Each time Gary exuberantly attempted to force the car down or to put more than one car on the ramp his mother became annoyed and scolded him. In this case the mother's expectations of her son's playing skills were unrealistic. Subsequent intervention did not centre on teaching Gary to conform to such rigid expectations but rather on helping mother to understand that her expectations of the child were unrealistic.

(3) Consequences. Learning theory states that a behaviour must be reinforced if it is to persist. As most children referred to the clinic exhibit persistent deviant behaviours we may conclude that somehow these behaviours are being reinforced or rewarded. Ideally, in examining the consequences of a deviant behaviour we hope to identify the reinforcers. For instance, by whining a child may gain positive reinforcement (for example, to sit on mother's knee or be given sweets) or he may avoid an unpleasant situation (such as having to tidy his room). In this second instance the unpleasant situation (tidying the room) functions as a negative reinforcer in that it motivates avoidance behaviour (whining). During observation we may see few instances of positive reinforcement.

Social behaviours are rarely reinforced continuously. Behaviours which result in intermittent positive reinforcements (such as mother only occasionally buying sweets for Kate when she screams in the shop) are generally much more resistant to change than those which are continuously reinforced (such as mother always lifting John when he holds his breath). However in observing the deviant family we will frequently notice that positive reinforcers are either infrequent, inappropriately used (in the above example, whining was reinforced by maternal attention) or their application is inconsistent and non-contingent (that is, unrelated to the child's behaviour). In some circumstances a deviant behaviour may be maintained by reinforcement from siblings or peers. It is important to identify these situations because during intervention we would not focus entirely on the deviant behaviour but would also need to modify the sibling or peer reinforcers.

CHILD PROSOCIAL BEHAVIOURS

If an intervention programme is to be successful we should ensure that prosocial behaviours replace any deviant behaviours which we attempt to reduce. During observation we should thus attempt to assess whether the child is capable of exhibiting the prosocial skills which we will require. Generally, it is advantageous to seek out prosocial behaviours which are incompatible with the deviant behaviours (for example, obedience is incompatible with disobedience because simultaneous occurrence of both behaviours is impossible). Reinforcement of these prosocial behaviours, combined with punishment of the deviant behaviour, will tend to speed up the intervention. It is important for the therapist to know whether he will have to teach the child these prosocial skills as well as remove the deviant behaviour. For example, does the demanding child know how to ask appropriately or has the encopretic child ever learned toileting behaviour? Deviant children are often observed to have poor peer relationships. As peers are important models to the child we should observe whether he has appropriate interactional skills. This would include looking at his ability to play co-operatively.

In order to establish prosocial skills we must find effective reinforcers. During observation we are particularly attentive to the child's response to social reinforcers, such as the parents' verbal and non-verbal approval. Behaviour therapists have too often assumed that praise or approval are effective reinforcers (Sajwaj and Dillon, 1976). Such reinforcers may never have been established in the young child and initially we may have to use material rewards. For the older child social reinforcers may not have the required potency—if this is the case we could perhaps supplement them with privilege gain. For example, being allowed to stay up late.

PARENT REWARDING AND PUNISHING

(1) Antecedents. We observe the behaviours or cues preceding the reward or punishment. One might assume that the precedents of reward are prosocial behaviours on the part of the child and the precedents of punishment are deviant behaviours. However, this is not always the case. Reward and punishment may not be contingent or dependent on the child's preceding behaviour. We may not observe any deviant behaviour by the child which we could say has led to punishment. Conversely, parents may reward the child even though he has exhibited no obvious prosocial behaviours. Occasionally parents will reward the child in expectation of future good behaviour; for example, mother might say, 'If I read you a story will you go to bed quietly?' Sometimes the parents do not specify exactly the behaviour which they are anticipating; for example, mother might say, 'If I buy you sweets will you be a good boy when Granny comes?'

(2) The response. We observe the parent reward or punish. This includes noting the method used. To punish the child, does the parent smack him, put him to bed or remove privileges? The frequency and intensity of reward and punishment are also worth observing and comparing. For example, parents may insist that sending their child to his bedroom is ineffective, although observation might reveal that the child only spends a few seconds there and that the punishment is not supervised. Often a first specimen recording contains very little evidence of appropriate reinforcement by the parent. We may find that many prosocial behaviours on the part of the child pass unrewarded. In this case we are noting parental non-responses. Similarly, we may assess that the parent uses punishment inappropriately for some behaviours. Perhaps the mother is ignoring a very deviant behaviour, such as destructiveness, and yet excessively punishing the child for occasional enuresis.

(3) The consequences. We observe whatever occurs at the end of a punishment or reward sequence. Appropriately applied punishment should have a suppressing effect on the deviant behaviour. Failure to achieve this effect may occur because the punishment was applied long after deviant behaviours had begun (as discussed above in examples of escalating aggression) or was too long after the behaviour had ended.

There is often considerable delay between an episode of low rate delinquent behaviour (for example, stealing) and eventual punishment. These behaviours frequently evade immediate detection because they occur outside the home. In the interval, the reinforcements for the stealing (such as delinquent peer approval, things bought with the money, etc.) often override any suppressing effect of late punishment. Unfortunately, it is often impossible to discover which reinforcers are important in the maintenance of deviant behaviours occurring outside the home. In other instances, when punishment is not having the desired effect an examination of the events immediately following the punishment may reveal an explanation. Perhaps the child is having more interaction with the parent at the time of punishment than at any other time. This occurs especially in situations in which the parent generally avoids the child, because he finds that unpleasant rows often result. In another case the mother may believe that she is punishing the child appropriately when she smacks him, but she may be unaware of the fact that within seconds of the punishment she usually allows him a reward such as cuddling or giving him a biscuit. Parents who tend to feel anxious about the use of punishment, sometimes out of guilt, attempt to seek the child's reassurance immediately after punishing him. Children who receive relatively large amounts of adult attention or reinforcements during or immediately following punishment may learn that punishment is one signal for reinforcement. It is possible that this is one of the ways in which masochistic behaviour develops. Sometimes parents are under pressure not to punish because the other children or significant adults create difficulties when they do so. During observation we may see these pressures operating. It may be that the parents have not reported this problem in the case history because it is too difficult for them to deal with. For example, the divorced mother of a 6-year-old child did not like to punish him when a male friend was present because he might disapprove. On further observation it appeared that she tended to ignore the child in the presence of the friend.

The parents' reward may not always be reinforcing to the child. Careful observation of the child's behaviour following events which are thought to be reinforcing will reveal whether or not this is the case. Assuming that an appropriate behaviour has been reinforced, then if deviant behaviours increase we can suggest that the presumed reinforcer is not in fact reinforcing. As with punishment, reward may not be sufficiently intense or it may be too delayed. Parents often overestimate their child's ability to link good behaviour with a later reward. For example, John's parents believe that they are rewarding him for obedience when they promise him a special treat at the weekend. However, John is only 6 years old and requires more immediate reinforcement. With this young age group it is especially important that both reward and punishment should be fairly immediate in order to be effective.

PARENT VERBAL STYLE

We have already alluded to the importance of the way in which parents give commands to their children. Do their commands clearly specify what the child is supposed to do, or are they indirect and vague? The verbal interactions. We have noticed that many parents of deviant in a similar manner. Notice should also be taken of the tonal quality of verbal interactions. We have noticed that some parents of deviant children often give commands and praise in a dull unassertive manner. This is discussed in more detail below. Since parents are continuously teaching and shaping their children's behaviour we should also examine the content of instructions and explanations. For instance, following a punishment do the parents give any social explanation for the punishment, and detail those behaviours which might be expected of the child in the future (rather than just saying, 'You will do it because I say so')? While few parents give elaborate explanations to their children following every punishment, in a treatment situation it is felt that such a step may hasten the child's understanding of what is expected of him. For example the parent might say, 'You will not play with your food because it is messy, it may upset other people at the table and it is bad manners'. Observing the parents playing with the child can be a particularly useful situation in which to examine (and later practise) parental instructional and other verbal interactional behaviours.

PARENT NON-VERBAL STYLE

This is an attempt to gain a tonal picture of parental interaction with the child. It involves looking at the intensity of their responses to the child. For example we may observe a mother playing with her child but notice that she appears very flat and disinterested. We should try to examine the non-verbal behaviours, such as cues in the parent betraying hostility (continued shouting and criticism), anxiety (avoiding the child, or inability to implement contingencies) and depression (lack of responsiveness). The amount of physical contact between parent and child should also be observed. It is useful to compare the styles of both parents and to observe the child's differing responses.

Key Ideas

The therapist explains the reasons for observation clearly to the parent and specifies exactly what this entails in terms of: time commitment; physical restrictions; postponement of the intervention programme.

The therapist observes parental ability to track or accurately follow behaviour in terms of its antecedents and consequences; that is, their ability to give clear instructions to the child and to consistently implement the contingencies of reward and punishment.

6

The Parent and Child as Observers

Ultimately success is dependent on the preparedness of clients to accept that they will be the agents of change. Involving parents and children in keeping observational records immediately demonstrates the active role expected of them in therapy.

Parent Observation

Parent and therapist observations differ in two main ways. The therapist observes the behaviours of all members of the family but, in the early stages of management, the parent observer mainly records data on the child's behaviour. Unlike the therapist the parent is usually asked to begin observations by looking at a few simple target behaviours (the reasons for this are discussed later). The model of the behavioural sequence which was presented in the previous chapter is still relevant but generally the parent observes behaviour at a simpler level.

Parents are always asked to make observations. Sometimes these are supplementary to the therapist observations but at other times the parent will be the principal observer. Although parent observations are simple and selective they have the following advantages which necessitate their implementation.

First, parents may feel more involved if we ask them to observe from the beginning. Their response, in terms of attempts to record, may help us to assess their motivation. This is especially important as they are the ones who will be implementing therapy. Secondly, it has already been stressed that faulty behaviour tracking is often a problem with the parents of deviant children. In teaching them to track behaviour we are providing them with a skill which is essential for successful intervention. Observation facilitates an understanding of the relationship between behaviours. For example, if parents are asked to record their child's disobedience they may become aware of the number of commands and unconsequated threats which they are issuing. As mentioned in chapter 3, parent recording may sometimes result in an amelioration of the presenting problem to such an extent that no further intervention is necessary. Thirdly, parent recordings form part of an ongoing assessment. They may continue to be used following active intervention, in order to detect any gradual deterioration in the child's behaviour. This enables quick preventative action if it is required. In some cases parent records form an intrinsic part of the intervention programme, for example when a points system is used the parents enter points on a chart each time a designated behaviour occurs (see chapter 10). Fourthly, in some situations therapist observations are either difficult or impossible. In these cases we must rely on the parent as the principal observer. The situations in which this occurs may be summarised as follows:

(1) Generally children over the age of 9 do not exhibit deviant behaviours in the presence of an outside observer during the initial sessions. In routine clinical practice it is unrealistic to wait for such a child to habituate to the observer's presence and therefore we rely on the parent recordings.

(2) When the deviant behaviours are low rate it is impractical for the therapist to maintain observation until these occur. For instance, the observer may have to spend considerable time in the home before seeing the encopretic child soil. However, in these cases of reported low rate deviant behaviours the observer should, where possible, take some initial specimen recordings in the home to ensure that unreported high rate problems are not also occurring.

(3) Some categories of low rate behaviours cause even more difficulty to the therapist observer. Characteristically these behaviours occur outside the structured settings of the home or school—examples include truancy, stealing, promiscuity and staying out late. Although we may ask parents to record these behaviours we realise that they do not have access to the immediate behavioural antecedents and consequences. For example, on one occasion a child may steal as a result of a dare from his peers and be reinforced by their approval. In this case the parents can only report on the circumstances of the deviant behaviour as far as they understand them, and on the method which they used in subsequently dealing with the behaviour.

(4) Even the most dedicated therapist will hesitate at the thought of observing the child who refuses to stay in bed at night. The parent

therefore usually observes nocturnal problems. However, in these circumstances the parent may not be fully alert (especially if the problem occurs in the middle of the night) and so his recordings may be unreliable. His later application of intervention techniques can also suffer for the same reason.

The therapist uses several criteria when considering parent observational assignments. If he is also observing he can, on the basis of his own observations, select target behaviours for parent recording. In circumstances where it is not feasible for the therapist to observe, he extracts the target behaviours from the case history. Other than primarily asking the parents to observe the child's deviant behaviours, we may sometimes be interested in parent self-recordings and spouse-to-spouse recordings. For example, in addition to recording obedience or disobedience in the child, the parents may also record their own or their spouse's frequencies of commands and approval. It is not advisable to introduce the use of this strategy in the early stages since parents may find it too difficult or threatening. The case of George in chapter 9 further illustrates the use of spouse-to-spouse recording.

Initially we ask parents to observe easily definable behaviours. For example, they might record tantrums and destructive behaviour. As they acquire observational skills we can extend their assignments to include a greater number of behaviours and also behaviours which are more difficult to define and observe, for example sulking. The total number of behaviours which parents can record with ease depends on the frequency and the complexity of the behaviours under observation. In assigning tasks to parents we must consider whether the time commitment is realistic. For example, a working mother or the mother of a large family is limited in the amount of time she can give to observations. Parents whose handling of the deviant problems has been highly inconsistent and disorganised are most likely to have difficulty in recording. With these parents our initial assignments should be very simple.

Training the parent to observe is important and is similar in process to therapist observer training. It may be accomplished using verbal, video tape or *in vivo* instruction. As before, we ask the parents to prepare the child for observation. It is important to ensure that the parents do not use the recordings as threats to control the child's behaviour. Parents sometimes tell their child that if his behaviour record is bad the therapist will remove him from home. Such statements may initially have a marked effect on the child's behaviour. However, when it becomes apparent to him that such threats are not being carried through then it is likely that they will lose their effect. We strongly discourage the use of such threats. Hopefully in therapy we will teach these parents to use realistic threats which can consistently be put into effect if necessary (for example, 'if you do that you will not be allowed to watch television this evening').

Generally, parents use four methods of recording. As these methods have been discussed extensively in the previous chapter we shall limit our remarks to indicating which method may be situationally appropriate.

(1) Specimen recordings. These are mainly used to record low rate behaviours.

(2) Event recordings. These are used by parents to record high rate behaviours. Certain times in the day may be delegated for recording and occasionally the parent may also record duration of the behaviour.

(3) Scanning. This method of observing high rate behaviours can be used by parents when they have a limited amount of time or when they are observing several children in the family. This is also a convenient method of post-intervention observation.

(4) Attitude rating. A measure of programme effectiveness may be introduced by asking parents to rate daily their feelings towards the child on a simple attitudinal rating scale.

In our clinical experience we have found great difficulty in persuading parents to maintain adequate records. This problem has also been mentioned by other authors, for example Wahler (1976). In most cases we find that the parent records have been completed, but for various reasons we have doubted the reliability of the observations. Our suspicions would obviously be aroused in the following circumstances: when the recording sheets look extremely clean and unused; when the parents have difficulty in finding the sheets or if they have left them somewhere comparatively inaccessible (for example, on the top of the kitchen cupboards). We notice this especially if we make an unexpected home visit. Finally, when the recorded rate of behaviours is discrepant with our own observations.

Why do parents fail to produce reliable records? When we first asked ourselves this question we decided that our preparation of the parents must have been inadequate. However, although we further explained the rationale of recording to the parents and arranged brief practical training in their own home we still could not increase the efficiency of many of our parents' recordings. We hypothesise that this recording failure is part of a more general and persistent motivational problem which is initially reflected in the parents' incapacity to cope with their child, which further manifests itself at the observation stage and which eventually is reflected in intervention failure. This problem will be further discussed in chapter 14. There are nevertheless a number of simple and practical measures which may help to increase parent output:

(1) Supplying parents with prepared recording sheets, which have an attached pencil and which are conveniently placed (for example, on the living-room wall).

(2) Simple frequency counters which the parents can easily carry may also be provided (Lindsley, 1968; Mattos, 1968).

(3) The therapist should, where possible, put assessment on a contingency contract. This entails informing the parents that intervention will not start until baseline records have been completed (the general use of contingency contracting will be discussed in chapter 11).

(4) The parents can be informed that data will be collected daily. This process will be facilitated if there is a telephone available to the clients.

(5) Following the introduction of parent recording the therapist can, if possible, conduct observational reliability checks at spaced intervals.

Child Recordings

Ideally, we ask children to take some records of their own. Obviously this is only practical with children who are of a certain age—usually over 7 years old. Whilst we may gain some information from these records we feel that their primary purpose is in motivating the child. Often children feel hostile towards the therapist because they have been referred to the clinic by their parents for deviant behaviour. Involvement of the child in the initial stages of assessment is probably associated with positive results in intervention. The child's viewpoint is valued if we consider his records in our intervention programme. In addition, children may find parent recordings more acceptable if they are asked by the therapist to make parallel recordings of their own. The authors have found the following kinds of child information to be useful:

(1) Child recordings of unpopular parent behaviours. For example, frequently asking the child to do messages; not allowing him to watch a full television programme; not giving enough pocket money. These

records are useful because they provide us with feedback as to the child's perception of the situation from day to day and they afford a more balanced picture of parent – child expectations. If we discover that the parents are making some excessive demands on the child (for example, housework) then we may be able to use this information later to help in drawing up a parent – child contract in which the child bargains changes in his behaviour against prescribed changes in parent behaviour. If possible, we ask the child to complete a daily attitudinal rating, parallel to the parent's rating.

(2) Child recordings of reinforcers. The child may be asked to keep records of things he enjoys doing. This has obvious implications for intervention.

(3) Child self-recordings. Bolstad and Johnson (1972) demonstrated that disruptive children in first- and second-grade classrooms were able to keep reliable records of their own deviant behaviours and report these, even though they resulted in negative sanctions. The majority of therapists have perhaps assumed that a greater level of sophistication was required for this process of reliable self-recording. The authors have only used self-recording with older children as a precursor to training them in self-control techniques. For example, an obese adolescent would learn to record her own eating behaviours before starting her self-management programme.

The parent prepares the child prior to therapist or parent observations. In contrast, the therapist prepares him for child observations. This is important because whilst the child may be reticent in discussing his parental difficulties with us, he would understandably be even more reticent with his parents. To help overcome this problem we emphasise to the child that his records will not be discussed with the parents without his permission. Although parents are usually informed that the child is recording we collect his information separately and discuss it with him individually.

Most commonly we ask the child to take specimen recordings. For example, if we wish to know which parent behaviours annoy the child we ask him to record what the behaviour was, how and when it happened, and the nature of his response. Once a number of parent behaviours have been clearly described the child may progress to keeping frequency counts on these behaviours.

Key Ideas

Asking parents and children to take observations affords a clear demonstration to them, from the beginning, that they are not abdicating their role to the therapist. The knowledge that they can make a valued contribution to the programme may increase their self-esteem and motivation. Learning how to observe also facilitates their understanding of the relationship between behaviours and ideally this is a skill which they can continue to use and develop long after the programme has been terminated.

PART II

PLANNING

7

The Decision to Intervene: Some General and Specific Considerations

In a clinical setting, clients are commonly referred either by their general practitioner, by other agencies (such as Educational Psychology and Social Services) or by themselves. The implication of any referral is that the referral source regards the child's behaviour with some concern. In view of this, our decision centres not on whether intervention is required but on the focus, intensity and duration of intervention. For example, a mother may verbalise concern that her 3-year-old child exhibits tantrums 3−4 times per week. At such an age this number of tantrums is not excessive (Patterson, 1975). Our action in this example may be more appropriately focused on reassuring the parent about the relative normality of the child's behaviour. An elaborate intervention programme focused on modifying the child's behaviour could be detrimental, as it may serve to reinforce parent anxiety. If detailed work is considered necessary it would be more appropriately focused on modifying parent anxiety, expectations, etc.

The Focus of Intervention

In the initial stages of intervention we usually focus on changing a few deviant behaviours or interactions occurring between family in- dividuals. The utilisation of research data about predisposing factors of family deviance, together with our own assessment, should assist us in reaching an early decision about where to concentrate our efforts.

It is not the purpose of this text to examine in detail the predisposing factors. This is more ably described in texts relating specifically to child psychiatry, for example Robins (1966), Rutter (1966), and Quay and Werry (1972). However, we will mention a few of those factors which we consider important. For convenience we have divided them into parent and child factors, although they are often found to operate in conjunction.

The parents

Some factors correlating with child deviance are: single-parent families (especially those resulting from marital or interactional breakdown); parents with chronic physical or mental ill health (Rutter, 1966); parents involved with many social helping agencies (Tonge, James and Hillam, 1975); parents with past histories of delinquency (Robins, 1966). It is important to note that the large majority of predisposing factors relate to family life and not to community circumstances (Craig and Glick, 1965). The low socio-economic grouping and esteem of delinquent families is probably a result, rather than a cause, of their deviancy.

Child deviance resulting from some of the above circumstances may often be regarded as secondary. Ideally our first steps may entail intervention with the parents. At a practical level this could involve ensuring that the family is in receipt of all social benefits to which they are entitled, obtaining them a home help or referring them for appropriate medical or psychiatric care. More specifically, we may have to start working with day-to-day management skills, marital communication, etc.

The child

Certain factors peculiar to, or directly affecting, the child may predispose him to deviance. Some of these are as follows: below average intelligence; chronic physical illness; brain damage; low reading attainment; hyperactivity (Rutter, Tizard and Whitmore, 1970); institutionalisation, of which a most important aspect is perhaps early sensory deprivation (Yarrow, 1961). Prolonged separations are also of importance (Rutter, 1972). However, the circumstances surrounding the separation are an important factor in many cases. Separations which result from home interactional difficulties are thought to be more damaging to the child than separations resulting from natural causes such as parental illness or death. These factors provide an indication about future management and the probable prognosis. For instance, the child of below average intelligence and the child with brain damage perhaps require more regularly consistent handling. The child who is failing academically may require special education, which hopefully will provide a situation where he is not exposed to persistent failure.

Much of the information which we have discussed above is derived from population studies of families and is reported in the form of group data. In clinical work we are managing individual families and thus we should apply the results of population studies with caution. For example, while one family may exhibit all the characteristics of a problem or broken family, occasionally intensive individual intervention in such a family yields surprising success. Usually, however, the less these general indications feature in the case history the better will be the prognosis.

ASSESSMENT DATA FROM THE CASE HISTORY

The sociological indicators discussed above rarely offer detailed and precise descriptions of what is 'normal' in terms of day-to-day interaction, nor do they describe the genesis of deviance at a molecular level. Only through our own observations can we gain an overall perspective of interaction within the referred family and thus decide where to focus intervention.

In some instances our observations may reveal a situation in which reduction of the child behaviour problems would not be the prime aim of intervention. The most common of these situations are as follows:

(1) Marital problems, especially those which involve conflict over child management, are often associated with child behavioural problems. In these cases each parent may well possess reasonable child management skills. Therapy directed towards resolving the marital interactional difficulties should result in improvement in the child's behaviour. In other cases of marital disharmony, not involving conflict in child management, the child may present with symptoms of insecurity (which may be typified by refusal to separate, eating difficulties, etc.). Again, in these cases, therapy focused on the marriage may resolve the child's difficulties. Rutter (1966) has demonstrated that in these disturbed environments the most important factor which protects children against developing problems is a good relationship with one of the parents.

(2) Where there is marked parental rejection of the child. It is

socially unacceptable for parents to openly reject children and therefore we may not become fully aware of this rejection until we discover, during intervention, that parental attitudes towards the child are immutable. Often at the onset it is understandable that the parents should feel negative towards their child; however, we would expect this to change as the child improves. In situations where this does not occur we may suspect rejection. Some of the factors leading us to this conclusion might include: persistent negativity associated with a lack of co-operation; over-use of the punishment techniques; persistent difficulty or failure in reinforcing the child; and failure in situations where the parents are known to have reasonable handling skills (as evidenced by management of their other children).

(3) Parental expectations of the child may be unrealistic. This is sometimes a major problem with the parents of retarded children. It may prove difficult to prevent parents from having very high hopes. Young and immature parents, especially those from problem families, are often found to have inappropriately high expectations of the child's behaviours. For example, they may expect their 3-year-old child to exhibit total love and respect—defiance or tantrums may result in extreme sanctions or rejection. These patterns of high expectations are often found in the parents of non-accidentally injured children (Smith and Hanson, 1975).

(4) Occasionally the problem may lie outside the family. For example, a child may be truanting from school because he has been placed in an inappropriate class and is failing academically, or we may discover that his form teacher has general classroom management difficulties. The child who is referred with behaviour problems from a residential setting may be symptomatic of a situation in which the staff are overworked and have management problems.

In the situations cited above the child's problem may be symptomatic or representative of other family or outside difficulties. However, in this text we are mainly concerned with the modification of deviant child behaviour which is considered to be the primary problem.

Selecting Initial Target Behaviours

In the majority of cases, parents complain of several problem behaviours. Selection of the initial target behaviours is partly determined by the following factors:

(1) Commonly assessment reveals that non-compliance (that is disobedience) is a problem although the parents may not have recognised it as such. For example, the parents may come to the clinic anxious to obtain help with their child's encopresis. Further investigation may reveal that the child is disobedient and has tantrums. A programme for managing the soiling requires the child to comply with parental instruction. Thus our first task in this (and in other similar cases) would be to increase compliance. Dealing with non-compliance can have far-reaching implications. Wahler and Nordquist (1973) found that a child's compliance related positively with the likelihood that he would imitate his parents. In this study the parents of the relatively disobedient children were taught how to use a simple punitive isolation procedure. No attempt was made to stress the importance of positive reinforcement for obedient behaviour. Interestingly, when the technique was put into operation and non-compliant behaviour reduced, the child exhibited a significant increase in the probability that he would imitate his parents.

(2) On some occasions it will be important for us to demonstrate early change, especially with parents who are anxious or doubtful about the programme. In these cases we focus on a narrow area of behaviour; for example, rather than concentrating on all disobedient behaviour we might at first deal with refusal to go to bed. The programme can be extended as the parents gain more skill and confidence. This approach is preferable to an initially over-expansive one which may fail and leave parents discouraged.

(3) Our objectives should be formulated before we change a behaviour. For example, John is referred for being disruptive in class; we could reduce his disruptive behaviour and yet have no effect on the amount of schoolwork he completes. In some instances treatment which focuses solely on increasing academic performance may not only achieve this aim but also be associated with a reduction in disruptive classroom behaviour. The reason is that while sustained schoolwork continues it is unlikely that disruptive classroom behaviour will occur, because the two behaviours are imcompatible. Similarly, in managing encopresis our objective should be the establishment of regular toileting. If we mistakenly set 'clean pants' as the objective we could create a further problem of constipation in the child (that is, by only rewarding clean pants and punishing dirty pants, the child might become constipated in an effort to remain clean). Occasionally, in altering one behaviour we may change a total situation and this change

is not always desirable. For example, we might alienate an adolescent from her peer group by altering her 'staying out late' behaviour. In treating Billy, a 6-year-old retarded child, we eventually focused on peer-directed aggression. Billy's mother was instructed to remove him from the play situation if he exhibited aggression. His peers, who seemed to find his company tiresome, quickly recognised the contingency and teased Billy in order to elicit aggression which precipitated his removal. Ideally, in this situation we should have focused on establishing Billy's play skills.

(4) When we discover that a child has learned and has since lost certain skills, such as appropriate toileting behaviour, we usually regard this problem as secondary. Our assessment should indicate some reasons for this lapse, for example recent parental marital problems. In this case it would be more appropriate to focus on the marital problem, although subsequent retraining of the child in toileting behaviour may be necessary. We would suspect any problem to be secondary if it has clearly emerged recently and if it entails deterioration in the child's behaviour, for example the re-emergence of tantrums or academic regression. If an assessment fails to reveal a precipitating factor it would seem permissible to focus initial intervention on the secondary problem. Often, during intervention, the precipitating factors may reveal themselves.

(5) It is well known now that some behaviours vary stably in relationship to each other; for example if several co-operative behaviours are exhibited by an individual, other co-operative behaviours have a high probability of occurring at the same time. Behaviours which vary in this manner are referred to as members of a common response class. While the response class concept has been well demonstrated, the potential of its therapeutic value has only recently received attention (Wahler, 1974; Kara, 1975). It is suggested that we may be able to modify problem behaviours in an indirect manner, by changing other behaviours which belong to the same response class. In other words we modify a behaviour which we have identified as varying stably with the target behaviour. For example, A and B are two behaviours which we think may belong to a common response class. If our hypothesis is correct, a modification of B (in terms of its frequency and intensity) should result in a change in A. The changes which occur in A (for example whether it increases or decreases) will of course depend on whether A and B co-vary directly or inversely. Wahler (1974) points to the possible utility of this method in the management of delinquent

behaviour. He has suggested that low rate delinquent behaviours (for example stealing, breaking and entering, truancy, etc.) might possibly belong to the same response class as high rate oppositional behaviours. If this is the case then successful intervention directed solely towards the high rate behaviours may indirectly be associated with a reduction in the low rate problems.

In working with delinquent children we often experience social pressure to focus initially on the low rate problems. These behaviours are notoriously difficult to treat. One major reason for this is that the reinforcers for such behaviours are relatively inaccessible. For example stealing may be reinforced by the peer group and many incidents go undetected (or the detection is delayed) because they occur outside the home. In managing high rate problems the opposite is true. We usually have direct access to the antecedents and consequences of these behaviours. Thus if Wahler's hypothesis is correct our task in managing the delinquent child who presents with both low and high rate problems may become slightly easier. During initial therapy this would entail ignoring the delinquent low rate behaviour occurring outside the home, while we focus our attention on the high rate home behaviour (for an example of this approach see case example in chapter 12). A successful focus on the problems occurring within the home should obviously be associated with an increase in parental effectiveness. Hopefully, this increase in parental effectiveness will serve to counterbalance the relative values of outside reinforcers for the child's low rate behaviours (for example, those supplied by the peer group).

Intensity and Duration of Intervention

The amount of time and effort which we invest in any case is decided by several factors:

(1) The nature of the therapy. Essentially, in behaviour therapy we are interested in changing behaviours which are readily observable and measurable. The changes are usually brought about by directively altering the parents' handling techniques. In establishing these parental skills it is often insufficient (except where parents efficiently and quickly grasp the principles or where the problems are minor in nature) to instruct parents on a weekly basis from the clinic setting. First, verbal instruction may not generalise to the practical situation—usually *in vivo* training using modelling and practice is required. Secondly, parents

who have just begun treatment often encounter some immediate difficulties which may not have been covered by the treatment instructions and practice. Any improvement or progress which has occurred can be lost if we do not resolve such difficulties immediately. For these reasons, intervention is ideally carried out in the home, initially on a daily basis. We suggest that successful outcome often depends on this level of treatment intensity.

(2) The agency restrictions. The average clinician cannot maintain this intense level of commitment to any family over an extended period. The duration of therapy therefore depends on agency restrictions and on other factors to be discussed below. If it is decided during assessment that long term maintenance may be necessary, we may have to enlist the help of another agency (for example, the Local Authority Social Services Department) in the follow-up stage of the intervention programme. As an alternative, Wahler and Erikson (1969) demonstrated that voluntary workers with no previous behavioural modification experience could be quickly trained to implement and maintain behaviour modification programmes with families. It is interesting to compare the time commitment reported by different authors. Patterson (1973) and Eyberg and Johnson (1974) (each with a research orientation), in treating behaviour problems, averaged respectively 30 hours and 12 hours per case. The authors have found an average time of 8 hours to be practical within their clinical commitment. Often the early sessions may last for 1–2 hours but thereafter visits to the home may only be for 15–20 minutes. Generally, active intervention would last no longer than 1 month, although some contact would be maintained with the family for 6–9 months. In the section on intervention we have detailed the time commitment in each case example.

(3) The nature of the problem and associated variables. By the time we reach the planning stage our knowledge of the parents, the child and his problem should give us some indication of the amount of time which will be required for our programme. On the basis of research observations Patterson (1973) has categorised parents into three types: (a) selective diffusion; (b) diffusion; (c) sado-masochistic.

With the first type of parent the problem seems to occur mainly between the parents and one particular child. This categorisation implies that the parents handle their other children normally and that they thus possess normal parenting skills. Provided motivation is present one could suggest that, in these cases, the intensity and extent of

72

therapy should be short, since it only involves strengthening skills already present. This is often the situation with children who are hyperactive (overactive and unable to sustain attention for very long) and behaviourally disordered. These children are frequently difficult to manage. Their overactivity and poor concentration often upsets the handling skills of even the most capable parents. George's case, which is reported in chapter 9, is a fairly typical example of the problems which these children can present. Our own experience is that cases which fall within this category often succeed within a short time.

In the second category we are faced with more widespread problems. Although one child only may be presented at the clinic, other children in the family usually have significant behaviour problems. The implication here is that the parents exhibit a relative deficiency in parenting skills—such deficits may also extend to areas of their general day-to-day management. Deficits of this magnitude suggest that our therapy, in addition to being intense, must also be applied over wider areas of family life and be maintained for longer periods, to ensure skill consolidation.

In the final category the problem centres not so much on each parent's child management skills, but on conflict between the parents about child management—in other words the child is exposed to a conflicting social learning situation. The inter-parent conflict usually reflects wider marital problems. Thus, as in the second category, we are again confronted with more widespread problems which have similar implications for the intensity and timespan of therapy. Further implications of widespread problems are discussed in chapter 14.

The duration of the behaviour problems will also affect the amount of time required. For instance, if non-compliance has been present for 6 or 7 years it will probably prove difficult to modify. Generally the behaviours of younger children are more readily changed than those of older children. Many of the reinforcers for older children lie in the outside environment (quite simply because they spend more time away from home than the very young child). Thus with the older child, whose problems have been present for a longer duration and whose social behaviours are relatively more complex in terms of their reinforcers being widely spread, we are often faced with longer therapy which requires considerable ingenuity.

Children presenting with conduct problems generally have a poorer outcome (and are more resistant to therapy) than those exhibiting neurotic symptoms (Robins, 1966). (Neurotic disorders are typified by behaviours such as refusal to separate, dependency, school-refusal, phobias, psychosomatic symptoms, etc.) This would seem to indicate that more intensive efforts should be concentrated on children exhibiting conduct problems. When confronted with 'diffusion' parents (in Patterson's sense) who present at the clinic with an 11-year-old conduct disordered child, often the only hope of achieving any success (if this is ever feasible) would be a massive and long term intervention programme which involves several professionals working in liaison, on a daily basis, over a number of years (Patterson, 1975).

(4) Pressure from other agencies. Robins (1966) suggests that court appearances may be detrimental to a child's future. Once a child has been labelled as 'a trouble maker', society often continues to see him as deviant and thus fails to make allowances for any behavioural improvements. This point was effectively demonstrated in the Wahler and Leske (1973) study reported in chapter 3. Similarly, expulsion from school may result in difficulties in the child's future placements. In view of these points we will often attempt to increase interventional intensity in the hope that imminent authoritative action can be avoided.

Occasionally other agencies will request the admission of a child to an in-patient unit for treatment. While it is often possible to modify a child's behaviour within such a setting (Phillips *et al.*, 1971), maintenance of change or generalisation rarely occurs when the child is returned to his natural environment (Wahler, Berland and Leske, 1975). This is due to the fact that the parents have not learned (or have failed to learn) those techniques which the residential staff have found to be effective. Admission of the child may ultimately result in extra work and cost, since we must eventually attempt to train the parents in managing the problem. However, in terms of the amount of work required, the in-patient setting has several valuable assets:

(a) With severe behaviour problems a short in-patient spell may serve to defuse an inflammatory home situation. During this time some preliminary work might be carried out with the parents.

(b) Again, in severe situations or where circumstances do not permit an efficient home programme (for example an unco-operative, interfering grandmother or where the family's distance from the clinic makes intensive home intervention impractical), admission of one parent and the child for treatment may prove to be the most efficient course of action. Alternatively, if the problem is one which is difficult to deal with at an out-patient level, admission of the parent and child may also be indicated. For example if a child presents with a night-time behavioural

74

problem, management may be more efficient where there is 24-hour staff cover.

It is our experience that programmes operated at an in-patient level will only work effectively if there is complete staff unison in the efforts to train the parents. Successful treatments of this type must be followed up carefully after discharge since the effects, even when the family is included, may not necessarily generalise to the home setting (Sajwaj, 1973).

(c) One weakness of home intervention programmes is that it is difficult to work with children who have peer interactional problems—access to the peer group is usually not feasible except perhaps in the school setting. It is important to note that a feature common to children referred to psychiatric clinics is that they often have peer interactional difficulties (Rutter, Tizard and Whitmore, 1970). Programmes to improve such skills are possible in the in-patient setting where there is easy access to other children of a similar age.

Specific Considerations with Regard to the Child

Our assessment of the child and his capabilities will aid us in planning the intervention programme.

(1) At what level should we start? This will mainly depend on the level of the child's prosocial skills. Before setting up contingencies for failure to do homework we must ensure that the child has the amount of concentration required for this sustained effort. If the child lacks this ability we may have to develop it by implementing a programme which progressively rewards increased amounts of sustained effort. We may initially reward him for only doing part of the assignment, rather than immediately establishing consequences which depend on the completed work assignment. Similarly, it would be insufficient to punish a child for coercive verbal demands without ensuring that he has the appropriate repertoire of approach and asking skills. One method of overcoming this is to rehearse the situation with the child so that when he then asks appropriately he is granted his original request. Later, selected rewards and punishments can be instigated in conjunction with continued practice of the appropriate behaviour.

If we discover that a child is not amenable to social reinforcement we may have to teach responsiveness by a shaping process. Initially, the child is materially rewarded for the target response, but each material

75

reward is preceded by social approval. Gradually, as the child responds to praise, we withdraw the material reward.

(2) For what level should we aim? Our assessment will have revealed any physical or mental limitations which the child may have. Children who are hyperactive and exhibit high rate coercive behaviour may not initially be amenable to psychological testing. In these cases we would set up a programme to reduce the high rate behaviours before arranging to have the child retested. It is then possible to gauge the child's capabilities more realistically. For example, with a child who is refusing to go to school it would be a waste of time to set up a programme designed to ensure his school attendance, before we assessed whether this particular educational setting is the most appropriate.

(3) How much should the child be involved in intervention? We have already stated that children with normal intellectual development may be taking observations from approximately the age of 7. These observations would be considered during our planning. For example, we cannot hope to use pocket money as a positive reinforcer if the child has realistically complained that the amount is inadequate. Our first step, therefore, would be to arrange for parents and child to agree on an appropriate amount of pocket money. Similar bargaining might take place over bedtime or coming-home time. Obviously more weight is given to the child's involvement as he gets older and gains more sophistication. From early adolescence we must look to the child himself as an agent of change. He is gradually establishing major reinforcers outside the family and the overall value of family reinforcers is relatively less. In these situations intervention plans should more often be geared towards self-control or self-treatment procedures.

(4) Which techniques should be employed? This decision is mainly dependent on what we said in the foregoing paragraphs; that is, on the child's present abilities, his potential and on his capacity for involvement in the programme. We have artificially divided the techniques into three groupings, which become increasingly more sophisticated. These techniques are not mutually exclusive and may be used in varying combinations. The first technique is the use of differential attention and 'time-out', which is a simple punishment isolation procedure. This is most commonly employed with children under the age of 7. The second technique is the use of a points system. This is generally employed with children between the ages of 7 and 12 and is often combined with the use of time-out. Thirdly, contingency-contracting, which involves the use of parent – child bargaining, is

employed with children in the age range of 10 upwards. The practical implementation of these techniques will be discussed in part III.

Specific Considerations with Regard to the Parents

Our assessment of the parents and their capacity will assist us in planning the intervention programme.

(1) Consideration of the parental understanding of the problem is important. In many cases we can anticipate that parents will either exhibit feelings of guilt or else they will have a rationalised explanation for the current problem. Common rationalisations are 'genetic' (for example, the divorced mother who says, 'Tom is just like his father', or the adoptive parents who believe that their child has 'bad blood'). Other rationalisations may involve causal explanations (for example, the child's deviant behaviour only started after a recent road accident, or the child is asthmatic and should never be disappointed). In the early stages of behaviour therapy it is not expedient to engage in long discussions with parents as to the origins of the problem. Such discussions do little to resolve the difficulties which are now present. Following assessment, we outline the problem to the parents in behavioural terms so that they can understand the rationale of the treatment which they will be implementing. The emphasis is on the present situation and on future plans. We impress on parents that the intervention procedure should provide a set of skills which will facilitate their future handling of the child. Usually, we hope, parental attitudes will modify as the programme progresses.

(2) What are the parental expectations of the therapy being offered? As with assessment we explain to parents how much of their time and effort we judge will be involved in the intervention programme. It is made clear to parents that they are not handing the problem over to us. They are viewed as the principal agents of change, and success mainly depends upon their commitment. With a particularly difficult problem this may in some cases entail either or both parents taking leave from work, so that a concentrated programme can be developed. Having explained to parents our expectations of them in the treatment, we ascertain what they expect from us. In many cases the child's capabilities may be relevant. For example, we should ensure that parents do not expect us to improve intellectual functioning in a retarded child. Other parents may simply expect us to reinforce their

own methods of child-rearing. For example, we may have to indicate that we do not regard it as appropriate to expect a 14-year-old girl to be home by nine o'clock every night.

(3) Parental attitudes to the method often require attention before proceeding. Occasionally parents view our techniques as mechanistic, superficial, punitive, directive and involving the use of bribery. Initially parents feel self-conscious and mechanistic when they have to consistently follow a set of programme instructions. These procedures will seem unnatural for two reasons. First, the parents will be asked to apply behavioural consequences which they have failed to apply in the past. These new behaviours may thus feel somewhat contrived. Secondly, in the early stages of the programme the numbers of rewards and punishments will be more frequent and consistent than those used by parents in normal situations. However, with practice and subsequent success this operational method feels less contrived and becomes more or less automatic.

We agree with parents who state that the method only deals with overt behaviours. However, we can indicate the link between behavioural and attitudinal (and therefore emotional) change. Once the problem is alleviated and prosocial behaviours are established, parents can phase out the programme. Confident in the knowledge of their new skills, parents may become more relaxed with the child than they were prior to intervention. Occasionally parents view the use of rewards (social or material) as bribery. It may be stated, for example, that it is the child's duty to hang up his coat and that he should not require a reward (even praise) for doing so. Other parents feel so negative towards the child that they express difficulty in reinforcing him at all. In these cases we may have to use material rewards until the behaviour improves sufficiently for the parent to feel more positive and then be able to supply social approval in a relaxed manner. It is explained to parents that prosocial skills are not innate—they have to be learned and, in order to be sustained, they require some reinforcement.

On occasions, parental attitudes to the method have been persistently negative and in these cases we have judged it impossible to run a successful programme. One father who had previously refused to employ the methods because he saw them in terms of bribery, changed his attitudes after seeing a television programme about behaviour modification. Parents who have moral qualms about the method may benefit either from meeting other parents currently engaged in treatment or else from exposure to visual material relating to past cases.

78

(4) As parents will be managing the treatment, success will be based partly on their capabilities and on the methods which we use to teach them the techniques.

First, the intervention techniques should be geared to their capabilities. For example, a mother of below average intelligence who has poor child handling skills, may be incapable of handling a points system which involves both the rewarding and removing of points and also the later exchange of points for privileges. We have found, more often than not, that we have tended to make treatments too elaborate, especially when points systems are being employed.

Secondly, the amount and length of supervision required depends initially on the parents' ability to grasp the principles as they are applied to a single problem behaviour and, later, on their ability to adapt the techniques for use with other behaviours. We have found on several occasions that anxious parents have difficulties with this latter point. In some cases prolonged supervision has been effective in increasing the parents' generalised use of the techniques, while in other cases relaxation techniques (which were taught to the anxious parent) have helped.

Thirdly, the type of supervision is important. When parents are highly motivated and we are dealing with a simple problem, verbal instruction may be sufficient. However, when managing frequent oppositional problems the additional use of role-playing and modelling will often greatly facilitate the treatment speed. Both Gardner (1972) and Nay (1975) have demonstrated that role-playing and modelling are very important components in teaching the required skills. Parent training manuals are very much in vogue, although Patterson (1973) has demonstrated that these alone are ineffective unless they are combined with some of the methods suggested above. The authors have found manuals to be helpful either in the training of new therapists or exceptional parents. A list of some manuals is provided in appendix A.

Other Significant People

In planning the intervention programme we may have to consider people other than the parents or the child.

(1) The success of the programme may depend on the co-operation or involvement of other adults who have frequent contact with the child. For example, grandmothers or single mothers' men friends.

Overlooking these adults may cause resentment and therefore result in direct sabotage—such as grandmother removing the child from time-out (an isolation procedure) or father not punishing behaviours which mother is punishing. At the least, ignoring other adults may damage the programme simply because of some misunderstanding on their part. For example, grandmother may continue to provide pocket money non-contingently and thus cause a 'reinforcement leak'.

In a residential setting it is particularly important to involve all members of staff. The literature on the use of points systems in institutional settings demonstrates the necessity for total staff involvement in the methods. There are also advantages in having more than one adult involved in the programme. Two people can discuss the management of difficult behaviours and they can monitor each other's responses. Ideally, we would attempt to build this monitoring into the programme in the form of contracting between the adults; for example, mother is fined by father when she fails to identify and reward her daughter's obedience.

(2) It appears more equitable also to involve siblings in the programme, who are of an appropriate age to the referred child. This usually eliminates any feeling of unfairness. The implementation of the programme will not greatly affect the sibling unless he is relatively deviant—which is often the case. Siblings of a disparate age to the referred child (for example, 4 years older) are not usually subject to the programme. This is because they would perhaps not respond to similar contingencies. Nevertheless, we must ensure that they have some understanding of the treatment and will co-operate during its implementation.

Older siblings may have strong negative feelings towards the programme, especially in situations where punishment occurs frequently in the early stages. We would try to dissipate this feeling by explaining our objectives and asking the sibling to aid us. He is told that he can help the deviant child to escape punishment (by encouraging and modelling for him prosocial skills). Occasionally, we have encountered siblings who refuse to accept that the referred child is deviant—this despite the fact that both our observations and parent observations demonstrate deviance. As these siblings do not accept the need for intervention we cannot expect them to be involved in the programme. The situation may become unmanageable if the sibling actually hinders the parents in carrying out the programme. In this case we could ask him to take his own observations on the target behaviours of the deviant child. If, following discussion of these observations, he continues to hinder the parents we may have to introduce a short period of separation. This may entail admitting the deviant child and one parent to an in-patient unit or sending the sibling to stay with a relative for a few days, until the gross behaviours of the referred child have settled. When a sibling can be so disruptive to a programme we must assess whether we should instigate a separate programme for him. In less extreme cases, following intervention with one child, parents often notice an improvement in the behaviour of their other children.

Key Ideas

General
Behaviour therapy, to be maximally effective, initially requires intense and active intervention, preferably in the home setting. In many cases this intensive, short term programme will be sufficient for the family to sustain improvement. In other cases we have to make realistic provision for long term maintenance.

Specific
In order for an intervention programme to be successful the parents of the referred child have to accept, and be capable of implementing, the plans. In selecting target behaviours, consideration should be given to several points:

(1) In the authors' experience the majority of cases demonstrate a degree of non-compliance, which must first be handled.

(2) A useful rule is to select a limited area for initial behaviour change and then to expand this if intervention succeeds.

(3) It is advisable to concentrate on behaviours for which we have access to the antecedents and consequences (that is, behaviours which occur in the home or in the school).

(4) It should never be a therapist's goal merely to deplete the child's behavioural repertoire. Simply removing a deviant behaviour does not automatically ensure that the child will acquire the incompatible prosocial skills. Ideally, we should plan to teach him these skills by shaping, modelling and practice.

8

Theoretical Considerations in Planning

The theoretical aspects of behaviour modification have not been emphasised in this text. Nevertheless the therapist requires a working knowledge of the major concepts underlying each of the treatment techniques. For example, the use of differential attention (that is, praise appropriate behaviours and ignore inappropriate behaviours) will only be successful if adult attention functions as a reward for social behaviours. Thus before applying any technique described in this text the therapist has to understand the basic theoretical principles involved in behaviour change. This chapter therefore includes discussions on stimulus control, punishment and reinforcement, extinction and the concept of generalisation.

Stimulus Control

In the classroom most children behave predictably. They exhibit a high level of work and attention and a low level of disruption. They have learned to discriminate that certain stimulus situations suggest particular actions. For instance, being in the classroom, the presence of a particular teacher giving an instruction and the sight of other children at their desks are all stimuli which are associated with a probability that the child will sit down and start to work. Similarly the deviant child's behaviours are under stimulus control. For example, being in a sweet shop, mother refusing to buy sweets and the experience that mother is less likely to punish in public may all be important stimuli associated with a high probability of tantrums. During the development of a tantrum the early interactional behaviours between the child and parent will predict whether or not the tantrum will terminate or escalate. For instance, if the parent's early behaviour is inconsistent or ineffective the child may escalate his behaviour because he knows (and this knowledge functions as a stimulus) that under such circumstances his tantrum is likely to be successful. All of the above stimuli (apart from the cognitive ones) are easily observed. Researchers such as Patterson (1973) have shown that seemingly innocuous stimuli, such as room size and number of people present, may be associated with an increased probability that a deviant behaviour will occur. Although the average therapist has insufficient time to conduct such a detailed stimulus analysis, he should never overlook the importance of altering the stimuli associated with deviant behaviour. In most instances this will involve changing parental behaviour; for example we might strengthen their commanding style.

Behaviour results from the interaction of both external and internal stimuli. These latter stimuli, which include emotions, cognitions and perceptions, cannot usually be directly observed by the therapist but they can be described in detail by the client, or else inferred from his actions. For example, if he is anxious he might sweat or complain of a headache. In therapy it is important that intense emotions are recognised since they are often associated with less effective behavioural performance. For example, the very anxious mother may have great difficulty in applying time-out. Apart from ensuring that our treatment programme is simple and clear, other more direct methods can be used to manage inhibitory internal stimuli. The major component of these treatment approaches involves teaching the parents to recognise the early stimuli associated with excessive emotions which cause them to behave ineffectually. As a first stage we might ask the parent to describe the situational, somatic, cognitive and emotive stimuli associated with their ineffective behaviour. In other words we are outlining the precipitating events, describing how the situation was perceived and what thoughts, feelings and bodily sensations occurred. Once these early stimuli have been recognised then it is much easier to plan effective treatment. Such a plan might involve asking the parents to keep self-records as well as training them in a relevant technique such as relaxation. Methods used in self-treatment (or self-control) are discussed in detail in a text by Watson and Tharp (1972).

Behaviour therapists have tended to neglect the importance of stimulus control and instead concentrate their efforts on the consequences of deviant behaviour. This approach is often successful because usually the major problem lies between the adult and the child. However, the success is partly dependent on stimulus changes which may occur indirectly. For example, when an adult begins to use punishment and reward more effectively the child's behaviour will change, not only because the behavioural consequences have altered but also because there has been a change in stimulus control. The child learns that in the adult's presence he must now exhibit different behaviours. In other words the adult's presence has come to represent a different stimulus situation.

Alteration of the predicting stimuli is not in itself sufficient to produce and maintain change. Reward and punishment are also usually required. For example, altering classroom rules, teacher's verbal styles and children's seating positions may have an initial improving effect. However, unless contingencies of reward and punishment are implemented, such changes will not necessarily persist.

Punishment and Reinforcement

DEFINITIONS

Punishment. Any stimulus or event which will result in the suppression of a behaviour, when it is made consequent on that behaviour, is known as a 'punisher'. Punishment can take two forms: (*a*) the application of aversive stimuli or (*b*) the removal of reinforcers. The application of aversive stimuli tends in practice to refer to physical punishment. The removal of reinforcers includes the removal of attention, loss of privileges or the implementation of time-out. Time-out is an abbreviation of the phrase 'time-out from positive reinforcement'. It signifies a cessation of all available reinforcers, usually for a short duration. When applied to the child this usually involves his removal to a corner or to his bedroom, where all available reinforcers (such as adult attention, his toys, television and peer attention) are unavailable. In contrast, when we remove privileges we are only eliminating specific reinforcers (such as loss of pocket money).

Reinforcement. For the purpose of definition, reinforcers can be divided into two categories:

(1) A positive reinforcer (synonymously referred to as a reward) is any stimulus which increases the probability that the child's preceding behaviour will recur. For example, if Jack is given pocket money when he finishes his house chores there is an increased chance that he will carry out these chores in the future, since this specific behaviour results

in reward. Generally we use reinforcement in three forms: material, social and privilege rewards.

(2) A negative reinforcer is any stimulus (usually aversive) which increases the probability that the behaviour which resulted in its removal or termination will recur. In other words the aversive stimulus is escaped or avoided. For example, each evening when bedtime comes, Ian refuses to go to bed and starts screaming. Frequently his parents, unable to manage or tolerate his screaming behaviour, allow him to stay up late. In this situation the stimuli associated with going to bed (that is the time, putting on pyjamas, brushing teeth, etc.) can be viewed as negatively reinforcing stimuli—Ian avoids them by screaming. Similarly the screaming is aversive to the parents and their avoidance behaviour, which is 'giving in', is reinforced. In this example it is probable that, following the screaming, Ian becomes involved in rewarding activities such as watching television, playing with his toys, etc. One can observe that the situation is 'double-edged'. The screaming resulted in avoidance of bedtime and gained access to rewarding activities. Further examination of many child—parent coercive situations will reveal both positive and negative reinforcement in operation at the same time.

It is important to recognise that aversive stimuli may result in either suppression of behaviour (that is, punishment) or the development of escape and avoidance behaviours (that is, negative reinforcement). These consequences are different, and therefore the terms 'punishment' and 'negative reinforcement' should not be confused. The effective use of punishment and reward depends upon a number of variables:

INTENSITY

Punishment. Intense punishment is more effective than mild punishment but the former is often associated with undesirable side effects. These include: the generalisation (or spread) of suppressive effects to other behaviours (for example, a child who has been exposed to severe and inconsistent punishment will often appear timid and unassertive); excessive emotional side effects (such as anxiety, fear, hostility and pain-elicited aggression); escape and avoidance behaviours may be generated (for example, a child may learn to skilfully lie his way out of punishment); modelling of the behaviour of the punisher may occur; and lastly it has been suggested that the person who punishes may become aversive to the punished child and thus lose his potential as a supplier of positive reinforcements.

While Azrin and Holz (1966) have indicated these adverse side effects of punishment, some recent literature has suggested that punishment can have an important role in the management of child problems. For instance, Taplin's (1974) analysis of Patterson's work with disruptive children, tends to suggest that time-out was an extremely effective component of the treatment. Further, we have already quoted the Wahler and Nordquist (1973) study in which it was found that time-out enhanced rather than lowered parental value as a positive reinforcer. In other cases, authors have reported that very intense forms of punishment were required in order to eliminate successfully some disruptive behaviours. For instance, Risley (1968) found that the only way he could reduce the dangerous climbing behaviour of a 6-year-old brain-damaged child was by the use of electric shock. Lovaas, Schaeffer and Simmons (1965) found, when teaching social skills to autistic children, that electric shock was essential in reducing some of the children's disruptive behaviours.

When punishment is to be used in therapy we should attempt to strike a balance and employ those techniques which are most efficient without producing side effects. For instance, the withdrawal of social attention has fewer side effects than does the use of physical punishment or time-out. However, there is little point in using the former punishment with a socially unresponsive child to whom adult attention is not reinforcing. In each individual case it is essential to examine the past punishment history and, on balance, select that punishment which we assess will be most effective.

We have found that the removal of reinforcers is normally more effective than physical punishment. First, the removal of reinforcers is associated with fewer emotional side effects (such as fear or anxiety). Secondly, we often find that it provides a successful and alternative method to parents who have previously employed physical punishment either inappropriately or without success. It is not uncommon to observe deviant children whose behaviour is unaffected by, or which even escalates because of, physical punishment. In these circumstances we might observe that the parents' initial punishments are weak and therefore ineffective. As they become more angry they may increase the level of punishment, but as the child becomes more upset he simultaneously increases his tolerance level and gradually habituates to physical punishment. In animal research Church (1969) has shown that pigeons will continue to respond normally following extremely intense punishments, provided that the punishment intensity has only been gradually increased over a period of time. Thirdly, there are obvious practical advantages to the use of time-out. It allows parents and child time to 'cool off', and also results in the child's removal from any source of reinforcement for his deviant behaviour (for example, parental attention). These advantages are discussed further in chapter 9.

Reward. As with punishment intense rewards are more effective than mild ones. Generally the rate of occurrence of a desired behaviour will be related to the magnitude of reinforcers which are consequent on that behaviour. Rewards of low intensity are simply not worth working for. For example, in considering social reinforcement it is often insufficient for parents to reward behaviour by merely saying 'good'. In most cases, and especially when new social behaviours are being established, more attention will be required. At the other extreme, when rewards of very high intensity are frequently used they may lose their potency. For instance, if desired child behaviours are frequently rewarded with large numbers of sweets it is possible that the sweets may lose their value as reinforcers. In some instances they may even become aversive. Such an effect is termed satiation, and it has been used as a therapeutic technique which is mainly reported in literature referring to adult problems. For instance, in the treatment of gamblers or transvestites (persons who dress in the clothes of the opposite sex), continued and prolonged exposure to the reinforcers for their behaviours may eventually result in the extinction of these behaviours. In the case of the transvestite this exposure would include providing him with unprohibited access to female clothing, and having him repeatedly and intensely carry out his cross-dressing behaviour.

CONTINGENCY AND CONSISTENCY

A contingency is a rule which stipulates that certain consequences (either of reward or of punishment) will be applied following the emission of designated behaviours. For example, John has a tantrum and his mother sends him to his room for 10 minutes—in other words the punishment is contingent on his tantrum. In a behaviour modification programme deviant behaviours should always be followed by punishment; however (for reasons which are discussed below), it is sometimes expedient that 'good' behaviour is not always reinforced. In this case the contingency will state how often good behaviour is to be rewarded (that is, it will lay down a reinforcement schedule). For example, John will be rewarded on every third occasion of compliance. Consistency in behavioural terms means the consistent use of the contingent principle, as when every time John has a tantrum his mother sends him to his room for 10 minutes.

Punishment. To have its optimal suppressive effect, punishment must be consistently applied following each episode of deviant behaviour. The less the frequency of this relationship the less suppressive will be the effect of punishment. It is an easy matter to observe that even the best parents are incapable of applying punishment to every occurrence of a specific behaviour, on a one-to-one basis. Even if this were possible it is not desirable. Hopefully a few punishments will invoke in the child a self-control response. In the future he may be less likely to adopt that behaviour because he knows it to be a punishable offence, and this in turn may elicit emotion which inhibits transgression. However, in the initial management of deviant behaviours which have been reinforced in the past it is important to ensure that punishment (where it is used) follows all episodes of the behaviour. Punishment which is non-contingent, or relates to behaviour only on a random basis, has more general suppressive effects on behaviour. Punishment of this type is less predictable and may result in excessive emotionality and behavioural helplessness. For example, a child who is not recognised as being retarded may be punished repeatedly for academic failure. When he tries to achieve results this is not recognised because his efforts are less successful than those of normal children. Consequently, because he has no control over his punishment he may become anxious and feel helpless. The use of non-contingent punishment is common in deviant families.

Reward. Continuous reinforcement is useful when establishing a new behaviour, but once it has been established then intermittent reinforcement is more effective in maintaining the behaviour at maximum strength. For example, in teaching a child to say 'thank you' we might at first praise each response. Later, when the response has been established, we would only praise it occasionally. The large majority of social behaviours (including the example just given) are maintained on intermittent reinforcement. The reasons for the strength of intermittently rewarded behaviour include the following. First, the occurrence of the reinforcer is not totally predictable and thus sustained effort is required to gain its access. Secondly, because the reinforcer is occurring infrequently it will maintain its incentive value. In establishing new social behaviours a most crucial question is, what should the ultimate frequency of reinforcement be? If reinforcements are too infrequent then the effort required to obtain them may not be worth while. Similarly, if the reinforcers are too frequent then the behaviour may not occur at a maximally sustained rate. For example, if a child is rewarded with a bag of sweets every time he washes the dishes it is likely that he might tire of sweets with a resulting decline in the frequency of dishwashing.

If children have been habitually exposed to non-contingent reward prior to the programme (that is, reward unconnected with their behaviour), they may later fail to recognise the causal link between prosocial behaviour and reward. This may be one of the reasons why reinforcement does not always seem to be an effective means of changing behaviour (see chapter 14).

TIMING

Generally, the sooner a punishment follows a behaviour the more effective it will be in suppressing that behaviour. Similarly, the sooner a reward follows a behaviour the more effective it will be in increasing that behaviour. However, in social circumstances this contingency does not always occur. For instance, reward does not always immediately follow a successful examination. In order that punishments and rewards should remain effective, some link or signal may be required between the occurrence of the behaviour and its eventual consequence. Broadly, these links are provided in two ways:

(1) External signals. For example, by doing chores a child may earn extra pocket money. Money has no inherent reinforcement value but it affords access to those things which we enjoy (for example, a child may buy sweets, toys, etc.). Thus in this case, money provides the link between the event and long term reinforcement.

(2) Internal signals. As we grow older we learn to evaluate our behaviour in terms of its future consequences. When an obese person begins a diet the ultimate reinforcer will be loss of weight. During the early stages of the diet, the knowledge that remaining on the diet will achieve this goal provides an internal reinforcement link between his current behaviour and its ultimate goal. Of course this knowledge, as everyone knows, is often insufficiently motivating. When this type of internal monitoring is effective we are exerting self-control.

In planning therapy we must assess whether immediate reinforcement will be required or whether delayed reinforcements can be employed. Generally, with younger children, retarded children and highly coercive children (who commonly have gained instantaneous gratification in the past), more immediate rewards are required. If we are working with an older child who lacks self-control, our programme should consider correcting this as well as directly reducing deviance and increasing prosocial behaviours. A useful working example of this process in operation is seen in the social skills therapy provided for delinquent children at Achievement Place (Phillips *et al.*, 1971). On entrance to Achievement Place the child earns or loses points which can be exchanged, initially on a daily basis, for privileges. As the behaviour improves he moves to earning and losing points which can be exchanged on a weekly basis. Eventually he moves off the points system altogether, although if his behaviour deteriorates he can drop back a level if required. In other words, as the child improves it is hoped that he will learn to evaluate his behaviour in terms of long range consequences.

Extinction

When the positive reinforcers for a behaviour are removed then that behaviour will gradually disappear or, in behavioural terms, extinguish. Initially, after the removal of reinforcers, there is often a temporary increase in the frequency of the behaviour, followed by a gradual and continued decrease in the rate. At a later time there may be small temporary reappearances of the behaviour. However, provided the reinforcers remain unavailable the behaviour will eventually disappear altogether. The time required for the extinction to become complete depends on the following factors:

(1) The completeness of reinforcer removal. In an experimental situation it is usually possible to completely prevent reinforcement but in social situations this is seldom possible. For instance, the reduction of adult attention for tantrums can never be complete. Because of this, extinction in social circumstances will tend to be relatively slower than in the experimental situation.

(2) The reinforcement history of the behaviour. If a behaviour has in the past been continuously reinforced then extinction will occur rapidly. If in the past it has only been intermittently reinforced then extinction tends to be slow. The main reason for this difference in speed lies in the fact that it is much easier for the child to recognise that reinforcement has disappeared, when the behaviour was previously continuously reinforced.

In clinical practice it is inadvisable to use extinction as the sole means of reducing deviant behaviour. First, extinguished behaviour will reappear rapidly if its reinforcers become reavailable. This is more likely to occur if a suitable adaptive behaviour is not provided as an alternative to the deviant behaviour. Secondly, the extinction of intermittently reinforced social behaviour tends to be a rather slow process. As we have already noted we often do not have the necessary control over social reinforcers to make extinction a totally effective technique. Thus, in therapy the extinction of deviant behaviour is usually combined with other techniques, the most important of which is the reinforcement of an alternative adaptive behaviour. Progress can be enhanced if this behaviour is incompatible with the occurrence of the deviant behaviour. For example, it is unlikely that a child will be both obedient and disobedient at the same time; alternatively, he is unlikely to exhibit sustained school work and disruptive classroom behaviour simultanously. The most important quality of the incompatible behaviour should be that it is a social skill. Deviant or coercive children's social repertoires tend to be stereotyped and narrow (Moore, 1975). For this reason we should resist the temptation to reinforce the child merely for non-occurrence of the deviant response; for example, rather than rewarding him for a time span of not shouting at mother we might reward him for speaking appropriately to mother. The development of incompatible behaviour should theoretically preclude the occurrence of symptom substitution.

In addition to extinguishing deviant behaviours by removing their reinforcers and replacing them with incompatible prosocial skills, we frequently punish the deviant behaviours because punishment usually speeds up extinction.

The extinction of inappropriate avoidance behaviours (for example, a dog fear or phobia) presents a different problem. Commonly the emotions such as anxiety or fear, which motivate the avoidance, prevent the subject from coming into contact with the phobic situation or object. While this persists, extinction of the fear responses is impossible. The therapeutic approaches used to manage this problem include:

(1) Flooding or implosion—that is, forced or prolonged exposure to the phobic stimulus.

(2) Graduated extinction—that is, gradual exposure to the feared stimulus. Using this latter technique a child who is dog phobic might be treated in the following way. We discover from the child what, in relation to dogs, makes him least anxious. This might include items such

as thinking about dogs or seeing a picture of a dog. From here, with the child's help we construct a hierarchy of about 10 steps which involve a gradual approach to the phobic object. When this is constructed the child is asked to carry out each step until he can successfully achieve this without anxiety. Eventually, we hope that he will be able to play with the dog. When relaxation training is used to assist this graduated approach we refer to the technique as desensitisation (Wolpe and Lazarus, 1966).

Generalisation

This is an important principle in behavioural change. If we change a behaviour and we note (*a*) that this behavioural change transfers to other settings or (*b*) that related behaviours exhibit similar change, then we can state that generalisation has occurred. For instance, the child may be deviant in the school as well as in the home. We hope that in changing the child's behaviour in the home we will also be positively affecting his school behaviour. However, generalisation across settings does not often occur (Wahler, 1969). Even within the home the child's behaviour may change with the mother but not with the father, especially if he has not been actively involved in the programme. Non-generalisation across settings may be partly due to the fact that the consequences for the child's behaviour vary across settings, and partly to the fact that the child is not yet controlling his own behaviours. The importance of self-control has already been mentioned in this chapter. Its relevance in deviant children is discussed in chapter 14.

A problem which has not been widely discussed in the literature is the parents' inability to generalise the techniques of behavioural change either across settings or from target behaviour to other behaviours. For example, a mother may learn how to cope with tantrums at home and yet be helpless when these occur in a shop. Again, we may teach parents techniques for successfully dealing with verbal abusiveness and yet they may be unable to use this knowledge constructively when the child refuses to eat his meal. The authors have found that parents who are low in self-esteem or over-anxious are especially prone to this problem of non-generalisation of learning.

Key Ideas

Behaviour therapy is a methodology—it is a disciplined system which conforms to a number of theoretical rules governing behaviour change. In practising behaviour therapy within this system we may use a number of techniques or procedures (such as time-out) which have been developed by behaviour therapists but which are not necessarily their exclusive prerogative. The authors believe that it is limiting, and possibly harmful, to apply these techniques randomly without understanding the theoretical concepts of the wider behavioural model.

PART III

INTERVENTION

9

Simple Contingency Management

In chapter 7 we outlined three general techniques which can be employed to modify child behaviour problems. The first of these is simple contingency management, which is commonly used with younger children who exhibit high rate behaviour problems such as non-compliance, tantrums and/or physical and verbal abusiveness. The term 'simple contingency management' refers to an intervention approach typified by the use of rewards and punishments which are both immediate and simple. The rewards are either social or material, and the punishment is either the withdrawal of attention or the application of an isolation procedure known as time-out. In this chapter we shall discuss each of the therapeutic procedures and then describe the practical implementation of the programme.

Reward

Prior to intervention we shall have selected deviant behaviours on which to focus. However, the elimination of deviant behaviour is not the complete goal of the programme. We also aim to shape up or reinforce prosocial skills in the child and to give him an increased repertoire of appropriate behaviours. Rewarding behaviours which are incompatible with the deviant behaviour is therefore an important part of the programme.

MATERIAL REWARDS
During assessment we ascertain whether material reinforcers (such as sweets, toys or pocket money) are required rather than social reinforcers (such as praise or cuddles). This occurs in two main circumstances. First, when parents have difficulty in praising the child, either because

they feel so negative towards him or because they lack the skills. As has been stated previously we expect negative parental attitudes towards the child to become more positive when change in the child's behaviour has been demonstrated through treatment. By this stage parents may feel more able and willing to praise and hug their child and material rewards can be reduced to normal levels. Parents who lack the appropriate skills of administering social reward must first use material reward. In the meantime we can teach them to praise effectively as outlined below, with the use of role-play and cueing during observation sessions. Secondly, we may initially require continuous material reinforcement when the child appears to be unresponsive to social reinforcement. In these circumstances material reward is preceded by a social reinforcer, so that a link is established between material and social reinforcement. Ultimately, as behaviour improves and social approval becomes effective, we eliminate some of the material rewards. Generally one material reward is given for every two to three social rewards.

During the programme we must ensure that material rewards fulfil the requirements of timing and contingency which we discussed in the previous section. Often, parents supply the reward some hours after the behaviour has occurred, mainly because it was not available at the time. For example, mother may say, 'That was very good, John, to ask to use the toilet. When we do the shopping tomorrow, I'll buy you some sweets.' In treatment we do not always supply the child with extra presents, sweets or money, but we often simply restructure regularly occurring material rewards (for example, pocket money or the weekly trip to the cinema) so that they follow 'good' behaviour. During treatment we would only increase the frequency of material rewards beyond the pre-intervention level if we had assessed that the child was being under-rewarded; for example, if his pocket money was significantly less than that of his peers.

SOCIAL REWARDS
In teaching parents to praise effectively we again stress the importance of timing, contingency and content of the praise. Social reinforcement should immediately follow the desired child behaviour. It should contain both a clear verbal and a non-verbal component. The verbal component will indicate the adult's pleasure, for example, 'That's good, I'm delighted', and should also contain an explicit reason for the praise, for example, 'I'm very pleased with you because you tidied your clothes away neatly'.

Parental facial expression and verbal tone should also indicate pleasure; for example, the phrases quoted above would not sound convincing if they were delivered in a monotone, associated with a general posture of boredom. The non-verbal component should frequently involve some positive physical contact such as a hug or a pat on the shoulder. Most importantly the parent must momentarily stop what he is doing and provide full attention to the child while giving face-to-face reinforcement. Simply saying 'good' to the child while walking past or when involved in some other task is of little value. As with material rewards we restructure regularly occurring social reinforcement so that it follows some desired response. For example, if parents are in the habit of reading to their child they should alter the situation so that they read to him following appropriate behaviour.

PROBLEMS IN REWARDING

Successfully managing to have parents praise their child's behaviour is one of the most difficult aspects of any programme. The authors have found that many parents seem to learn the punishment techniques more rapidly and effectively. However, we anticipate that following the initial days of intervention parents will be rewarding at a frequency of at least four rewards to every one punishment. In our attempts to promote reasonable levels of reward we recommend the following measures:

(1) In situations where adult attention and social reinforcement have been low we may attempt to schedule certain basic interactional requirements of the parents—for example that they regularly allocate a time to play with, or talk to, the child. This basic requirement is non-contingent (independent of the child's behaviour) and is introduced by us in an attempt to create a minimal level of positive interaction between parent and child.

(2) With parents who have inadequate verbal skills we may draw up a list of a variety of verbal praise statements and practise these statements with the parents.

(3) Initially, parents are instructed actively to seek out good behaviour in the child and to keep a list of times when he was reinforced. This provides parents and child with visible proof of his 'good' behaviour.

(4) Additionally we ask parents to create situations in which there is a high probability of the child exhibiting a socially appropriate behaviour. If non-compliance is the target behaviour then the parents would ask the child to do tasks which he is likely to do. Unfortunately

most deviant children are often completely non-compliant in the early stages of the programme. In this case we have to accept that the first few days' records will reveal high frequencies of punishment.

Punishment

The two main forms of punishment used in simple contingency management are withdrawal of attention (or ignoring) and the application of time-out.

WITHDRAWAL OF ATTENTION

Generally this technique is used in the following circumstances:

(1) Ignoring deviant behaviour in very young children is fairly effective. With children aged 4 and under, time-out is rarely necessary.

(2) Withdrawal of attention is used to punish certain behaviours which concern the parents but which do not appear to be grossly disruptive. These behaviours would usually fall into an attention-seeking category, for example, sulking, taking too long at a meal or crying when put to bed. They are not the result of a disobedient interchange and do not contain directed aggression or destructiveness. As will be discussed later we also use ignoring to deal with deviant behaviour exhibited while the child is in time-out.

(3) During the treatment we initially focus on a few deviant behaviours. In the early stages, in order to prevent confusion and to allow maximum concentration on the target behaviours, we usually instruct parents to ignore other deviant behaviours. Once the parents have developed more confidence they may consider appropriate consequences for these behaviours and put them into effect.

(4) Even with target behaviours parents may sometimes be uncertain whether punishment is justified. For instance, does the child's behaviour constitute non-compliance? Did he break the plate on purpose? On these occasions we advise the parents to ignore the incident. Occasionally a parent may become very anxious and feel unable to administer the time-out procedure. In such a situation we again advise the parent to ignore the current episode. If this problem occurs frequently we may have to reconsider our initial management plan. We could either simplify the programme or else concentrate directly on helping the parent to cope with his anxiety.

It is surprisingly difficult to ignore deviant behaviours. This is especially so in families which have been used to a high rate of angry interchanges between the parents and children. We must ensure by some means that the parent neither watches nor addresses any remarks to the child when he is exhibiting the designated behaviours. It may help to suggest that the parent engages in some purposeful activity during this time, for example a specific household task, or else that he retires from the child's view. Often parents verbalise concern that the ignored child will proceed to exhibit more aggressive behaviours which they cannot continue to ignore. For example, the child may break ornaments or threaten the mother with a poker. In these circumstances there is little alternative to implementing the time-out procedure. The child who cries persistently at night presents us with another type of problem. Initially, in such cases when screaming is prolonged, parents may worry that there is something wrong with the child and therefore feel unable to ignore his behaviour. In such situations it may help to set the child's bed in a position where it can be viewed secretly through the open door of his room. If this is impossible we suggest that the parents go to observe the child infrequently, briefly and with the minimum of verbal or non-verbal interaction.

Although the withdrawal of attention is a simple and mild form of punishment it has several disadvantages. As it is fairly mild it may have differential effects. For example, it has been noted that on occasions ignoring increases rather than decreases deviant behaviour (Sajwaj and Dillon, 1976). When the withdrawal of attention is effective it usually takes longer to produce change than does the implementation of time-out. This is of considerable importance as parents may become somewhat discouraged if they do not see some change after a few days' intervention. Finally, it seems inappropriate to expect parents to ignore the more disruptive and aggressive behaviours. It is unlikely that authorities outside the family will ignore physical aggression and disruption. Thus for the more highly aggressive behaviour we favour the use of time-out.

TIME-OUT

The major principle behind time-out is that consequent on deviant behaviour the child is removed or isolated from any reinforcers which may be available at that time. Considerable space is devoted here to the discussion of time-out. This is because it has been shown to be one of the most effective components in managing child behaviour problems (Taplin, 1974). However, the success of time-out depends upon careful selection of the appropriate location; upon the correct implementation of the procedure; and upon ensuring that it is not abused by the parents.

(1) *Location*. In selecting time-out location we seek the least reinforcing place for the child. Texts often suggest the use of the child's bedroom or the bathroom. We tend not to favour these places. Commonly there are toys in the child's bedroom (they are reinforcers) and there are obvious hazards in leaving a child alone in the bathroom. In addition these areas are usually far removed from the supervising adult and we have found this causes anxieties in the parents. They will often verbalise concern that the child will further misbehave, for example destroy furniture or climb out of the window. Thus we prefer to select areas such as the kitchen corner, the living-room corner or the hall. In these places the parents can ensure that the procedure is being correctly adhered to. Time-out is not designed to frighten the child, and parents should be deterred from using a frightening location such as the cubby-hole under the stairs or a dark room.

(2) *Duration*. Most authorities are agreed that between 5 and 15 minutes is sufficient time-out duration. Our impression is that with younger children a shorter time is effective, for example with a 4-year-old child 3−5 minutes is often sufficient, whereas with an 11-year-old child we would consider 10 minutes appropriate. White, Nielson and Johnson (1972) have shown that the length of time is less important than the consistency with which this is applied. In this research it was demonstrated that short duration time-outs became ineffective if they were later used in conjunction with longer duration time-outs. We have encountered situations in which parents tend to vary the time-out duration depending on the perceived intensity of the deviance and on how much it happens to upset them at that particular moment. For example, Kate is put into time-out for 3 minutes for tearing her own book but gets 6 minutes for tearing her library book. Again we stress that if parents have used an isolation procedure prior to intervention we must carefully consider the previous durations involved before we employ time-out.

Often children will cry and scream when first put into time-out. It is possible that, if the child is released following a fixed time, any crying or screaming which immediately preceded the release will be reinforced. To avoid this possibility we can use either of the following methods. First, with older children, commence timing the duration of time-out only when the child becomes quiet. Secondly, with younger children, commence timing the duration immediately the child goes into time-out (whether or not he is quiet) but wait for a quiet moment before releasing him.

Time-out is an effective form of punishment and also a safe one. It allows the opportunity for highly charged emotions to diffuse and may, in some instances, decrease the risk of battering (see discussion on non-accidental injury in chapter 12). However, it is important to ensure that parents do not abuse the system and conveniently 'forget' about the child who has been sent to time-out.

(3) *Implementation of time-out.* We have adopted and developed a three-stage procedure—the three-step contingency. The stages are as follows (figure 9.1): stage 1—the child is commanded to do something or to stop doing something; stage 2—the child is rewarded if he complies; if he has not complied within a reasonable length of time (which is judged according to the content of the command) then a second command is given with a punishment warning; stage 3—the child is rewarded if he complies; if he has not complied within a further reasonable time he is sent to time-out.

As always, considerable emphasis is laid on the verbal and non-verbal style of the parents. The commands should be given in an

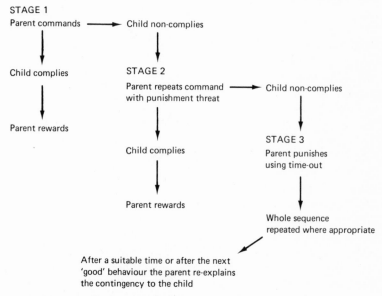

Figure 9.1 The three-step contingency procedure for implementing time-out

authoritative manner and should clearly specify what is expected of the child. In the early stages of intervention, parents are asked to overact the commanding style. It is hoped that in so doing they shall aid the child in discriminating a change in parental consequating. If stage 3 is reached then the child is asked to go to time-out. At this stage the parents should not allow any argument to develop about the time-out but simply ensure that it is carried through. The only verbal exchanges now allowed are restricted to the parents informing the child that he must remain in time-out until he has been quiet for 5 minutes (or whatever time has been decided upon). At the end of this duration, the child is informed that he may come out. If the original command was one which required the child to complete a specified task then the whole procedure is repeated. The ultimate goal is compliance and child reward. Following this eventual reward the parents are asked to re-explain to the child the new house rules and the reason for his punishment. If the time-out was used for a refusal to stop deviating, for example swearing, then the re-explanation should follow 10–15 minutes after time-out. This explanation is important because it actively engages the parent in teaching the child appropriate behaviour and it also helps the child to discriminate the new situation and thus avoid high frequencies of time-out.

(4) *Problems in implementing time-out*. Initially, time-out rarely runs as smoothly as in the above outline. If it did we would suggest that there was little need for it in the first place. We frequently encounter (*a*) refusal to go to time-out, (*b*) refusal to remain in time-out and (*c*) refusal to leave time-out.

(*a*) Refusal to go to time-out. In the majority of cases initial refusal is almost inevitable. With younger children we suggest that the parents should physically remove them to time-out. Obviously they must be able to effect this quickly and without argument or overt anger. If the child is older, or the parents are incapable of physically implementing the punishment, then we advocate a response-costing method. The practical use of response-costing is discussed in more detail in the next chapter. In the present context, response-costing might involve the parent stating that 1 minute extra will be added to the time-out duration for every 15 seconds that the child refuses to comply with the punishment. Again, this should be stated without overt anger or argument. Once 15 minutes has been added to the time-out duration and the child has still not complied, the parents could if necessary remove time from privileges, for example television viewing or staying up late. The parent will inform the child that he will go to bed 5 minutes earlier for each refusal. Parents should ensure that any time penalties lost in this way are recorded and put into effect later. Once maximum time penalties are reached (these are always set prior to intervention) the parent then simply ignores the child until he complies. Where this procedure has been followed correctly we have yet to encounter a case which has run to the set maximum time penalties. We believe that, in addition to the actual punishment procedure, the changes in parent consistency and verbal style contribute significantly to an increase in child compliance. However, it must be remembered that these parental changes alone (that is, without the use of punishment) are insufficient to effect large and sustained improvement in the child's behaviour.

(b) Refusal to remain in time-out. If the child was physically removed to time-out then the parents continue this physical restriction until he sits quietly on his own. At this stage they begin timing the duration. Above all, parents should be prepared for the initial trauma of this procedure. They must be sure not to show anger or to argue when the child shouts and screams. We suggest that these first episodes of time-out must be supervised by the therapist, at least until the parents feel more confident or the child has learned to sit quietly. In some cases the initial time-out episodes may last up to an hour or more. In one case, where initial time-outs were of long duration due to the child's refusal to sit quietly, we employed an older sibling as a confederate to model the time-out situation. This was to demonstrate to the deviant child that he was only required to sit quietly for a few minutes. We believe that this procedure contributed to the reduced duration of subsequent time-outs. With older children, when a response-costing method has been employed for the initial refusal, the parents continue to use it for each episode when the child leaves time-out (for example, 1 minute could be added to the time-out duration). If the child remains in time-out, but is not quiet, then the duration does not begin until he is quiet.

(c) Refusal to leave time-out. When the duration of time-out has expired the parent informs the child that he may leave, but he should not persuade him to do so. Parents often find it upsetting when their children remain in time-out after the required time has lapsed. They impute from this that time-out is having little effect on the behaviour. Often associated with this is a blasé child attitude to time-out. The child may leave, saying, 'I don't care, it doesn't matter to me'. Parents are instructed to ignore this attitude and concentrate only on ensuring that the procedure is fulfilled. After a few days it will be possible, by reviewing the observational data, to assess whether time-out is having the desired effect.

Implementation of a Contingency Management Programme

Generally, the above techniques are not detailed to the parents until the day therapy begins, as prior discussion may lead them to try some of the techniques unsuccessfully. Following the description, we practise a few of the implementation sequences (for example the three-step contingency procedure) to ensure that the parents have a clear idea of their use. Stress is placed on verbal style, initial overacting, consistency and timing. The parents inform the child of the new rules which are then put into effect.

The therapist observes the parents operating the contingencies. Each interchange is discussed with the parents and they are reinforced or remonstrated for correct or incorrect implementation. The therapist also cues the parent if he fails to respond appropriately to the child's behaviour (for example, if the child tidies his toys but mother is unresponsive; in this case the therapist cues the mother to reward). Another example may be when mother warns the child four times not to tear his book, but fails to take consequating action when he continues to do so. In this case the therapist reminds the mother that her commanding level is too high and that she is not adhering to the three-step contingency procedure.

Frequently in the early stages of implementing time-out, parents need the therapist to reassure them that the child will eventually settle if they persevere. Generally we attempt to spend 2–3 hours in the home during the first day. In order that our time is maximally effective we may ask the parents to give 5 or 6 commands per hour to the child, which they will consequate. The amount of time spent in the home on subsequent days depends on how successfully the parents are managing. If our formulation has been correct and the parents are co-operative our own observations and the parent observational data should reveal that behaviours are changing. When dealing with young children (that is, under 8 years of age) this will become apparent after approximately 3–4 days. Therapist time spent in the home may then be reduced. Further visits may be necessary only to check on parent data, to discuss specific problems and to encourage the adaptation of similar strategies to other behaviours. In cases where there is initial success, parents are usually able to generalise the contingencies to other behaviours. If the treatment goes well after approximately 2 weeks we usually suggest to the parents that they may relax the contingencies if they so wish. Parents should understand that if problems increase again they can revert to the methods employed in the treatment.

Common Problems in the Use of Simple Contingency Management

Few cases run as smoothly as this chapter might lead one to suppose. In fact many more cases fail than succeed. As failure is a large problem we have devoted a separate chapter to it (chapter 14). At the moment we shall discuss some of the problems of contingency management.

(1) Parent failure to generalise the skills across behaviours. Occasionally we meet parents who are capable of implementing a programme to deal with the target behaviour (for example, tantrums), but when the child exhibits a new and different behaviour (for example, aggression to a sibling) the parent is unsure of what to do. If the situation is left unsupervised the behaviours can deteriorate and the parent appears to lose all his newly acquired skills. In these cases we have often assessed that the main problem is high anxiety in the parent. We have coped with this problem in two ways. First, by training the parent in the relaxation techniques (Wolpe and Lazarus, 1966). Whenever the parent feels anxious about managing the child's behaviour he is instructed to leave the situation, relax himself as trained, reconsider the problem and then proceed to deal with it. Secondly, with highly anxious parents we may provide a longer supervised follow-up. In doing this it is hoped that, in time, the parent will have dealt with a sufficiently wide number of problems in order to feel confident in tackling new ones without anxiety.

(2) Parent failure to generalise the skills across situations. Dealing with behaviours which occur outside rather than inside the home often presents the parents with difficulties. Again we believe that parent anxiety plays an important part. It seems that children are quickly able to detect this anxiety. In situations where the techniques can be operated, for example a friend or relative's house, then they should be put into effect. Where this is impossible, for example in the supermarket, then the parent should issue a warning that time-out will occur when the child returns home. If this warning is ineffective the parent

should return home and implement the time-out. With an older child, response-costing, as discussed in the next chapter, is a useful method of coping with behaviour problems which occur outside the home. We encourage parents who are concerned about their child's outside behaviour to set aside time to expose him to these situations. In this way the parent can focus fully on the child's behaviour and then reward or punish as appropriate. Obviously it will help if the therapist initially accompanies parent and child on these outings.

(3) Parent failure to adhere to the contingencies. Often parents fail to comply with the programme rules. For example, they may fail to reward or they may leave the child in time-out for longer than is required. If cueing parents in their management is ineffective then we need some further motivating factor. We have found it beneficial to set up a contract between husband and wife in which each partner levies a fine on the other if he/she fails to reward or punish appropriately or correctly. Commonly used fines have been cigarettes or money. If the mother is a single parent or if the father refuses to co-operate, a contract between the mother and therapist may be required. The contract could involve gain or loss of therapist time according to the mother's adherence to the programme.

Case Example using Differential Attention to Cope with Tantrums and Crying

Synopsis
A family known to us at the clinic asked for our assistance in managing their 3-year-old daughter, Jean. Jean had been suffering from gastro-enteritis and had just returned home from hospital where she had spent 1 week. The mother complained that Jean was having frequent tantrums, continually following her around the house and demanding that the mother carry her. At night time, Jean refused to go to bed and screamed until lifted—this usually happened after 20 minutes' screaming. There were other problems in the household but these are not dealt with here.

Observation
This was carried out in the home setting and specimen recordings were taken by the therapist. During observation time father was at work and the older sibling at school. Mother was asked to continue with her usual

chores. Observations taken over a period of $1\frac{1}{2}$ hours revealed the following sequence. Each time mother attempted to leave her seat, Jean followed and demanded to be lifted. If mother refused to pick her up, Jean screamed until she complied, usually after about 2–3 minutes. While Jean was being carried by mother, or was following her, mother constantly reprimanded her. At the beginning of the observation period, Jean's toys were strewn about the floor. On each occasion that mother picked up any of these toys, Jean screamed and mother dropped the toy within 2–3 seconds. Jean also screamed when mother turned on the radio or attempted to read the newspaper. This screaming stopped when the radio was turned off or the newspaper laid down.

Plans

Following this observation we decided to proceed directly to a management plan. The following strategies were adopted:

(1) Mother was asked to ignore Jean's demands to be carried (instructed to pretend she was not there).

(2) Mother was also asked to ignore Jean's screaming behaviour and to continue with the chores. To facilitate this, mother and therapist drew up a list of tasks which she could do in the next few hours: tidy upstairs, go to the toilet (this had been a problem as Jean was insisting on accompanying the mother), wash the dishes, tidy Jean's toys, read the newspaper, or listen to the radio.

(3) When Jean stopped screaming, mother was instructed to approach her, talk to her, cuddle or play with her. If the screaming recommenced mother was instructed to again ignore the child.

Intervention

The plans were put into immediate effect and therapist observations recommenced. When mother went upstairs, Jean followed her demanding to be carried. Later, when mother came downstairs, Jean remained on the landing and screamed for 15 minutes. Mother began to tidy the toys and Jean came into the same room where she screamed for a further 10 minutes. Immediately Jean was quiet, mother was cued to pick her up and cuddle her. However, mother could not continue to give Jean undivided attention so she left her after 5 minutes and went into the kitchen to wash the dishes. Jean started to scream again. As instructed, mother ignored this behaviour but again cuddled Jean when she stopped screaming. The procedure was continued over a 2-hour period during which the screaming was reduced to occasional episodes lasting for a few minutes. At the end of this session, father returned from work and the day's programme was reviewed and discussed with him.

A plan was evolved for coping with Jean's bedtime behaviour. The parents were instructed to put Jean to bed after playing with her for a short time and to ignore the subsequent screaming. If Jean came downstairs she was to be returned to bed without any interaction. It was explained to the parents that they could check on Jean at night if her prolonged screaming caused them concern. However, they were instructed to confine interaction to the minimum and not to engage in argument or discussion. Therapist observations taken the next day revealed that daytime behaviours were improved. The mother's event records showed only two tantrums on that morning. Further, mother had generalised the principles. Jean had demanded an early lunch, which mother found inconvenient, so mother stated that she would have lunch at the normal time. She ignored the subsequent tantrum and Jean took her lunch 1 hour later. Visits were made on the subsequent 2 days and observation showed that the daytime behaviours had maintained their improvement. Night-time crying was now only lasting 5–10 minutes. Over the next 2 months, parent records revealed continued and maintained improvement. This case, which was regarded as fairly straightforward, required about 5 hours' therapist time.

Case Example employing Differential Attention and Time-out to Cope with High Rate Oppositional Behaviour

Synopsis
George, a 7-year-old child, was referred to us with a wide range of behaviour problems. His parents were unable to cope with his disobedience, verbally abusive behaviour, messy eating habits, physical aggression and hyperactivity. The family's social life was curtailed as both parents felt unable to take George out visiting or to entertain their friends. George had even coerced his parents into bringing his breakfast to bed each morning.

George had two older siblings—a girl aged 13 and a boy aged 9—neither of whom had ever presented behavioural problems. The parents' marital relationship appeared to be satisfactory. The case history indicated that George's behaviour problem had begun shortly after he was 2 years old and had gradually worsened since then. There was no history of brain injury or physical illness and he had not presented any problems at school.

Observation

In the 10 days following the initial interview, 4 observation sessions, each lasting 1½ hours, were conducted in the home. During these sessions both parents and siblings were present. The observations substantiated most of the above-mentioned complaints about George's behaviour. Both parents were inconsistent in dealing with George and they exhibited high frequencies of commands (on some occasions 30–40 commands per hour) which they failed to consequate. They rarely carried out threats, often omitted to label or praise socially appropriate behaviour and any social approval which was employed was used in an attempt to reduce disruptive behaviours, for example, 'That's a good boy, George; sure you wouldn't hit Daddy with the poker'. Over these observation periods, approximately 90–95 per cent parent–children attention was directed towards George; his two siblings only receiving 5 per cent.

Plans

As the problems were multiple it was decided initially to modify only one behaviour. As non-compliance was the major problem we decided to focus on it with an intensive programme. Intervention was to be carried out in the home under several hours' direct therapist supervision over a period of 4 days. In order to make maximum use of this time the parents were asked to stay off work and George was kept from school. The parents were instructed in, and practised, the sequence for time-out. They were asked in the early stages to overact their commanding and rewarding styles. In selecting rewards we decided initially to use material rewards in addition to attention and praise, as we assessed that George was relatively unresponsive to social approval. At first the parents were to use three social rewards for every material one. The following is a list of the rewards used: social approval, sweets, crisps, fruit, trip to shop with mother, ride in car with father and trip to harbour with father. The latter three rewards were known to be valued activities. The punishment to be used was 5 minutes' time-out in the kitchen corner. Physical force, to remove the child to time-out, was to be employed if necessary. Duration in time-out was only to begin when George was sitting quietly on his own.

Intervention

At the beginning of the first day of intervention the parents explained the rules to George. Following these instructions he was immediately non-compliant (he refused to stop jumping over the furniture) and his mother took him to time-out. George screamed and kicked and required physical restraint for 20 minutes before he quietened and duration could be timed. There were two further time-outs that afternoon which lasted 45 and 35 minutes, respectively. No occasions for reward were observed. It was during this first day that the therapist's presence was most critical as the parents needed continual encouragement during the implementation of time-out. In view of the long punishment times we suggested that the parents use George's brother as a confederate to model time-out. On succeeding days the length of time-out reduced dramatically, varying between 5 and 15 minutes. George also began to exhibit many instances of compliance for which he was rewarded.

During these 4 days it became evident that the mother was more successful than the father in managing the contingencies. We frequently had to cue the father to keep to the instructions. In order to facilitate further improvement in the father's style we drew up the following contract. The parents agreed to monitor each other's behaviour towards George. When one partner's behaviour deviated from the programme rules (for example, by giving a third command, failing to implement time-out or failing to praise) the other partner was to levy a fine of 5 cigarettes. This contract was operational for 2 weeks. Initially, the father was losing 25–30 cigarettes per day, while the mother lost only 5–10 per day. Over 3–4 days the father's style improved considerably.

After a period of 4 days' intensive intervention, George's compliance increased dramatically. Visits were then carried out once a week, with daily telephone calls made in the intervening days, during which time any problems which arose were discussed. In the succeeding days the parents began to generalise the programme instructions. For example, at meal times they removed George from the table when he was disruptive (and if he persisted with this behaviour he was put into time-out); if he messed the bathroom he was asked to clean it and on refusal to do so was sent to time-out—this cycle was repeated until he complied. Disruptive behaviour in the evening resulted in George being sent early to bed. The parents also noted that the older siblings' behaviour had improved and they believed that this resulted from their own increased consistency in handling. One month later the improvement was sustained, but George remained hyperactive and showed a very short attention span. He was rarely able to remain still and concentrate on one activity for longer than 30 seconds at a time. As behavioural methods are not usually very successful in managing hyperactivity we prescribed a drug (methyl phenidate) which ameliorated this problem considerably. At one year follow-up the behaviour improvement was sustained.

Key Ideas

In setting up a simple contingency management programme we concentrate on the timing, content and consistency of the reward and punishment, and on the parental implementation of these procedures. In the authors' experience, parents generally learn how to punish more readily than they learn how to reward. The therapist initially rehearses the implementation sequences with the parents and then cues them as they operate the contingencies with the child. Parental verbal and non-verbal style is especially important. For example: social reinforcement should clearly indicate the parent's pleasure and also contain an explicit reason for the praise; commands should clearly specify what is expected of the child and state the consequences; if the third stage in the three-step contingency procedure is reached then the parent should not engage in further interaction with the child, but simply ensure that the time-out is implemented. Later, during explanation time, the parent rehearses or models the situation with the child and re-explains the contingencies.

10

Points Systems

During the mid-1960s behaviour modifiers began developing monetary systems, mainly for use within institutional settings, where large-scale behavioural programmes required clearly defined and easily administered procedures to cope with daily behaviour management (Allyon and Azrin, 1968). In more recent years the successful application of these programmes has been demonstrated in the home setting (Christopherson *et al.*, 1972). Points (or tokens) are earned when the child exhibits previously defined behaviours. Later these points (or tokens) are exchanged for previously defined rewards. For example Denis, a 10-year-old child, frequently refused to keep his room tidy, continually swore and rarely helped in the house. In attempting to change these behaviours a system was devised whereby he earned points for keeping his room tidy and for helping his mother in the house, and he lost points for swearing. At the end of each day, Denis could exchange the points (which were recorded on a chart) for some basic privileges such as watching television, earning pocket money and being allowed to stay up later at weekends.

Generally, we use points systems with children who are over 7 years old. For these children, immediate reinforcement, either social or material, is often no longer sufficient. They require more sophisticated reinforcers, such as being allowed to attend a youth club. Often this type of privilege cannot be employed instantaneously, and we therefore use a stimulus, that is a point or token, to bridge the time lag between the occurrence of the behaviour and the eventual reward.

Setting Up a Points System

In setting up a points system we must select the behaviours to be rewarded, the behaviours to be punished and the privileges which the child will be able to earn. Finally, we assign points to the selected behaviours and arrange for earned points to be exchanged for the privileges.

BEHAVIOURS TO BE REWARDED

In most instances it is insufficient to reward the child for simply not exhibiting the deviant behaviour; for example, if the complaint is that Jack often fights with his younger brother we could award points for lapses of time during which Jack does not fight. It would, however, be more socially appropriate to award the points when he plays co-operatively with his brother. In selecting behaviours to be rewarded we look for positive behaviours which are incompatible with the deviant behaviour and which can be observed and dealt with directly and consistently. In practice we focus the rewarding of points on two categories of behaviour.

(1) Regular task-oriented behaviours. In children of school age and upwards, regular task-oriented behaviours, such as doing homework, keeping one's room tidy, washing the dishes, etc., assume more importance. As children have a daily opportunity to exhibit these co-operative behaviours, they can regularly earn points. In order to facilitate their capacity to earn points we should ensure that the environment is conducive to completion of the task within a pre-determined time. For instance, a place and time should be fixed for homework so that it is carried out in a non-distracting setting and at a time when highly preferred child activity (such as a favourite television programme) will not occur. A list is drawn up of the regular task-oriented behaviours which the parent expects the child to exhibit. Provided we judge these expectations to be reasonable this list can be regarded as the minimal level of co-operative behaviours which we hope the child will eventually achieve.

(2) Extra task-oriented behaviours. During planning we also draw up a list of extra tasks for which the child can earn further points. For example, whilst Mary's parents always expect her to make her own bed, they acknowledge that she is being especially co-operative when she cuts the grass. When extra tasks are being selected for the points system the child is generally more involved in the selection. Any observational records which he has kept about unapproved parental behaviours are considered. For example, he may complain that he is asked to take too many messages. In the following chapter we shall discuss how the child

and parent might bargain these extra tasks against extra privileges.

In addition to the advantages already mentioned the use of task-oriented behaviours helps to simplify the design of the points system. We can usually predict how frequently these behaviours might occur each day, and thus when points are being assigned to them we will have a reasonably accurate idea of the potential total points which can be earned daily. From this sum we can approximately evaluate the relative costs of the rewards and privileges. However, when we are managing behaviours such as obedience on our points system, this simplicity is not always possible. For instance, it is more difficult to predict the frequency of obedience from day to day and thus the total potential points which can be earned daily.

BEHAVIOURS TO BE PUNISHED

Commonly we employ three forms of punishment within the points system.

(1) Response cost (that is, loss of points). This occurs in three main situations. First, when the child fails either to carry out or to complete the regular tasks assigned to him he loses a previously specified number of points. Secondly, points fines are generally levied for less serious high rate behaviours, such as each instance of swearing, arguing, etc. During planning we shall have decided to which behaviours this contingency applies. Thirdly, when time-out is being employed a child loses points for failing either to go to time-out or comply with the rules of time-out (see chapter 9).

As a punishment, response cost has several distinct advantages over physical punishment and time-out. First, response cost results in the loss only of preferred reinforcers, whereas time-out results in the loss of all reinforcers. Secondly, following response cost the child can usually work harder to correct for points lost (or not earned). Time-out is time lost, because during time-out the child cannot adopt the socially appropriate behaviours which we are attempting to increase. Thirdly, response cost has less emotional side effect than time-out. For a full discussion on response cost see Kazdin (1972).

(2) Failure to earn points. The child is not fined for failing to do extra tasks, but he does fail to earn points and therefore privileges.

(3) Time-out. This is still usually employed in dealing with high rate antisocial behaviours such as non-compliance, physical aggression, tantrums, etc. It is used in conjunction with the points system for two main reasons. First, as mentioned in the previous chapters, in highly

explosive situations it allows a 'cooling off' period for both parent and child. Secondly, it provides a technique which the parent can use to disrupt or suppress escalating aggression. A clear definition of those high rate behaviours to which time-out will be applied should be reached in the initial stages of the programme.

REWARDS AND PRIVILEGES

These are selected from parent and child interviews and from the child's recordings (where these have been kept). Privileges are divided into two categories:

(1) Normal routine privileges. Most of the reinforcers used are privileges which a child of that age might regularly expect, for example preference over certain television programmes, reasonable amounts of pocket money, trips out with parents, etc. Whether these have occurred non-contingently in the past is relatively unimportant. What is important is that now these activities are made contingent on earning points. For example, John now has to earn a required number of points before receiving his usual pocket money.

(2) Extra privileges. When talking to the child about privileges it is common for him to mention activities which he enjoys but which are viewed as rare treats, for example being taken to the pictures or to a football match. Bargaining with the parents for inclusion of special privileges, contingent upon high points earned by the child, can be very useful. Bargains which meet some of the child's expressed desires may help to motivate him to increase his prosocial skills.

It is also important to consider when privileges might become available. Some privileges are long term (the child being allowed to make his own choice of the next article of clothing to be purchased) and others are short term (extended television viewing that evening). In many deviant children, especially those who exhibit high frequencies of successful coercive behaviours, it is unlikely that self-control has been well developed (that is, the ability to postpone gratification until later—see discussion in chapter 14). In these children it would probably be valueless to select only long-term privileges. In such cases reinforcers should be selected on at least a daily basis. Through points exchange we make both daily and weekly privileges available. It is hoped that by encouraging the child to save points we shall foster the development of self-control.

In assigning points to behaviours it appears to be advantageous to use large numbers of points rather than small numbers (Kazdin, 1972). For example, instead of assigning a particular behaviour 1 point and a privilege 3 points, they are assigned 20 and 60 points, respectively. There is also evidence to suggest that points fines do not necessarily have to be high, relative to points reward, in order to have maximum suppressive effect. The number of points earned for each socially appropriate behaviour should therefore be much greater than the relative number which are costed for each deviant behaviour. For example, keeping one's room tidy may earn 60 points, whereas failure to do so may only result in a loss of 10 points. Whilst this small loss will provide definite negative feedback to the child, it will not seriously detract from the points earned for prosocial behaviours. This points weighting gives constant emphasis to prosocial behaviours. With these provisions in mind we would assign points as follows:

(1) From our baseline data we assess the child's present prosocial skills level and set initial behavioural goals which are within his current capabilities. Achieving a correct balance of points gain may be an initial problem; for example, the child may either find it too difficult or too easy to earn the required points. However this balance can be altered in succeeding days.

(2) We establish a total number of points which will give access to all privileges. This number is quite arbitrary, for example, 1000.

(3) We list the privileges, assigning them points which bear relevance to their value to the child. The sum total value of these will be equal to the total which we decided in (2) above; for example, see figure 10.2 on page 128.

(4) In another chart we list the behaviours to earn points. We can generally predict the daily occurrence of these behaviours (for example, the child has only to do homework once or dry the dishes after the evening meal) and thus we assign them points values, the sum total of which should approximate to the total in (2) above. The number of points assigned to any one behaviour will depend on its relative importance in intervention; for example, see figure 10.2.

(5) We list behaviours to lose points. As stated above, these fines are kept small.

EXCHANGING THE POINTS FOR PRIVILEGES
Points are usually totalled and exchanged for privileges at the end of

each day. However, if a points system is employed with a young child the points may have to be exchanged immediately or at the end of each half-day. In deciding on the times delegated for points exchange we are assessing the child's ability to delay gratification or exert self-control. Points systems can be used explicitly to achieve this aim by gradually lengthening the time between earning and exchange. Usually a number of rules on points exchange are devised:

(1) Points not exchanged (or saved) at the arranged time are cancelled. This is to prevent points hoarding. In situations in which the child has earned a large number of points but has not exchanged these over a few days, we can envisage that his behaviour may deteriorate as he has now sufficient points to buy privileges for the consecutive days without having to exhibit socially appropriate behaviours.

(2) Points which are saved (where this provision is made) are not to be used for anything other than a specified number of long-term privileges.

(3) Once privileges have been purchased by the child then the parents must honour them.

The designated time for points exchange is useful in that it provides an opportunity for parents and child to meet and discuss his behaviour during the preceding interval. In the last chapter we noted that discussion about deviant behaviour should not occur at the time of the deviance, but that it should follow later (for example, after the next appropriate behaviour, a few minutes after time-out or during points exchange). In these circumstances parents explain to the child why certain behaviours are appropriate and others inappropriate. Reasons such as, 'Because I say so', must be avoided. It is important to state clearly why the behaviour is deviant (for example, 'Not doing your homework will result in you falling behind with schoolwork and getting into trouble with the teacher') and to describe and encourage the appropriate prosocial behaviour for that occasion. Any changes in the programme are also discussed at points exchange time.

Daily Maintenance of the Points System

Following the introduction of the points system, therapist home visits are frequent, in most cases daily. These visits continue regularly until we are fairly certain that the treatment is operating effectively. At these appointments several aspects of the system are reviewed.

Each points gain or loss is discussed.

(1) Points gain. It must be remembered that the points themselves have no intrinsic worth. Their value is that they can be exchanged for privileges, they cue the parent to exhibit social approval, and they provide the child with positive feedback about his behaviour. In awarding points the parent should praise the child, specify the behaviour and immediately enter the point on the chart.

(2) Points loss. Parental verbal style is equally important when removing points. The child should have been informed of the contingencies prior to implementation, and so when he deviates the parent merely indicates the deviation (for example, failure to make his bed within the set time) and fines the child. He does not argue about or discuss the points loss. In the case of negative behaviours or refusal to go to time-out, an initial fine is levied and the parent continues to fine while the behaviour continues. During one behavioural sequence a parent may fine up to a predetermined maximum, which is usually approximately one-quarter of the potential daily points.

During the therapist's daily maintenance visits each of the points interchanges is fully discussed with the parents and child. Any which have proved difficult or faulty are rehearsed correctly (for example, if the parent and child have argued about the validity of a points fine at time of implementation) and the points exchange time is also discussed. We ensure that the parents re-stipulate, where necessary, the requirements being made of the child, and give clear explanations as to why behaviours are appropriate or inappropriate.

PROGRAMME ADJUSTMENTS

The following programme adjustments are often required in the early stages.

(1) If the child is easily earning the required points we can first increase the privilege costs. For example, being allowed to watch a valued television programme may now cost 60 points instead of 40. Secondly, we can increase the required performance level of one or several of the target behaviours. For example, if an encopretic child was initially being rewarded for going to the toilet we can now require that he has a bowel movement at the toilet in order to earn the same points. Thirdly, extra behaviours can be incorporated in the system. In most points recording sheets which the authors have used, several columns were left vacant for this purpose. The parents are encouraged to

implement this stage themselves. They will have to define the behaviour, assign it points and adjust the values of other behaviours.

(2) If the child is having difficulty in earning the required points we can decrease the skill level required in the target behaviour or reduce the number of behaviours being recorded in the programme.

(3) If the child shows no inclination to earn points we should consider whether the points exchange time is occurring soon enough and whether the privileges are sufficiently reinforcing. Extra privileges should be routinely added to the list at intervals in order to provide variety and to encourage the child.

Phasing Out the Programme

When the behavioural goals have been established for 2—3 weeks we can consider phasing out the programme. Perhaps the most effective way of doing this is to gradually increase the distance between points gain and their exchange. Thus, from earning and exchanging points on a daily basis, the child moves to earning and exchanging over a 2-day period. Later we can move to a weekly system in which the points earned over one week are exchanged for the next week's privileges. The points records will continue to furnish information about the child's behaviour, and if any deterioration occurs we can move back to the previous level. This method of phasing out has an advantage in that it may foster the development of self-control. When the weekly level has been stably established the system can be dropped altogether. However, parent records are still kept to detect any deterioration. Those successful points systems which we have operated have usually lasted about 2 months and have entailed 10—14 hours of therapist time in implementation and follow-up.

Further Uses of Points Systems

SCHOOL-TO-HOME REPORT CARDS

It is often difficult to carry out intervention in the classroom setting. Teachers are usually unable to devote extensive time to the management of one child. However, with sufficient teacher co-operation the therapist may carry out a few observations in the classroom and define the behaviours to be changed. Following this the teacher is asked to record the presence or absence of these behaviours on a card. The parents collect this card every day or else ask the child to bring it home. In this latter instance it is important to regularly check with the teacher to ensure that the card has not been altered by the child. The parents provide the consequences for the classroom behaviour by operating a points system at home. The second case example in this chapter illustrates the use of a school-to-home report card points system.

MANAGING PROBLEMS OUTSIDE THE HOME

When parents and the child are outside the home (for example at the park), deviant behaviour may prove both difficult to deal with and embarrassing to the parents. Points rewards and fines can provide a way of managing such behaviour. With younger children, however, there may be no alternative to direct consequences such as smacking the child, removing him to the car or fining him immediately during the trip; for example, no sweets at the supermarket.

USAGE IN SMALL RESIDENTIAL HOMES

The use of a points system in small residential homes may help to set a unified procedure for dealing with deviant and prosocial behaviours. This is important as often there are a number of staff working on different shifts. Several general house rules (for example, do not destroy furniture, no verbally abusive behaviour) and task requirements (for example, make own bed, help in the kitchen) can be established and maintained on the basis of a points system. Any behavioural problems or social skills deficits (for example, lack of co-operative play skills), relevant to an individual child, may be incorporated in the programme. For further information on the use of a points system in residential homes see Phillips *et al.* (1971).

Case Example Demonstrating Use of Home Points System

Synopsis

Bruce, who is 9 years old, was referred to the clinic by a health visitor because of a range of difficulties which had been present for 3 years, but which had intensified recently. These problems included:

(*a*) Disobedience. The areas of disobedience which upset his mother most included his refusal to go to bed on time at night (9.30 p.m.); to keep his room tidy; to take simple messages; to come home on time in the evening; to tidy his toys away.

(b) Verbal abusiveness. This usually followed maternal requests or commands. The remarks included shouting, 'No, I won't', 'Get lost', 'Why should I?' or 'Do it yourself'.

(c) Destructiveness. Bruce frequently broke toys shortly after acquiring them. The destructiveness extended to breaking his siblings' toys, frequently after arguments or fights with them.

(d) Poor sibling and peer relationships. Rarely was Bruce able to sustain co-operative play with his two siblings for more than several minutes at a time. On average there were 2–3 arguments with them each day. Also, he tended to tease or distract them by lifting their toys, disrupting games, changing the television channels repetitively or nipping and pinching his siblings while they were watching television. They were often reluctant to involve Bruce in their games. It was difficult to obtain specific information from the parents about his peer relationships. However, an interview with his schoolteacher revealed that he was a 'loner', principally by exclusion. The peers rejected him since he always wanted to lead or dictate games activities. However, he continued to attempt to coerce their behaviour by disrupting many of their activities. In class, he would pinch other children, take their pens or hide their books. In the playground he often ran off with the football or was verbally aggressive. While his teacher saw his behaviour as problematic, she was not over-concerned. Academically he was average.

Bruce's developmental history revealed little other than the fact that he had always been active and irritable. His mother had experienced some difficulties with his feeding and his toilet training. His two siblings were aged 10 and 5 years. They had not, in the past, exhibited any behavioural problems. The parents had been married for 12 years and were not having any marital problems. Both found difficulty in managing Bruce and both were keen to resolve the problem. In the past they had tried physically punishing Bruce, restricting privileges and ignoring his deviant activities. They felt helpless in that none of these methods had been effective. The mother felt particularly negative towards Bruce since he was disrupting so much of their family life. However, two points relating to the parents did seem important. First, they had few friends and engaged in few social activities. Secondly, the mother was of foreign extract and seemed to have different child-rearing attitudes. She tended to be strict with the children and disapproved of many of her neighbours because they were too lenient with their children. However, her husband supported her disciplining of the children. In spite of this strict background both parents interacted positively with the children; for instance, they regularly played games with them and read them stories.

Observations

A few observational sessions were conducted in the home. The mother and her 3 children were present. These revealed little in relation to Bruce's deviance, in spite of attempts to intensify the situation by having the mother issue him several commands, plus instructions to try and make him 'look bad'. He was totally obedient and demonstrated normal social skills. However, it was noticeable that in games situations the mother directed less attention and praise to Bruce than to her other children.

Two observational sessions were conducted in the child's classroom. During these he interacted minimally with peers. He did, however, spend a considerable time standing beside the teacher's desk and staring around not doing any work. On several occasions he was told to get on with his work or to go and sit down. These commands had little effect on his behaviour. The teacher did not attend to his disobedience. It was noticed on 4 occasions, during the observational sessions in the school, that when Bruce was praised for working he carried on working for longer spells than would have been anticipated—he seemed to be most responsive to adult approval.

During the week following the completion of these observations the mother was asked to keep some behavioural records of Bruce's behaviour. The results are as detailed in figure 10.1. The father was also actively involved in these recordings.

Planning and interaction

The management of the case was planned in two stages. The first stage was set at a simple level and involved an attempt to reduce three high rate behaviours and to increase three incompatible prosocial skills. The goals were assessed to be within Bruce's current behavioural capabilities. Providing stage 1 was successful it was planned to implement, as a second stage, a school-to-home report card system in an attempt to modify some of the peer relationship behaviours. During stage 1 we decided to employ a points system in conjunction with time-out. It was thought that the use of a points system would provide the parents with a

	BEHAVIOURAL EPISODES						
	MON	TUES	WED	THURS	FRI	SAT	SUN
Non-compliance	X X X	X X	X X X	X	X		X X X
Verbally abusive	X		X X X X			X X X	X
Sib. fighting	X	X X X	X	X X X X	X X X	X	X X
Destructiveness	X			X X		X X X	
Stealing			X				

Figure 10.1 Parent observations of Bruce's behaviour during the week prior to intervention

method of reward which would carry them over their initial difficulties in supplying social approval. It would also facilitate a link between Bruce's behaviour and potent reinforcers which were not immediately available to him (such as a weekend outing).

We decided with the parents that Bruce and his older sibling should be involved in the programme. In the case of the younger sibling, the time-out procedure was to be employed without the additional use of a points system.

Stage 1

The three behaviours selected for initial reduction were (a) disobedience, (b) fighting with siblings and (c) destructiveness.

(a) Disobedience. Initially we decided to focus on some specific areas of disobedience. These included failure to comply with requests which related to the following: messing with food; being verbally abusive to parents; refusing to tidy away toys; refusal to go to bed.

(b) Fighting with and annoying siblings, especially where this involved physical and verbal aggression towards them. It did not include 'rough' play.

(c) Destructiveness, especially where it resulted in broken toys, damaged furniture or ornaments.

The behaviours to be reduced were all punished by the use of 10 minutes' time-out, which was administered downstairs in the kitchen corner. Failure to go to time-out resulted in a loss of 25 points for each 30-second period of refusal. If refusal still persisted, following 6 minutes (that is 12 response costs), then the subsequent refusals were ignored and the response cost points for the 6 minutes (that is, 300) were removed.

The behaviours to be increased were (*i*) obedience, (*ii*) co-operative sibling behaviours and (*iii*) care of toys and personal possessions:

(*i*) Obedience, which was divided into two categories. First, compliance following instruction to stop exhibiting those behaviours mentioned under disobedience. Compliance in these situations resulted in praise from the parent, and the child also avoided the contingency of time-out. Secondly, compliance following requests to exhibit socially appropriate behaviours; for example, 'Please help with the dishes', or 'Please go for a message'. Instances of this category of obedience earned the child points, as illustrated in figure 10.2.

(*ii*) Co-operative sibling behaviours. Points were earned following 10-minute episodes of uninterrupted play between siblings or 10 minutes of non-disruptive lone activity when another sibling was present. Ten minutes was selected since the history and parent recordings suggested that co-operation had rarely lasted for any longer than this time.

(*iii*) Care of toys and personal possessions. There were 4 opportunities to earn points in this way during each day and these were as follows: changing and putting away school clothes on return from school, having toys tidied away before the evening meal, and again changing and putting away clothes and toys at bedtime. Points were not earned if the parent had to ask either child to tidy toys or change clothes.

The daily opportunity to earn points for each of these behaviours was limited. Compliance could earn points on 6 occasions each day, co-operative behaviours on 4 occasions, etc. (see figure 10.2). This artificial and limiting rule was incorporated in order to facilitate easy calculations of the costs of reinforcers relative to the total daily points earnings (see the discussion earlier in the chapter). The points system is also slightly atypical in that we were rewarding prosocial behaviours (that is, co-operative behaviours and compliance) of which the daily rate of occurrence was difficult to predict. However, in this case the main function of the points system was to provide the parents with a rewarding sequence which did not initially stress praise, as they found this difficult with Bruce. In addition it provided a continuous record of targeted child behaviours.

The reinforcers used included social approval, material rewards and privileged activities. The two latter types of reinforcers were selected from separate interviews with Bruce and his mother. They included: pocket money (maximum of 10 pence per day); permission to stay up an extra hour in the evening; a family game (usually Monopoly) after the youngest sibling had gone to bed; access to favourite toys (which were otherwise locked away); access to a favourite dessert after the evening meal. The points value of each reinforcer is illustrated in figure 10.2. Both children were able to gain access to these reinforcers using the points earned during that day.

Points gain and loss were recorded, immediately following the designated behaviours, on a chart placed on the kitchen wall. At 6.30 p.m. each evening the points were added and the two children were allowed to select those privileges which they wanted for the next 24 hours. In addition, feedback was given on the last 24 hours' performance. The points allocation and privilege costs are detailed in figure 10.2. Points not used within 24 hours of being earned were cancelled (to prevent points hoarding).

Daily maintenance of the system

Prior to the implementation of the system Bruce's mother came to the clinic to practise the time-out and rewarding sequences. These were conducted using a confederate child. Emphasis was focused on consistency, verbal styles, etc. (as already discussed in the preceding chapter). Also, the points sequences were discussed in detail until we were certain that these could be carried out with ease. The system was also discussed (though not practised) with the father on two occasions.

Two weeks following the initial visit the system was put into operation, having been explained to both children. In the initial 4 days the elder child gained all his privileges while Bruce had only enough points to gain 1–2 privileges on each day. It seemed that most of the points losses were centred on his refusals to go to time-out following disruptive activities with his older brother. From discussions there appeared to be two main problems. First, the older child was tending to play more on his own, seemingly to earn his points without disruption from Bruce. Secondly, Bruce did not co-operate in any play initiated by the older brother. He always wanted to win in games, he would not share favourite toys and wished to dictate the rules of the games. Two changes were made. First, points gained for co-operative behaviours were made contingent only on play together. Secondly, the mother was to spend 20 minutes each day watching and directing their play. During

WEEK 1	COMPLIANCE = 50 pts per episode Max possible = 300 pts per day	CO-OPERATIVE SIB. BEHAVIOURS = 100 pts per episode Max. possible = 400 pts per day	CARE OF PERSONAL POSSESSIONS = 100 pts per episode Max. possible = 300 pts per day	TIME-OUT REFUSALS = −25 pts for each 30 second refusal Max fine in one series = −300	NO. OF TIME-OUT EPISODES	TOTAL POINTS
MON	50, 50, 50, 50, 50, 50	/	100, 100, 100	−200	3	400
TUES	50, 50, 50, 50	100, 100	100, 100	−250	2	350
WED	50, 50	/	100, 100, 100	−100	1	300
THUR	50, 50, 50, 50, 50	100	100, 100, 100	−200	2	450
FRI	50, 50, 50, 50, 50	100, 60, 100 ＊	100, 100 100	/	1	810
SAT	50, 50, 50, 50, 50	100, 50, 100	100, 100, 100	/	2	800
SUN	50, 50, 50, 50, 50, 50	100, 80, 100, 100	100, 100, 100	−25	1	955

Monday's points are earned between 6.30 pm on Sunday and 6.30 pm on Monday. Tuesday's points are earned between 6.30 p.m. on Monday and 6.30 p.m. on Tuesday, etc.

REWARDS

(1)	Pocket money (10p)	= 200 pts
(2)	Staying up 1 hour later	= 200 pts
(3)	Games with parents	= 200 pts
(4)	Access to toys per 24-hour period	= 200 pts
(5)	Favourite dessert	= 100 pts

＊At this point, in order to facilitate the shaping up of co-operative behaviours one lot of 100 points was divided into 10 units of 10 points each. Each unit was used to reward individual components of co-operative play. See text for full description.

Figure 10.2 Week 1 of the points system for Bruce

this time 100 of the points set for co-operative behaviours (see figure 10.2) were divided into units of 10 points. The mother awarded 10 points for each co-operative behaviour observed. For instance, in a game, points were given when Bruce awaited his turn, told his brother it was his turn, played the game according to the rules, did not get upset when he was losing, etc. On each evening, when points were exchanged, particular emphasis was placed on these behaviours. After several days of this regime Bruce's points started to increase to maximum. This stage was maintained over a further period of 2 weeks (3 weeks in all). After this time the mother and father felt much more relaxed and able to praise Bruce.

It was then decided that the present points system should be implemented on alternate days for a further month. The improvement was sustained and the parents gradually phased out the points system. It was noticeable that the mother seemed much more relaxed and confident when talking about Bruce's behaviour.

Three weeks after the beginning of the points system we returned to the school. The teacher stated that she had not noticed any change in Bruce's behaviour in class.

Stage 2

We felt that it was still important to focus on the peer behaviours and then, following the phasing out of the home programme, a school-to-home report card was initiated (design very similar to the one outlined in the next case study). Points were gained for working on his own without interrupting the other children (during work assignment times) and interacting appropriately during periods when the children were allowed to talk together (for example, art and crafts). Points were lost for disruptive activities with peers. The chart was completed by the teacher 4 times each day, signed at the end of the day and given to Bruce. This was returned to the parents by the child. These points were used to earn privileges which had been available on the home points system. School peer behaviours appeared to improve right from the start of this programme and were sustained.

At a 6-month follow-up, though the parents were not recording, they reported that Bruce's behaviour remained improved and there was also improvement in the behaviour of the two siblings. In all, approximately 15 hours' therapist time was used in this case.

Case Example Demonstrating Use of School-to-Home Report Card Points System

Synopsis

Geraldine, who is 9 years old, was referred by the general practitioner to the clinic with academic difficulties. Her mother complained that she did not know when homework was set and that Geraldine did homework infrequently and even then she usually left it uncompleted. Her teacher had complained that Geraldine was badly behaved and rarely completed classwork assignments during the day. No other behavioural problems were reported.

Geraldine is the eldest of 3 girls. Neither of her siblings had presented any behavioural problem. The marital and home situation appeared satisfactory, although this assessment was based on the mother's account. In spite of making several appointments we never managed to meet the father.

An interview with Geraldine's teacher in the initial stages revealed that Geraldine was usually given 3 homeworks per week but she rarely submitted more than 1 per fortnight. During the past week she had not completed any classwork assignments. It was stated that she also distracted other children by continuous talking and out-of-seat behaviour. The teacher felt that Geraldine had difficulty in concentrating and that her parents were uninterested in her academic work. In contrast the history given by the mother suggested that Geraldine could sustain activity; for example, she enjoyed television and watched it or played with her toys for periods up to half an hour, without activity changes.

Observation

Three observation periods were conducted in the classroom, initially using specimen recording and, later, time-sampling. Over these sessions we found Geraldine to be on task only 15 per cent of the time observed. On each occasion she left the classroom for approximately 5 minutes, and according to the teacher this occurred several times each day. Thirty per cent of the time she was out of her seat. On these occasions she was either out of the classroom or else approaching and talking to other children. There was very little attempt on the teacher's part to control these behaviours or to insist on academic tasks. This pattern was also exhibited by several other children in the class, although not to the same degree. Systematic observations were not carried out on other classmates. As we suspected the occurrence of other behaviour problems in the home we asked the mother to keep records of compliance and non-compliance. However, these observations gave no indication of high rate non-compliance. Records of homework behaviour were not taken as the history gave sufficient information on this problem.

Planning

Following initial observations and later discussions with the teacher it was clear that she did not feel she had the time to initiate any general classroom management procedures. We have already mentioned that this is often the case when a teacher believes that the major problem lies with one child or with only a small number of children. However, Geraldine's teacher agreed to co-operate in a school-to-home report card points system. We planned to use this system to facilitate the following:

(1) Reduction in classroom deviant behaviour and increased academic performance. Three behavioural categories were defined. First, attending to teacher when she was teaching the class, and participation as appropriate. Secondly, completion of academic assignments. Before setting goals for the quantity and quality of academic work to be attained we must ascertain that these are realistically matched with the child's capability. We had not, in this case, carried out either an intellectual or academic attainment assessment, as the school had records of such tests—the latter were in fact conducted annually. These records indicated that Geraldine was of average intelligence and was about $1\frac{1}{2}$ years behind on reading and maths. This assessment matched the teacher's expectations of Geraldine's academic capabilities. However, prior to intervention Geraldine had not been completing assignments at this expected level. Our goal was therefore the accurate completion of these regular assignments set by the teacher. Thirdly, deviant behaviours were defined according to what the teacher considered to be class rules. These included not being out of seat without permission and no talking by children, except when they had completed assignments or were given permission.

(2) Communication about homework with mother.

(3) Completion and improvement in the standard of homework. The conditions most conducive to homework were discussed with Geraldine and her mother. It was decided that Geraldine should do her homework in her bedroom immediately after the evening meal. Mother was to check the homework when it was completed.

The classroom behavioural requirements were also discussed with

SCHOOL RECORD CARD

TREATMENT WEEK 3

DAYS	Present or absent	Last night's homework Arith.	Last night's homework Eng.	Morning class Attention	Morning class Class assignment	Morning class Behaviour	Afternoon class Attention	Afternoon class Class assignment	Afternoon class Behaviour	Number of homeworks set	Homework completed on time	Helped or not with homework Arith.	Helped or not with homework Eng.	POINTS
MON	✓	not given	30	10	10	20	10	10	10	2	20	N	N	120
TUES	✓	10	20	20	20	10	0	0	10	2	20	N	N	110
WED	✓	10	20	20	20	10	10	10	10	1	20	—	N	130
THUR	✓	not given	30	20	20	10	20	10	10	1	20	—	N	140
FRI	✓	not given	20	ABSENT						—				/

		Last night's homework RATING		Afternoon class RATING		Homework / Mother report
		Good 30 / 20 / 10 / 0 / Poor −10		Good 30 / 20 / 10 / 0 / Poor −10		On time 20 / Not on time −10
						H = Mother help N = No mother help

REWARDS

(1) Pocket money (max. 5p/day)   30 points = 1p
(2) Crisps or sweets   = 30 points
(3) Staying up half an hour extra   = 40 points
(4) Saving (recorded by mother)   1500 points = £1

Figure 10.3   The school-to-home report card used in managing Geraldine's classroom and homework problems. The reverse side of the card provided space for teacher's and mother's signature. The use of different coloured headings in the original card had the effect of making the card appear less complex

132

Geraldine. Initially she felt that these were too stringent, but following discussion on her classroom behaviour, plus her complaint that she was being 'nagged' by her teacher and parents, she agreed that some changes might be appropriate. She was asked to select privileges and pleasurable activities which were to be earned for the appropriate behaviours. For a list of these privileges see figure 10.3.

A points card was drawn up as shown in figure 10.3. One card was provided for each week. The card was given to the teacher every morning and she made recordings at lunch-time and at the end of the school day. Each classroom target behaviour (that is, attending to teacher, completion of academic assignments and reduction in deviant behaviours) was rated on a 5-point scale. We had to use this rather general measure as the teacher felt that event recording or scanning would be too time consuming. It was hoped that requiring the teacher to complete the card twice a day would increase the reliability of her observations. The points which could be earned for each behaviour are shown on the card. On return home each day Geraldine presented the card to her mother who combined these points with the ones which Geraldine earned at home (by completing homework within the prescribed terms). The points were exchanged for privileges which Geraldine selected from the available reinforcers.

Intervention

Ten days after the assessment had begun the programme was put into effect. The system was checked once a week in the classroom and twice a week with Geraldine and her mother. Over a 2-month period there was considerable improvement in homework completion and quality. Although the class behaviour did improve it was not a large improvement. On the basis of the weekly observation it appeared that Geraldine's behaviours now equated more to the general classroom standard. Observations taken at the end of the first and second weeks indicated that Geraldine now exhibited 23 per cent on task behaviour and 20 per cent out-of-seat behaviour. On these two occasions she did not leave the room. It was felt at this stage that further improvement in classroom behaviour could not have been achieved without the implementation of a programme applied to the whole class. In the situation, however, this was impractical and it was not further considered. At the end of 3 months the card was only to be used on alternate weeks. No deterioration was observed during weeks when the card was not employed. At 3 months the system was stopped and at 6-month follow-up the improvement had been maintained.

Factors believed to have been important in maintaining improvement were as follows:

(1) The mother now had some idea of the regularity of homework assignments. She ensured that Geraldine completed her homework under the appropriate conditions and she appeared to be taking more immediate interest in her daughter's academic behaviour.

(2) The mother now maintained a closer liaison with the school. In the interval between the 3 and 6 months' post-intervention she had visited the school twice to check on Geraldine's performance in class.

(3) The teacher was habitually paying more attention to Geraldine's performance. In addition, the principal's interest in the case probably played some part in maintaining the effects.

This programme, while not as successful as we might have hoped, was set up without many problems. Its relative success (certainly at the 6-month stage) probably hinged on the reliable communication system which had resulted between principal, teacher, mother and child. Three other cases in which we have attempted this type of approach have failed, we believe, mainly because of the inability to establish this type of communication.

Key Ideas

The operation of a points system has several general advantages:

(1) For children over the age of 7, immediate reinforcement may no longer be sufficient. They require more sophisticated privileges, which often cannot be employed instantly, hence the use of a point to bridge the time lag between the occurrence of the behaviour and the eventual reward. Privileges should become contingent on earning points.

(2) Response cost (that is, the form of punishment peculiar to the points system) results in the loss only of preferred reinforcers, and the child can compensate for points loss by further adopting prosocial behaviours. Time-out, on the other hand, results in the loss of all reinforcers and whilst the child is in time-out he is denied the opportunity of exhibiting prosocial behaviour.

(3) Points systems are potentially useful in helping the child to develop self-control, to acquire task-oriented skills, and to shape up social skills which may have been deficient.

(4) Awarding points cues the parent to exhibit social approval and provides the child with immediate and positive feedback about his behaviour.

Bargaining and Contracting

Disputes between two parties are often solved by discussions which lead to a mutually acceptable bargain. In the process of reaching this reciprocal agreement some compromise is frequently required from each party. The bargain reached can be formalised as a written contract. For example, a 12-year-old boy caused his parents concern because he frequently stayed out late. The boy felt that his parents were unreasonable in asking him to come home too early and in their refusal to allow him to attend evening cinema at the weekends. Following discussion with both parties an agreement was reached whereby he was allowed to stay out until 9.30 p.m., provided his parents knew where he would be after 8.00 p.m. If he kept these times, it was agreed that he should be allowed to go to evening cinema at the weekends. If he failed to keep his bargain one evening, then he was to remain at home the following evening and would lose the weekend cinema privilege. This agreement was written out and signed as a contract by both the parents and the child.

We mentioned briefly in the last chapter how a child might be involved in the setting up of a points system. For example, he could select some of the privileges and rewards, and his views on what behaviours might be expected of him would also be considered. In such a case the points system acts as an implicit bargain between the child and his parents. In this chapter we discuss the drafting and the use of a more explicit bargain (a contract) between parents and child.

Generally we have described the use of bargaining and contracting with older children. However, as bargaining skills are so important in everyday life we suggest that the competence of this skill should be assessed in the large majority of parents referred to the clinic. Where necessary the components of the skill should then be taught. Obviously it is difficult to bargain with a 6-year-old highly oppositional child.

However, once opposition has been considerably reduced then the parent can use bargaining in the shaping up of prosocial skills; for example, when John hangs up his coat, then he can go out to play. It would be naïve to suggest that equality exists between parent and child in the bargaining situation. However, the parent, as an authority figure to the child, can teach him by using and modelling the skills involved in the bargaining process.

Establishing Bargains and Contracts

A clear contract is usually the result of a process involving three stages. These stages include, first, the definition of the problem and the requirements of each party; secondly, negotiation or bargaining of behaviour changes and their consequences and, thirdly, the clarification and establishment of a contract. In the first stage the therapist interviews parents and child separately. This is because children may easily acquiesce when their parents and the therapist are present, and the result could be a contract which features more of the parents' ideas than those of the child. The second and third stages are carried out between the parents and the child with the therapist acting as a mediator. Ideally two therapists should be involved, one representing the child and the other the parents. Obviously when engaging in both single and family group interviews it is important to maintain confidence where this is requested.

STAGE I. DEFINING THE PROBLEM AND THE REQUIREMENTS OF EACH PERSON

On the basis of the case history and observations the therapist will have selected a number of behaviours which could realistically be targets for change. He then sees the parents and child separately. The parents are asked to list which child behaviours they wish to see decreased and those which they wish to see increased. Usually, the first list is comprised of those behaviours which cause the parents most concern. As mediator, the therapist helps the parents to make a realistic selection, that is, to select a few behaviours which are amenable to change. For example, Joan's parents primarily wish to decrease her stealing and increase appropriate peer group relations. In this case it would be more realistic to work with the home problems which assessment has already uncovered, such as carrying out regular household chores and playing co-operatively with siblings. These behaviours would be more amenable to change because we have access to their contingencies and, as we previously hypothesised, changes in such home behaviours may result in changes in the more difficult problems which occur outside the home (such as stealing and poor peer relationships—see paragraph (5) under the heading 'Selecting initial target behaviours', in chapter 7).

Once the target behaviours have been selected with the parents the therapist then estimates the extent of change which they expect and their willingness to compromise. When this has been clarified the child is seen and informed of the parental requirements. Although she may feel that these are excessive, she can weigh them against her own list of desired privileges and estimate what she would consider to be an appropriate reward for carrying out the requests and what might be a fair consequence for failure to do so. For example, Joan may suggest being allowed to have her friends in to play records, consequent on keeping her room tidy. She may agree to do extra chores, such as washing the dishes, for failure to complete her task (that is, tidying her room) on time. The therapist should ensure that the rewards and punishments remain within reasonable limits. Before turning to negotiation we also discuss the list of parent behaviours which the child finds aversive. Often these parent behaviours relate to the child's problem behaviours. For example Karen, who regularly fails to complete her homework, may complain that her parents continually 'nag' about homework. In this case parental behaviour change would be an integral part of the programme, as we would expect to modify the total homework interaction between parents and child. In other cases the child's complaints relate to the restriction of potential reinforcers. For example, he has to be in bed before 9.00 p.m. or he only gets 10 pence pocket money per week. If it seems reasonable to alter these restrictions then we should consider their negotiation with the parents. When parental agreement to changes of the above order can be negotiated then the value of compromise is demonstrated to the child.

Having defined the requirements of both parties we are ready to enter negotiations. If the initial steps have resulted in large discrepancies between parent and child requests then we should hold further single interviews until the discrepancies have been reduced to a reasonable level.

STAGE 2. NEGOTIATION OF BEHAVIOURS AND CONTINGENCIES
This can be the most difficult stage in the contracting process. Some

flexibility is needed by both the parents and the child in smoothing out discrepancies in their mutual requirements. The therapist guides these discussions between parents and child in a positive direction in order to avoid argument or breakdown. In many instances the therapist will have to take the part of the child, either because the child is initially reticent in the joint interview or else to balance the weight of the parents' authority. Siblings of a similar age should also be involved in these discussions, as for the sake of fairness the new contingencies will often also apply to them. Usually, if they have no behaviour problems, the new regime will not greatly affect them. However, if they are dissatisfied with the contingencies then the bargaining process can be extended to them.

First, problem behaviours are discussed. It is usually in this area that the child is being asked to compromise, therefore particular attention is paid to his viewpoint. For example, he may think that he is being asked to do too many tasks or that the tasks are scheduled for the wrong time. He may agree, for example, to do his homework regularly if he is allowed to do it immediately after the evening meal, rather than after school. In this case we should ensure that the shift of time will not clash with any other highly valued activities, such as watching a favourite television programme.

Secondly, if the child has verbalised complaints about the parent then these can be discussed at this stage. However, caution is required as parents may feel threatened by such criticism from the child. One of the major weaknesses of the whole procedure is that we have no way of implementing contingencies for desired changes in parent behaviours, unless both parents agree to manage this on a contract between themselves (see the section on parent – parent contracts below).

Thirdly, rewards and punishments are discussed by the parents and child (just as they discussed problem behaviours) until a negotiated settlement is reached. It is usually in the area of privileges that the parent is being asked to compromise, therefore particular attention is paid to his viewpoint. For example, he may regard the child's requests as precocious or unfitting. Often privilege levels (for example the amount of pocket money or the child's bedtime) will be reached by the therapist discovering the norm in the child's peer group and then encouraging the child to negotiate for this level with the parents. Punishment is usually in the form of response cost (that is loss of privileges) or the imposition of an extra task. The child may be allowed to win back lost privileges by completing extra tasks. Generally, in behaviour therapy, we aim to terminate each sequence by rewarding the child. This is because punishing or suppressing behaviour is totally insufficient unless these behaviours can be replaced by prosocial skills. Allowing the child a 'second chance' after punishment (for example, the chance to win back lost privileges or to comply following time-out) affords him the opportunity of practising and being reinforced for appropriate behaviour. In defining and selecting rewards and punishments we suggest that it is preferable to avoid consequences which take the form of privileged interactions between the child and parent, for example a trip to the football match with father. Failure to earn such privileges may add a degree of negativism to the total parent–child interaction, whereas our long-term aim in any therapy is to increase the quality and positiveness of such interaction.

STAGE 3. THE CONTRACT

The contract is reached by the parent and child. The therapist is not a party to it, therefore he should not impose his own ideas (which may be culturally inappropriate) on the agreement. The final agreement is summarised by the therapist and documented. The contract should define the behaviours to be changed and state the contingencies for each behaviour. This document may then be signed by parents and child. Simply drawing up a contract is not a complete therapeutic solution (Weathers and Liberman, 1975). Contracts will only succeed if the parties involved have the ability to implement the agreed contingencies. Instruction, rehearsal and modelling may be required. For example, Nick's parents realise that they should tell him to tidy his room before he goes outside to play, but they may be unable to contain their anger when he fails to comply with this request. We may need to practise appropriate parent consequating behaviour. In coping with problem behaviours, parents are always advised not to argue or debate with the child at the time of the behavioural infringement, but rather to impose consistent contingencies. We should also ensure that the child is capable of carrying out the behaviour for which he will be rewarded. For example, Mary would practise putting on her school uniform to ensure that she is able to reach an acceptable level of tidiness and therefore gain her contracted privileges.

When we have ascertained that the contract is viable it can then be put into operation. The agreements are recorded and tracked each day on simple charts which are posted in some significant place in the house. If several behaviours are involved then a points system may be incorporated in order to facilitate the operation of the contract. Initially progress should be followed intensely. Concentration is focused on the problem behaviours and parental implementation of the contingencies. The terms of the contract may be reviewed and further contracts, incorporating more behaviours, can be arranged when appropriate. As stressed before, it is most reinforcing to initially select behaviours which seem amenable to change and then, once parents and child have learned the skills, to move on to more difficult behaviours.

Teaching Skills of Negotiation and Contracting

Therapists should find it relatively easy to set up a contract with families who co-operate in treatment. However, whilst a therapist-facilitated contract can operate effectively it may deprive the family of learning the skills involved in the process. Therefore, as a second part of the programme we should focus on teaching the families negotiation and bargaining skills. This procedure is initiated once our primary contracts have been reasonably effective under supervision.

From a list of behaviour problems we select one to be discussed. This problem should be one which does not cause the parents too much anxiety or anger. As negotiating skills shape up, we move to succeedingly more difficult problems in future sessions. The parents and child are given a set time (for example, 10 minutes) to discuss the problem and reach a mutually agreed settlement. During this time some recording of the proceedings is kept. Video taping is the most valuable method as it provides a store for feedback of both the verbal and non-verbal components of the discussion. In the absence of video taping facilities the therapist could use tape or cassette recordings, plus notes. At the end of the designated time the discussion is stopped and the interaction is reviewed with the family. The focus is on the behaviours exhibited during the period (verbal and non-verbal) and also on the progress of the interchange. For example, we ask whether the problem was defined, negotiated and contracted.

In reviewing the session we will be interested in the presence of behaviours which hinder the problem solving process and of behaviours which facilitate it.

(1) Negative verbal behaviours. Some examples of unproductive verbal behaviours would be: criticising, 'Don't be stupid'; complaining,

'You're always on my back'; or side-tracking, 'You never wanted me anyway—I was just a mistake'.

(2) Negative non-verbal behaviours. Some examples of unproductive non-verbal behaviours would be: shaking finger, looking away, shaking head or obviously refusing to listen. Often the use of such negative behaviours leads to retaliatory behaviour on the part of the other person and may finally result in either the end of the discussion or else side-tracking.

(3) Positive verbal behaviours. Some examples of productive verbal behaviours would be: summarising the other's statements, 'You feel that John is allowed more freedom than you are'; stating one's present case non-critically and giving clear reasons for it, 'I believe that John is entitled to more freedom than you, Liz, because he is two years older and he is more able to take care of himself'; responding positively to positive cues or agreement from the other, 'As we agree that John is better able to take care of himself, we could ask him to take you along to the Saturday night dance or else you could go with a group of girls—I just worry about you going out on your own at night'; or relevant responses which remain on the topic.

(4) Positive non-verbal behaviours. Some examples of productive non-verbal behaviours would be: watching and listening to the other's suggestions; appropriate voice level; establishing eye contact; appropriate facial expression.

Having pinpointed these positive and negative behaviours the whole discussion is then reviewed with the family. Negative interchanges are examined and each person is asked how he felt during the interchange. This may help the individuals to become more aware of their own behaviours and the effect they have on others. Hopefully the individual may learn to control his responses before the stage of an argument and consequent breakdown of the discussion. More appropriate ways of phrasing feelings are modelled. For example, rather than saying 'Don't be stupid', we may say 'Sorry, I don't understand what you are trying to say'. Any positive interchanges are praised.

Following this exercise the family discussion period is repeated with all the points mentioned kept in mind. The recording is again monitored step by step. This continues until we reach a stage where there are few negative interchanges and many positive ones, and when problem-solving is established on a contractual basis. Following this the next problem on the hierarchy can be discussed. Later, assigned discussion tasks can be given to the family to carry out in the absence of the therapist. As sessions progress the family are asked to review the discussions themselves, allowing the therapist mediator gradually to withdraw.

When individuals are having great difficulty in reducing negatives a fining system can be introduced in an attempt to increase motivation. For example, a fine of 3 pence for every negative behaviour (negative behaviour being defined for that family). Fines can go to other family members. In teaching contracting the sessions should be conducted regularly and intensely (for example, twice a week), so that advances will be given a chance to consolidate through recognition and repeated practice. Each session lasts approximately $1\frac{1}{2}$ hours. Although we have had reasonable success in cases where the therapist has mediated during the bargaining and has later drawn up the contract, we have rarely succeeded in enabling families to generalise these skills so that they can later bargain and draw up contracts without the therapist's help.

In introducing the concept of bargaining and contracting we have concentrated on its use between parents and their children. The procedure involved is important in many other situations outside the family, for example employer – employee or teacher – student. To conclude this chapter we shall examine the use of contracting as a therapeutic measure for other aspects of family management.

Therapist – Parent Bargains

The relationship between client and therapist in any therapeutic situation is usually governed by a number of implicit or explicit terms; for example, the client accepts the form of therapy, he will keep regular appointments, and he will undertake assignments which the therapist requests. In return the therapist will provide his skills until there is agreement to terminate therapy. These basic understandings are essential to success. It is our impression that often the terms of therapy are not clearly specified and we suggest that prior to intervention a bargain should be reached with the clients, according to the method already outlined.

Definition
The client should specify the problem and what improvement he expects. The therapist should specify the nature of his approach, how

often and where he will wish to see the client, and what assignments he may require the client to complete (such as observation).

Negotiations

At this stage, agreement on the improvement anticipated and on the intensity of the therapy can be reached. Consequences for success or failure to comply with the terms of the bargain may be negotiated. Obviously these consequences tend to be one-sided in that they focus on the clients' side of the bargain, and therefore the therapist must ensure that the client is capable of fulfilling his commitments. Clients may only agree to assignments because they believe this is a socially acceptable response. One way of guaranteeing that the client will be provided with a service is to stipulate that he will have a designated number of therapeutic sessions, made available within a certain timespan. This time limit has the added advantage that it may help motivate the client to use therapeutic time to its maximum advantage. At the end of the designated number of sessions, therapy may be extended if both parties agree that reasonable progress has been made.

Most commonly, the consequences stipulated by the therapist are ones which make the continuation of therapy contingent on completion of task assignments, keeping of appointments, etc. Whilst we have employed this method there is sometimes reason to doubt the reinforcing value of therapy to the clients. For instance, a family which has experienced failure at the hands of various helping or counselling agencies may fail to see further therapy as reinforcing. Some workers (mainly American) have employed alternative reinforcers such as money. For example, a sum of money is deposited with the therapist by the client at the onset of therapy and is returned gradually according to completion of each stipulated stage of intervention. This approach presents certain practical difficulties when operated within our system of socialised health services.

Parent – Parent Bargains

We have mainly found parent – parent contracting to be useful in two situations. First, where there are parental marital problems and, secondly, where one or both parents are having difficulty in maintaining consistency in dealing with the child's behaviour. In managing marital problems the contracting principles and the method of teaching bargaining skills which we have already outlined is still applicable. As this text does not specifically discuss the management of marital problems we refer the interested reader to Azrin, Naster and Jones (1973) and Knox (1971). The management of parent consequating difficulties by contracting follows similar principles. Parents may agree to monitor each other's consequating behaviour with the child, and levy on their partner fines or rewards which have been previously stipulated (for example the loss or gain of money, cigarettes, a favourite television programme or an evening out). The use of parent – parent contracting is illustrated in the case of George described in chapter 9.

Case Example Illustrating Use of Contingency Contracting

Synopsis
Terry, a 13-year-old girl, was referred to the clinic with several behaviour problems which were as follows:

(1) Coming home late 2−3 nights each week. Terry's parents expected her to be home by 9 p.m. but the time on these late evenings varied between 10.30 and 11.30. p.m.

(2) Refusal to help with household chores. Terry did not keep her room tidy or make her own bed; she would not take messages and refused to help with chores when her mother was out.

(3) Failure to do homework.

The problems had only manifested themselves in the preceding two years. The behaviour tended to occur more in the mother's presence, although the father also appeared to be inconsistent in his handling. Even though the father was concerned about Terry and would on occasion support his wife's decisions, he clearly felt that the management of the problems lay between his daughter and his wife. Terry was in good health and did not have any other problems. School contact indicated that she was of average ability. Her past and developmental history did not reveal any abnormalities. Terry had one sibling—a brother of 18 who was working. He was a quiet boy who did not seem to present any problems. The parents' marital relationship appeared to be stable.

At the initial interview Terry made the following complaints: she did not get enough pocket money; she was expected to return home too early in the evening; she was not permitted to go to a local Friday night disco for young teenagers; her mother was always asking her to do things at awkward times, for example when she was watching a television programme; her mother continually nagged her about the above episodes.

Observation

Since it was judged that home observation would reveal little, we asked both Terry and her mother to observe and keep records of the problem behaviours. The father was not present at the first visit but at a subsequent interview in the home he agreed to participate in the record-keeping. The mother was asked to record Terry's behaviour as follows:

(1) Time Terry returned home each evening.

(2) Refusal to help with household chores, take messages or keep her room tidy. Failure to comply with each request was recorded as one episode.

(3) Episodes of verbal abusiveness to mother. A recording was to be made for each time Terry swore at mother or called her names.

(4) Whether or not homework was completed.

Baseline records were taken for one week. They revealed that Terry had been in at least 1 hour late on 3 occasions, that she refused to do tasks on an average of 5 times per day, and that episodes of verbal abusiveness had averaged about 6 times per day. During the observation period, homework was completed each evening.

Terry was asked to write commentaries (rather than keep frequency counts) on her mother's behaviours. This was implemented because it was felt that Terry had been somewhat reticent at the first interview. The problem areas which she was to describe and comment on were as follows: (*a*) unreasonable requests by mother; (*b*) things which mother does or says which make you feel angry; (*c*) anything else which makes you feel angry at home.

Some examples of Terry's comments were as follows: 'Was asked to go for message when I was in the middle of watching a television programme. I would have gone if she'd waited till it was finished. I always watch this programme'; 'Am not allowed to do the dishes because I use too much washing-up liquid—the next evening I was asked to do them'; 'Was asked to go for a message when I was in the middle of washing and dressing'; 'Was not allowed to keep my light on to read, when I went to bed at 10.30 p.m.'; 'Mother refused to give me 10 pence for my regular magazine'.

These comments, together with the mother's observational records, were of considerable value in providing further information on the problem areas. Terry's records revealed that she was often asked to carry out tasks at what would seem to be inappropriate times and that her mother was inconsistent in giving pocket money (for example, she often gave Terry pocket money following deviant behaviours in the hope that her behaviour would improve).

Planning
Initially we decided to focus on modifying the following behaviours:
(1) Coming in on time each evening.
(2) Verbal abusiveness to mother.
(3) Keeping her room tidy.
(4) Carrying out chores or requests made by mother.
In addition we decided to examine, discuss and reach agreement on two other areas which appeared to cause Terry concern:
(5) Pocket money.
(6) Permission to go to the Friday evening disco, which many of her friends attended.

Intervention—establishing the contract
Initially, each problem listed above was discussed with Terry and her mother separately. Following a definition of each one's viewpoint they were then interviewed together. The problems were defined until an agreement was reached as to what both parties considered appropriate or inappropriate, and what the consequences for each behaviour should be. The therapist role was to direct the discussion in stages and to avoid making explicit suggestions. The contracting lasted approximately 3 hours and was conducted over an afternoon. The following contracted agreements were reached by Terry and her mother.

(1) Coming in on time. Terry is to stay at home 1 evening per week in order to have her bath and wash her hair. On other evenings, on completion of homework and provided that she remains in the neighbourhood, she may stay out until 9.30 p.m. When her parents are aware of her exact location she may stay out until 10.00 p.m. If the rules are followed for the preceding week then Terry will be allowed to attend the local disco on Friday evening, from which she must return by 11.30 p.m. Failure to comply with the rules will result in loss of the next evening out.

(2) Verbal abusiveness to mother. Being verbally abusive to mother includes such things as telling her to 'shut up', calling her names, telling her to mind her own business or making rude signs or swearing in front

of her. For each instance of verbal abusiveness, 5 pence is to be deducted from Terry's regular pocket money. On each occurrence, mother is to indicate that Terry has been abusive and then state the fine. Attempts to argue are to be ignored and further abusive behaviour will be similarly fined.

(3) Keeping room tidy. After the evening meal, mother is to check Terry's room to ensure that it is tidy. Clothes are to be hung up, books and magazines neatly piled and the bed made. If the room is tidy, Terry is allowed to continue with whatever she is doing. Articles left lying around are to be confiscated for one week. The bed must be made before Terry is allowed to continue with her regular activities.

(4) Carrying out chores or requests made by the mother. It is agreed that Terry should only be asked to do 2 chores or messages each day. Apart from exceptional circumstances these are to be carried out within 1 hour of the request. Failure to comply with these rules is to result in a 10 pence fine. Compliance to these requests is to result in a random (approximately 1 in every 3 times) reward of 5 pence on completion of the task.

(5) Pocket money. Terry is to have £1 pocket money per week, which becomes available on Friday evening. Any fines during the preceding week are deducted from this money. Terry is allowed to spend the money as she wishes.

(6) Disco on Friday evenings. Terry is allowed to go to the disco each Friday evening according to the stipulations already mentioned in the contract. Her parents will agree to this privilege only if Terry observes the following rules: she is to be home by 11.30 p.m. and failure to comply with this rule is to result in a loss of this privilege for 2 weeks.

Following the drawing up of the contract, Terry and her parents were given copies of the agreement and asked to consider it within the next 2 days. They then agreed to put the contract into effect. At this stage, approximately 2 hours were spent with the mother discussing and modelling her commanding, praising and punishing styles. Particular emphasis was placed on not 'nagging' about tasks, rule infringements, etc.

Implementation of the contract
During the first week of implementation the family was visited daily. During this first week Terry lost 2 nights out through returning home late and she was not allowed to attend the disco. She also lost three-quarters of her next week's pocket money by being verbally abusive and

by failing to take messages on 3 occasions. Terry's reports indicated that her mother was still 'nagging' repeatedly about these infringements. Time during the therapist's visits was mainly spent in going over this 'nagging' behaviour with the mother. During the second week, Terry's behaviours began to improve dramatically and the mother seemed to be reducing her level of nagging. The improvement was reflected in the more co-operative way in which Terry and the mother conversed. At the end of this week Terry was able to go to the disco and lost only 15 pence pocket money. In view of the dramatic improvement the mother took Terry out and bought her some clothes on this second weekend.

The improvement persisted and at 1 month the parent and child observational recordings were stopped. At a 6-month follow-up the family all stated that the improvement had been maintained.

Key Ideas

Often an intervention programme functions in the form of an implicit bargain, either between client and therapist or between parent and child. In this chapter we have discussed the drawing up and use of a more explicit bargain, that is, a contract. However, simply drawing up a contract is not a complete therapeutic solution. Contracts will only succeed: if a few behaviours which are amenable to change are selected; if, during the first stage, discrepancies in the mutual requirements of both parties are reduced to a reasonable level; and if the parties involved have the ability to implement the agreed contingencies. Before putting the contract into operation we may need to practise appropriate parent consequating and ensure that the child is capable of carrying out the behaviour for which he is to be rewarded. Contracting is only an initial step in the solving of behaviour problems and once the contract has been established we must focus on the implementation of agreed contingencies.

Although a therapist-designed contract can operate effectively it may deprive the family of learning skills involved in the process. As a second part of the programme we should, ideally, focus on teaching the family negotiation and bargaining skills.

Delinquency and Non-Accidental Injury: Some Aspects of Aetiology and Management

Antisocial Behaviour Problems

In this text the terms 'antisocial' and 'delinquent' are used to refer to behaviour (such as stealing, lying, promiscuity, fire-setting, and breaking and entering), which when adopted, either inside or outside of the child's family environment, will carry strong social sanctions and the possibility of legal proceedings. These problems are often referred to by behaviourists as low rate problems. Commonly, antisocial children also present other, high rate, behaviour problems, such as tantrums, physical aggression, verbal abusiveness, non-compliance and poor social interactional skills.

It is impossible to provide an extensive coverage of the many research findings pertaining to delinquency. Thus the views presented below are related mainly to the authors' reading and personal viewpoint.

Characteristics of the Antisocial Child and his Family

FAMILY CHARACTERISTICS
The families of antisocial children tend to be larger, to come from lower socio-economic classes and to frequently have a history of antisocial behaviour. Their pattern of interaction tends to be undisciplined,

inconsistent, primitive, hostile and interpersonally conflictual (Robins, 1966). The family's behavioural style often leads to rejection and isolation by their subculture. Frequently they are referred to as problem families (Tonge, James and Hillam, 1975).

SCHOOL AND ACADEMIC CHARACTERISTICS

In school the antisocial child is frequently found to challenge adult authority and to display poor academic attainments. Rutter, Tizard and Whitmore (1970) have demonstrated that many of these children are severely behind in reading skills. In most cases this backwardness cannot be attributed to low intellectual ability. Explanations offered for this finding include poor concentration ability and low achievement motivation. Maloney, Maloney and Timbers (1975) have shown that antisocial children, committed by the juvenile court to residential care, had frequently demonstrated a gradual deterioration in academic attainments and an increase in the rate of truancy over the few years prior to their committal. They do not offer any explanation for this finding.

SEX DIFFERENCES IN ANTISOCIAL BEHAVIOUR

All studies known to the authors agree that antisocial problems are much more common in boys than in girls. The reasons for this are difficult to establish and must at least be multifactorial. In considering the male preponderance in child psychiatric disorders, Rutter (1975) discusses various points of possible importance. First, as male children are physically more delicate than female children, Rutter questions whether they are more psychologically vulnerable. Secondly, there are temperamental differences in the two sexes which may contribute to the discrepancy in child psychiatric disorders. For example, preschool boys are generally more aggressive than preschool girls. Thirdly, biological factors, such as the presence of an extra Y sex chromosome, have been found to be associated with male aggressive behaviour. Thus, we might deduce that the normal single Y sex chromosome may predispose males to behave aggressively. Lastly, social stereotypes and attitudes about the sexes are important in shaping behaviour. Parental expectations of how a male or a female should behave are demonstrated in the handling of their children.

While each of the above factors partially explains the sex differences in antisocial behaviour, it is probable that their contributions are relative and the result of interaction.

Peer relationships in antisocial children tend to be deficient. Frequently, they are characterised by lack of popularity and co-operation and by fighting and coercion.

THE FUTURE OF ANTISOCIAL CHILDREN

Robins (1966) has demonstrated that children with several antisocial problems are likely, as adults, to display further antisocial and criminal behaviours, to have poor work records and interpersonal relations, frequent marital problems and to produce antisocial offspring. Children involved in legal proceedings and institutionalisation (for delinquency) tend to have the worst prognosis. The appearance in court and its consequences were found to be related to parental adequacy and social class. Having parents who are adequate and of middle class appears to afford the child some protection from court appearance.

Aetiology of Antisocial Problems

Various hypotheses and theories have been put forward in an attempt to explain the aetiology of antisocial behaviours. A limited selection of these is presented below:

INHERITED AND CONSTITUTIONAL ASPECTS

The work of Chess, Thomas and Birch (1968) suggests that temperamental characteristics which can be observed at birth may be important in the development of later behaviour problems. In the New York longitudinal study these researchers isolated a small group of children who had been reported by their parents as difficult from birth. Temperamentally they differed from other children in that they exhibited irregular habits (sleeping and eating), withdrawal or distress in new situations and a slowness to adapt to change. Seventy per cent of this group later developed behaviour disorders. The researchers suggested that the ensuing behaviour problems resulted from an interaction between parental behaviour and child temperament.

Another temperamental trait which parents have found difficult is a child's inability to concentrate and persist (Thomas, Chess and Birch, 1968). Rutter, Tizard and Whitmore (1970) report that poor concentration is often found in children with reading backwardness. These researchers tentatively suggest that such academic failure may in some cases be an important aetiological factor in the development of antisocial behaviour. The importance of temperamental factors lies in the behavioural outcome of any interaction between parent and child temperaments. Patterson (1973) has noted how easily children can shape up aggressive behaviour in their parents. Probably parents with limited handling skills (as is often the case in delinquent families) may be less able to cope with temperamental clashes and thus be more readily shaped by their child.

Some physiological investigations, for example see Borkovec (1970), have revealed that some delinquent children appear to exhibit less autonomic (emotional) reactivity than normal children. For instance, they will show less anxiety or stress when observing another child being punished. Inheritance may play some part in autonomic reactivity. Eysenck (1957) suggests that antisocial persons inherently condition (that is, learn), less well than normal persons. However, Weiss, Krasner and Ullman (1960) demonstrate that conditionability is a function not only of inherent variables but of many situational variables.

While inherent variables are probably important in the genesis of some behavioural problems, their contribution is almost certainly nonspecific (in the sense that they do not lead to specific behavioural syndromes). For example, the epileptic child is predisposed to present with behavioural problems but we cannot predict what form these will take (for instance, whether they will be tantrums, truanting, destructiveness or disobedience). The behavioural outcome will depend on the interaction of the inherent factors with the social environment.

SOCIAL CIRCUMSTANCES

Since the majority of antisocial children come from the lower socioeconomic groups we might assume that factors associated with these groups (such as poverty, overcrowding and poor stimulation) are causal in the development of delinquency. This is not so. Robins (1966), Craig and Glick (1965) and Jephcott and Carter (1955) all stress that it is the family characteristics which seem to be most predictive. For instance, middle class antisocial children frequently show disturbed family backgrounds, whereas lower class children with normal family backgrounds are unlikely to exhibit delinquency. The theory that the antisocial behaviour is learned from other members of the socioeconomic class is also unlikely as many delinquent or problem families are unpopular in the community and culturally isolated (Tonge, James and Hillam, 1975).

The excess of delinquent problems in the lower socio-economic classes can be explained in several ways:

(1) The factors associated with being a problem family (for example, poor work record, debt and increased physical illness) will tend to result in a drift down the social scale, and will also inhibit movement up the social scale.

(2) Families from lower socio-economic classes appear to be less able to provide or to stimulate services which might avoid these problems (for example, better schooling).

(3) Society's attitudes are generally less tolerant of deviant behaviour in the lower socio-economic group. For instance, Robins (1966) found that antisocial children coming from unemployed and dependent families were more likely to be sent to a correctional institution than were similar children from self-supporting families. This prejudice draws attention to the number of problem families within the group.

LEARNING ANTISOCIAL BEHAVIOUR

Many antisocial children have been heavily exposed to inconsistent discipline, deviant models and repeated experience of failure.

(1) The inconsistent use of rewards and punishments. McCord, McCord and Zola (1959), in a prospective study of delinquency, reported that parental consistency in disciplining their children was the major factor which differentiated delinquent and non-delinquent children. Regardless of whether the home was warm or punitive, if disciplining was consistent then child delinquency was unlikely. Thus, those factors which contribute to inconsistency in the parent will be likely to contribute to delinquency, for example parents lacking appropriate social skills, 'broken' families, sick parents and single parents. Inconsistencies in discipline may result in the child's failure to develop appropriate social behaviours and their associated internal cues (such as guilt or anxiety). In this way the development of self-control is hindered. As the rewards and punishments used in disciplining are inconsistent and often non-contingent the child may fail to see their association with his behaviour and therefore social approval or disapproval from his parent may become completely ineffective (Sajwaj and Dillon, 1976). The inconsistent and non-contingent use of punishment and reward may also lead to a state of behavioural helplessness in the child. In other words, because the consequences are randomly related to his behaviour, he will tend to view them as being beyond his control. Under such circumstances the child's deviant

behaviour is likely to remain unchanged. For a fuller discussion on learned helplessness refer to chapter 14.

(2) Exposure to deviant models. Modelling and imitation are important methods of learning. The normal child learns most of his social behaviours by observing and imitating. A young child's major models will be his parents and his siblings. As he grows he will model the behaviours of other adults (teachers, neighbours, relatives, etc.) and peers. The child who comes from a problem family will be exposed to inappropriate models—his parents will often exhibit high levels of aggression, inconsistency, arguing and conflict. Since he is a member of a problem family he will have less access to outside appropriate models. First, his coercive behaviours (learned in the family situation) will tend to isolate him from his peers, and thus he will fail to learn appropriate play and co-operative skills. Secondly, because his family tends to exist in cultural isolation there will be less access to appropriate adult models. It has been suggested that modelling the behaviours of delinquent peers is an important factor in the evolution of delinquency. However, Robins (1966) found that belonging to a delinquent peer group had little effect on the prognosis of antisocial behaviour. This suggests that the delinquent peer group may not be of much importance to the antisocial child as a source of learning. Modelling is dependent on the reinforcement value of the model. Where this is high, then the model's behaviour will tend more often to be imitated. In the problem family, reinforcement value among family members will tend to be low, and thus while modelling may occur its overall importance will probably be less. The significance of this is discussed further in chapter 14.

ACADEMIC FAILURE AND ANTISOCIAL BEHAVIOUR

Rutter, Tizard and Whitmore (1970) demonstrated that many anti-social children had reading ages well below those which would have been predicted by their intelligence (as measured by intelligence tests). There is argument as to how this finding relates to delinquency. Is it cause or effect? The answer to this question cannot be simple and it is probable that academic failure is related in several ways. Rutter (1975) suggests three possible mechanisms. First, temperamental characteristics may predispose the child to both reading difficulty and antisocial disorder. Secondly, the characteristics of families which predispose a child to antisocial disorder may also predispose him to academic failure. Thirdly, academic failure in itself may result in the child seeking reinforcement in antisocial or delinquent behaviours.

Treatment and Outcome

There is no documented evidence that therapeutic intervention of any kind affects the outcome of delinquency (Robins, 1972). Some findings on the outcome of behaviourally oriented intervention strategies are given below.

(1) Patterson (1975) reports that intervention with behaviourally disordered families (in which the children are frequently referred to as predelinquent) often produces immediate behavioural changes which are not sustained at long term follow-up. An analysis of Patterson's data by Kent (1976) suggests that only 7 out of the 27 cases reported by Patterson could be regarded as moderately successful, in spite of an average of 30 hours' intervention time per case.

(2) Studies conducted at Achievement Place (see Phillips *et al*, 1971) demonstrate that substantial changes can be effected in the behaviour of delinquent children whilst they remain in a residential setting. However, these workers have yet to publish extensive long term follow-up results. Wahler, Berland and Leske (1975) conducted a study in a short term, intensive, behaviourally oriented correction centre and found that while behaviour changed considerably within the institutional setting, it was not maintained following discharge of the child. At 1 year, approximately 80 per cent of these delinquent children had had further involvements with the police or were felt to be in need of further treatment. It is clear that successful intervention must, at the very least, entail massive and long term intervention programmes which consider the child, his family, school and social surroundings. Research currently being conducted by Wahler is perhaps nearest to this approach. His therapeutic programmes include home and school intervention, summer programmes for under-achievers and communication skills training groups for parents.

Society's response to the delinquent child presents problems to any intervention programme. Once a child has been labelled as delinquent it is probable that he will continue to be viewed as deviant, and thus fail to gain reinforcement for considerable changes in his behaviour. Perhaps at this point in time our efforts should be directed more to recognising the precursors of delinquent behaviour, so that intervention can begin at an early age, before the child's learning becomes well established. Methods of motivating the parents of such children to seek out and co-operate in intervention will also have to be found. Certainly it has been our experience that such parents come for advice only when the child's behaviour has caused considerable social problems, and that once in therapy these parents also exhibit a high drop-out rate.

Within our own clinical setting the multi-model approach suggested above is difficult because of the shortage of time available for intensive work with individual families. There is little time to follow up and investigate the many drop-outs from treatment (which are common in the antisocial group). Further, those who do remain in treatment frequently fail to show any persistent changes. Below, we report two cases which will help to illustrate our approach to these problems. The first case was regarded as a success but was not typical of the antisocial group. The second case was a failure.

An Indirect Approach to Managing Delinquent Behaviour

Synopsis
Jack, a 10-year-old boy, was referred to the clinic with the following problems:

(*a*) Breaking and entering. Three episodes were known to the parents in the 4 months prior to intervention.

(*b*) Fire-setting. Two episodes known in the previous 6 months.

(*c*) Stealing. Jack had stolen small amounts of money from his mother once or twice per week. In the month prior to intervention, neighbours had reported on three occasions that they thought Jack had taken money from their homes.

(*d*) Staying out late. On average, Jack stayed out until approximately 11 p.m. once a week.

(*e*) High rate problems were reported in the home. These were non-compliance, tantrums and verbally abusive behaviour.

The parents had become concerned about Jack's antisocial behaviours approximately 6 months before referral. In an attempt to manage these problems they had employed physical punishment, restricted his pocket money and had kept him at home—all to no avail.

However, in some ways the history in this case did not exhibit all of the common characteristics which we might expect to find in the histories of antisocial children. Contact with Jack's school revealed that he was up to standard in attainments and there had been no truancy. Father was in steady employment, the marriage appeared stable and there were no other obvious family problems. Jack had a 4-year-old sister who exhibited no problems.

Observation

It was recognised that there was little point in applying contingencies to the low rate antisocial behaviours, as the parents rarely discovered these until much later and so they were unable to control the reinforcers. An indirect approach was adopted (refer to discussion on response class in chapter 7). It was hoped that successful management of the high rate behaviour problems in the home would indirectly affect the low rate problems and also increase parent reinforcement value, in which case Jack might be more liable to respect his parents' ideas of 'right' and 'wrong'.

During baseline, the parents took daily frequency counts of disobedience (or non-compliance) and verbally abusive behaviour. The occurrence of these behaviours was later graphed (figure 12.1). No therapist observations were taken as Jack was considered to be too old for this strategy. Once the points system was implemented, it replaced the frequency counts as the main form of observation and recording.

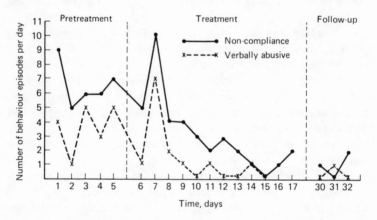

Figure 12.1 Graph depicting Jack's non-compliance and verbally abusive behaviours before, during and after treatment

Planning

Following discussions with the parents and child, the following plans were adopted:

(1) Non-compliance, tantrums and verbally abusive behaviours were to be followed by time-out. Refusal to go to time-out was met with successive points losses for each 1-minute refusal.

(2) Behaviours such as keeping room tidy, coming in by 8.30 p.m.

each evening, doing one set chore per day for mother, helping mother with other chores in the house (at her request), doing homework on time, were all handled with the aid of a points system.

(3) Points earned could be saved for weekend privileges (for example, going to the pictures or the swimming pool, being allowed to watch a late film on television on Saturday) or else exchanged at 7 p.m. each evening for daily privileges (for example, pocket money to a maximum of 10 pence, watching television until bedtime at 9.30 p.m., being allowed to stay up half an hour later, use of the record player). Points not saved were 'good' for 24 hours.

The parents were instructed in the use of time-out, points awarding and fining. These were practised with the therapist. The final contingencies were again discussed with Jack and his parents, and a points chart was constructed and posted on the kitchen wall (figure 12.2).

Intervention
During the first week of intervention the mother was seen on each weekday and on two occasions father was also present. The behaviours of the preceding day and the manner in which they were handled were discussed. The parents operated the contingencies excellently, and needed very little encouragement. They verbalised enthusiasm about the improvement in Jack's behaviour. The points system was kept in operation for about 1 month after which the parents gradually stopped using it. This occurred before we had decided to phase out the programme. Contact was maintained with the family for a further 6 months. At this time, none of the antisocial behaviours had recurred.

During follow-up we noted one problem which we left unsolved. Jack stopped associating with many of his previous friends with whom he had engaged in delinquent activity. Ideally, we might have attempted to encourage the development of relationships with other children. However, the parents discouraged this idea by frequently quoting various delinquent activities associated with the other children in the neighbourhood.

Total therapist time involved in this case was approximately $9\frac{1}{2}$ hours.

Day	Bedroom tidy Check 5.30 pm Tidy = 200 Untidy = -50	Homework complete by 7.30 pm Complete = 200 Incomplete = -60	Home on time last evening On time = 200 Each 5 mins late = -50	Helping with chores in house = 100	Required chore Complete = 150 Failure to complete = -50	Refusal to go to time-out = -30 for each minute	Total points for day	Points saved for weekend events
Day 1 WED	200	200	200	—	-50	-120	430	80
Day 2 THURS	-50	-60	200	—	-50	-210	0	—
Day 3 FRI	200	200	200	100	150	—	850	250
Day 4 SAT	-50	200	-50	100	150	-60	290	—
Day 5 SUN	200	200	200	—	150	—	750	150
DAY 6 MON	-50	200	200	100	150	—	600	100
DAY 7 TUES	200	200	200	—	-50	-30	520	20

REWARD COSTS

(i) Watching T.V. = 150
(ii) Staying up half an hour later = 100
(iii) Use of record player = 150
(iv) Pocket money (1p) = 20
(v) Pictures at weekend = 400
(vi) Late night T.V. film at weekend = 250
(vii) Swimming at weekend = 150

Figure 12.2   Points system for Jack—treatment week 1

A Case of Failure in Managing Delinquency

Synopsis

Chris was 11 years old when he was first referred to the clinic with the following problems: frequent fighting with peers, staying out late and stealing from relatives and neighbours. When with his mother at home he was disobedient, bad tempered (he had tantrums when he did not get money), verbally abusive (using obscene language), and destructive with toys and clothes. At school he was 2 years behind in reading. Although Chris did not play truant from school he frequently missed days through vague physical complaints.

Chris was born illegitimate and had been reared by his grandparents until he was 9 years old. At this time his grandparents refused to look after him any longer as he was 'impossible' to manage. The mother, who had recently married, then took over the care of Chris. She described her own childhood as unhappy because of frequent rows and separations between her parents. The mother had been referred to a psychiatric hospital, where she was described as an immature personality. Her marriage did not seem to have any problems to date. Her husband, stepfather to Chris, was in stable employment and he appeared to have no past problems. However, he probably contributed to some of the problems with Chris, as he believed that his wife was mismanaging the child, and therefore he was over-punitive towards Chris (for example, he stopped pocket money for 6 weeks at a time, occasionally made Chris stay in his bedroom for hours on end and sometimes he would not allow Chris to watch television for days).

Observation

Attempts to get baseline recordings failed because Chris was too old for therapist observation and the mother failed to keep frequency counts of the high rate behaviours. We had to rely on discussion of each preceding day's events to provide us with information about the problem behaviours and their current contingencies. These discussions revealed:

(1) The mother was inconsistent. On some occasions she would allow deviance to pass and on other occasions she became very angry with Chris. Her reaction did not seem to be related in any way to the seriousness of the deviance.

(2) She frequently gave Chris pocket money (without the stepfather's knowledge) on the grounds that he would behave himself.

(3) She complained about the child's lack of affection and stated that

she often succumbed to his demands in the hope of winning his affection.

(4) She frequently used threats which she had no intention of keeping; for example, informing the police about his behaviour and threatening to have him removed from the family.

Planning

Despite the mother's failure to keep baseline recordings we decided to proceed with a management programme. As stepfather worked until 8 p.m. he was not often seen and could not easily be involved in the programme. Our approach was basically similar to that adopted in the previous case. Time-out was to be used for the high rate problems such as disobedience, verbal abusiveness and tantrums. A points system was devised to manage coming in on time, keeping clothes tidy, doing chores and washing himself. The mother was unable to manage the points system and so it was dropped.

Intervention

The use of time-out and social approval (mixed with material reinforcers) effected positive behaviour changes in the child within 1 week. During this week many hours were spent in the home, with the mother, re-enacting and practising ways of handling non-compliance. Special emphasis was placed on helping her to keep calm and not to argue, rationalise or reason with Chris once he had deviated. During this time we also made 3 appointments for the mother to attend the clinic, but she failed to keep them. We had planned to use these clinic meetings to role play and video tape some of the mother's behaviours in the hope that the role play and discussion would facilitate her learning. Two weeks after implementation of the time-out contingencies both parents reported considerable improvements in Chris's behaviour in the home. However, at this time a reported episode of stealing from a neighbour set the mother back to her old style of consequating, and several afternoon sessions were spent in the home working through this. After 4 weeks of intervention the parents were left to manage on their own for 4 days, and again both the mother's style and Chris's behaviour deteriorated. Progress see-sawed at this precarious level for $3\frac{1}{2}$ months, at which time the first author had to leave the clinic for a period. The family were referred to another therapist who made several clinic appointments to see them, but they failed to keep any of these appointments.

Somewhere between 25 and 30 hours' therapist time was invested in this case, and there was never any evidence of sustained improvement. It is possible (although the authors consider it most unlikely) that had continued behavioural intervention been possible the improvement might have persisted. However, it is impractical to suggest that such an intensive programme could, in any case, have continued *ad infinitum*.

This case illustrates some of the major difficulties in managing antisocial problems: (*a*) parental inability to keep records and success-fully track behaviour; (*b*) low parental motivation (as evidenced by failure to keep appointments or take records), in spite of the fact that the child's current behaviours were likely to get him into trouble with the law; (*c*) failure of demonstrated change in the child's behaviour to persist; change, incidentally, which was recognised by the parents but which did not seem to motivate them further.

Non-Accidentally Injured ('Battered') Children

The non-accidentally injured or battered child (we dislike the latter term because of its negative connotations) is currently of considerable emotive and topical interest. Over the past 4 years we have been involved in the management of some of these cases. Our clinical impression of the majority is that the injury is not just part of a specific syndrome which occurs in isolation, but rather that it is only one feature of those wider problems which typify the 'problem family' and which we have already discussed in the section on delinquency. A recent research report by Smith and Hanson (1975) substantiates our views. This report stressed the following findings about the parents of non-accidentally injured children:

(1) They used more physical punishment than normal parents.

(2) Interaction with their child tended to be inconsistent and undercontrolled, for example if the child cried they were either overresponsive or else unresponsive. Love-withdrawal was frequently employed as a consequence for deviant behaviour. Generally the parents tended to be careless over the child's well-being.

(3) As children, many of these parents had been harshly maltreated; however, their childhood had not been without affection (as one might expect).

(4) The parents exhibited high levels of neuroticism, depression,

hostility and marital difficulties. In addition, mothers tended to have few friends.

Treatment in typical cases poses enormous problems, not so much in terms of therapeutic sophistication but more in relation to the massive amount of time and effort which is required. Ideally, treatment often has to focus on teaching the parents household and child management, marital and other interactional skills. The time which would be required to successfully manage all of these areas is not available to most therapists working in regular clinical settings. It is perhaps more important, at this moment in time, for the therapist to recognise those cases which are atypical and which will respond to the amount of help which he can realistically offer.

We suggest that behaviour modification has much to recommend itself in the management of some of these families. This claim is based on the fact that many of their problems result from inappropriate or deficient interactional skills. However, we are unaware of any reports which either substantiate or disprove our claim about the efficacy of behaviour therapy in this area. Long term follow-up data on non-accidentally injured children are not available. Nevertheless, their outcome is probably similar to that of some other children who have not been battered but who originate from problem families. To the therapist the main importance of the physical injury (apart from the legal or medical results) lies in the fact that it is an indicator of child–parent problems. The outcome will be determined by the long term effects of the daily learning situations and emotional interactions between the parent and child. It is these factors which may result in the child himself growing up to become a non-accidentally injuring parent, who has psychiatric, marital and other social problems.

Below, we report on two of the cases which we have seen over the past 3 years. The second case we regard as relatively successful. However, it is important to note that it was atypical in that it did not exhibit the usual degree of family pathology. In this respect the first case, which was a therapeutic failure, was more typical.

Case Example Demonstrating Failure in Management of a Non-Accidentally Injured Child's Behaviour

Synopsis
Bob, an illegitimate 5-year-old child, was referred to us following his

removal into care by the local Social Services Department. He had lived at home with his 24-year-old unmarried mother and 2 siblings, aged 1 and 3 years. This case had been taken to court on three counts:

(1) The child was thought to be at risk of being non-accidentally injured.

(2) He was beyond parental control—he exhibited a wide range of oppositional behaviours which included disobedience, tantrums and physical aggression.

(3) It was also suspected that there was a risk that Bob might seriously injure his baby brother. In court a Fit Persons Order (Children and Young Persons Act, Northern Ireland, 1968) was granted by the magistrate.

The Social Services Department had been involved with this family over a number of years and on several occasions had taken Bob into care at his mother's request. Each episode was precipitated by mother–child handling difficulties. The two younger children had not as yet given any cause for concern; however, our own involvement with the family would lead us to suspect that these children may eventually present with behavioural problems.

The family lived in a flat which was sparsely furnished. The front door, much of the furniture and some of the windows were broken. The mother was constantly in debt. Over the years she had persistent interactional difficulties with her parents, neighbours and the various helping agencies involved. Her interactions were characterised by frequent rows, resentment and, on some occasions, physical aggressions. She had cohabited with 4 men over the period of 4 years. These relationships were similarly difficult.

Following initial assessment, Bob was admitted to the psychiatric in-patient unit for further assessment.

Observation

Initially in the in-patient setting Bob was non-compliant, often swore at staff, exhibited frequent tantrums and was physically aggressive to younger children. These problems settled down over a 10-day period with firm and consistent handling, thus demonstrating that management was not too difficult.

During the first 3 weeks Bob was observed on 8 occasions (lasting about 1 hour each) with his mother. On 4 of these occasions he was taken home and observed there. The following findings are considered to be the most relevant:

(1) During each session there was a high level of interaction between Bob and his mother. When there were no behavioural problems they chatted continuously. Much of the mother's interaction was childlike and immature. For instance, she frequently asked Bob for his opinion on her problems or other events concerning her life. She often teased him persistently until he became angry—arguments regularly took the form, 'Yes, you will', 'No, I won't', 'Yes, you will', etc.

(2) Physical punishment (that is, a hard smack) was used on several occasions. These punishments did not consistently follow deviant behaviour. Sometimes, when teasing Bob, the mother would suddenly smack him for becoming angry, at other times she would tease him further. On occasions, when angry, the mother would stand and swear insults at Bob. While a relatively large proportion of the mother's interaction with Bob was positive (in terms of talking to him and giving him attention) this was not contingent on Bob exhibiting good behaviour, and he rarely received any reinforcement for appropriate behaviour.

(3) The mother's attempts to discipline Bob were usually unsuccessful. Attempts to make Bob comply were characterised by repetitive commands and unconsequated threats. Usually, the longer these interchanges lasted the more angry and aggressive the mother and child became.

During Bob's stay in hospital the mother visited regularly. She frequently brought him large quantities of sweets and lemonade. Clearly, while she was very fond of Bob she was quite incapable of managing him.

Planning

Following a discussion with the mother we decided to focus initially on increasing obedience following requests to carry out simple tasks (for example, fetching the paper), and to stop disruptive behaviours (which included swearing, physical aggression to mother and fighting with the younger children). The consequences for these behaviours included social and material rewards and time-out. They were to be implemented as described in chapter 9. The treatment sessions lasted about $1\frac{1}{2}$ hours and were conducted twice weekly on days when mother visited the in-patient unit. The mother and child were supervised on each occasion, either by a social worker or a social work student. These persons were responsible for demonstrating, modelling, instructing and keeping records of each session.

Intervention

Treatment was continued over a 4-month period without success. Approximately one-quarter of the treatment sessions went well. Mother showed that she was capable of exhibiting appropriate punishing and rewarding skills. Below is an excerpt from one of these sessions. 'Mother asked Bob to fetch her a book—he complied immediately (to mother's surprise). Therapist cued mother to praise Bob—she did so in a pleased manner—mother and child talked for 4 minutes about a forthcoming holiday—Bob then went off to play with a group of children—therapist discussed the above sequence with mother—praised her—Bob started to fight with Morna (a 3 year old)—mother requested him to stop—mother again repeated the request and threatened time-out—Bob was non-compliant—mother approached him and told him to go to time-out—he complied—therapist praised sequence.' In another session mother appeared to have forgotten her success. 'Bob came out after 5 minutes' time-out—he immediately started to fight with another child—mother asked him to stop—he did not—mother angrily repeated the request—he did not comply—she now said that she would not have him out for the weekend if he did not stop—Bob swore at mother—she went over and hit him (during this time mother ignored therapist's attempts to redirect the behavioural sequence).' In the later treatment stages Bob went home for short weekends. The mother reported frequent behavioural difficulties and therefore sessions were also conducted in the home setting. These did not have any impact on the success of weekends.

After 4 months and approximately 40 hours' supervised therapy, although we realised that the mother could learn the techniques, there were no signs that she was in any way consolidating the skills. The case was re-referred to the Social Services Department.

Perhaps the core of this case lies in the mother's inability to become motivated by both present and long term events (see chapter 14). For instance, any success she had was not sustained either by its immediate effect or by the likelihood that failure would probably result in Bob being taken into long term residential care. It would also be somewhat naïve and presumptuous of us to think that our very narrow treatment focus would change a few behaviours in a mother with widespread interactional difficulties.

Case Example Demonstrating Success in Management of a Non-Accidentally Injured Child's Behaviour

Synopsis

Don, a 6-year-old child, was referred to us by the local Social Services Department after being non-accidentally injured by his mother. Court proceedings had been taken and the child was put on a Fit Persons Order (Children and Young Persons Act, Northern Ireland, 1968). Since the injury was first detected, Don had been residing away from home in a Social Services children's home. A discussion with the mother revealed that Don, who was an only child, had always been difficult. As a baby he was very unresponsive and cried persistently. The mother stated that from approximately the age of 3, his behaviour became increasingly difficult. He was frequently non-compliant, had tantrums and was unresponsive when mother attempted to play with him. In the months preceding the injury Don had begun to soil himself. The more Don's problems increased, the more anxious and punitive the mother became. She felt that the soiling (which had also been occurring at school) had led directly to several episodes of severe physical punishment. The most recent beating had left large bruises over the child's legs. This was noticed and brought to the attention of the Social Services Department by the principal of Don's school. There were other significant family and marital problems. These included:

(1) The father was unsupportive. Although he was in stable employment, he was out most evenings, either drinking or fixing and servicing neighbours' cars. He rarely helped with the management of Don. When major decisions in regard to the house were required he often went to his mother for advice, rather than his wife. He had frequently been critical of his wife's appearance, her child handling and house management skills. The mother was sexually frigid.

(2) During the previous year the mother was under additional stress. Her father had been dying from a serious illness and consequently she had been visiting her own home regularly each day. These visits had been at the expense of housework and they were resented by her husband.

Following Don's injury his mother became guilty and depressed. She was admitted to a psychiatric hospital, where she was treated with brief psychotherapy and antidepressants. When she was first seen by us, she had been out of hospital for approximately 1 month.

Further assessment and observation

Since the Social Services Department was anxious about Don being at home for any length of time (in case of further injury) we decided to carry out further assessment and initial treatment in the child psychiatric in-patient unit. Both mother and Don were admitted.

Observations of the mother and child interacting revealed that she was unable to manage his deviant behaviour. Rather than persisting in attempts to make Don comply, she withdrew. On these occasions she seemed anxious and sought reassurance. In play situations she was unresponsive and did not readily become involved in the child's activities. The husband was observed interacting with Don on several hospital visits. His chat to the child was brief and he referred any behaviour problems directly to his wife. He was not observed playing with Don.

Planning and intervention

We decided that therapeutic success in this case would require treatment of both parent–child and parent–parent interaction. Since the child was under a court order and was 'in care' we felt that his problems required priority. We focused initially on two areas of child management. First, managing disruptive behaviour, and secondly, increasing the mother's play skills. The plan for managing disruptive behaviour follows the type of programme approach outlined in chapter 9 (that is, after setting basic rules, behaviours were managed using time-out and social and material reinforcers). In teaching the mother play skills we divided these into verbal and non-verbal components. First, maternal stance and expression while playing (for example, we wanted mother to get down to play with Don and show interest and pleasure). Secondly, verbal behaviours during play. We assessed that the most important of these were reflecting (this included commenting back to the child on what he was doing), showing Don how to do something, making requests of him and displaying interest (for example, 'tell me what you are doing', 'is that good fun?'). The therapy was to be carried out as often as possible during the day and it was the nurses' responsibility to supervise and shape the maternal behaviours. Incidentally, while the mother was in the in-patient unit she was as far as possible treated as a member of the staff. For example, she ate with the staff and had regular duties with other children as well as Don, although she did not attend ward case discussions. This type of involvement is important, since parents coming into a child psychiatric in-patient unit are likely to feel anxious and threatened. During each day a 1-hour session was set aside in which the child management skills were coached intensively. These sessions were run by the unit psychologist and the first author.

The first part of the programme was rapidly successful. Within 4 days the mother was confidently managing disruptive behaviour and was happily engaging in play. She stated that she was now, for the first time, enjoying Don. Two weeks after treatment had begun it was considered that the mother was quite capable of managing Don at home. Interestingly, there had been no problem of encopresis. Plans were now made to discharge mother and Don and begin to involve father. Three sessions were conducted in the child's natural home, during which the father was coached in the methods. Some bargains were made between father and mother in relation to child management. First, father was to be responsible for looking after the child when his wife was cooking meals and also during one other hour of each day. Secondly, he was to be responsible for putting the child to bed twice each week. Each bargained episode successfully met was worth 15 minutes for an agreed night out with his friends. Thirdly, both parents agreed to levy a small fine on each other for failure to follow the three-step contingency (see chapter 9). Fourthly, mother agreed that she would only visit her own home on 3 occasions per week. Extra visits were to cost her £2 each. Improvement continued at home and the father became successfully involved. However, at the beginning of a new school term there was a re-emergence of the encopresis. A simple programme which involved regular after meals toileting, associated with a small financial reward for successful toilet use, was quite sufficient to extinguish this behaviour (see chapter 13 for a discussion on encopresis and its management).

Seven weeks after the child management programme had begun we turned our attention to the marital difficulties. Initially, we focused on the verbal interactional problem and later on the sexual difficulties. Work on the verbal skills was conducted in two ways and involved teaching the parents to increase positive verbal statements and reduce negative verbal statements. In each therapy session crucial conversations of the past few days were reviewed and re-enacted. Following a reduction of any negative content and an increase of positive content, they were replayed. This process was repeated until the interacting was felt to be satisfactory. Secondly, parents conducted daily exercises in which they were to sit down and verbalise on a reciprocal basis as many positive statements as they could, over a 5-minute period.

After a further 2 months (which involved 12 therapy sessions) attention was turned to the sexual problems. Since the mother's frigidity was associated with anxiety a desensitisation approach was adopted. This was conducted in the following manner:

(*a*) A hierarchy of sexual behaviour, ordered in terms of increasing sexual anxiety, was constructed.

(*b*) The wife was taught and asked to practise deep muscular relaxation.

(*c*) The husband was taught to relax his wife and then how to present the sexual hierarchical items for her to imagine.

(*d*) When the skills had been learned the couple were asked to conduct the therapy at home. Each session was scheduled to last approximately between 20 and 40 minutes depending on success. In the first half of the session the husband relaxed his wife and then asked her to imagine scenes from the hierarchy, beginning with those associated with least anxiety. These were repeated until they could be imagined without anxiety. In the second half the satisfactorily imagined scenes were practised in real life.

It is difficult to estimate the amount of success achieved in the verbal interactional skills. However, it was felt that these were consolidating and still improving when therapy ended. The frigidity was satisfactorily extinguished over a 1-month period. At the time of writing, 9 months after initial intervention (with the child's problem behaviours), there are no reported child or marital difficulties.

This case of non-accidental injury appeared to result from a mixture of factors. First, a temperamental clash between mother and child, poor maternal and paternal child management skills (which were undercut by the mother's lack of confidence) and poor spouse child-management support. Secondly, the stress of the maternal grandfather's terminal illness, and lastly the marital interactional difficulties. Interestingly, it is now the wife rather than the husband who appears more confident and capable. Fortunately, this role-reversal has not been detrimental to the marriage.

13

School-Refusal, Enuresis
and Encopresis: Some Aspects of
Aetiology and Management

In this text we have concentrated upon the management of behaviour problems which fall primarily into an oppositional category. Clinically we have not so often been involved in the treatment of children who present with problems in which anxiety or fear seems to play a major part. Our method of history-taking may tend to minimise the importance of anxiety or high arousal. In the assessment section (part I) we suggested that complaints like 'My child is very anxious', can be broken down into overt behaviours such as, decreased appetite, refusal to go to school, poor sleep, etc. In examining the behaviour at this level it is often possible to offer firm and consistent proposals for management, which will remedy the presenting problem. However when anxiety or arousal is very high, either in the parent or the child, it may inhibit their capacity to follow instructions. For instance, it is well known that intense anxiety reduces the performance of a student in an examination.

Our own view of child anxiety is that the child learns such behaviours from the parents (for example, he may observe parental discomfort in certain social situations) or else that the anxiety is the child's response to specific parental behaviours (for example, the parents may demonstrate extreme concern when the child eats less than usual). While constitutional or genetic components (such as inherited emotionality) may play some part, we believe that these are of minimal importance. Moreover, from a therapeutic aspect little can be done to remedy inherited characteristics.

In cases where anxiety is not thought to be too severe, either in the child or the parents, the implementation of one of the management programmes already outlined in the text (for example, differential attention or a points system) may be appropriate and sufficient. However, in the presence of sustained and marked anxiety such strategies will not succeed. This is because the anxiety or fear will be relatively more motivating than the rewards or punishments which we might select. We must therefore consider other methods, such as desensitisation, for extinguishing or reducing the anxiety associated with the problem behaviours.

School-Refusal

In this section, school-refusal is presented as a model around which to discuss anxiety problems. Refusal to attend school is sometimes referred to as school-phobia. This latter term infers an actual fear of approaching the school. Whilst this may be an important factor in some cases, in the majority the problem is a fear of separation from the home, that is, separation anxiety. In other cases, both fear of school and of separation may be contributive. Employing the term school-refusal, rather than school-phobia, allows us to infer wider aetiological factors.

School-refusal must be distinguished from truancy. The child who plays truant differs from the school-refuser in several says. First, truanting is often associated with other conduct or delinquent problems. Secondly, the family background of the truant tends to conform to the pattern already outlined in the section on antisocial problems. Thirdly, anxiety is not one of the major problems in truancy. The parents of the school-refuser are usually aware of the problem, whereas the parents of the truant may not be because the child tends to prevent them from discovering his absenteeism. This rigid division between school-refusal and truanting does not, however, hold for all cases. Many cases will present in which mixtures of symptoms of anxiety and delinquency occur. In such 'mixed' disorders, the response to treatment and the prognosis seem more closely to match delinquent or antisocial disorders.

CHARACTERISTICS OF SCHOOL-REFUSERS

School-refusal in its 'pure' form, as described below, is not a common clinical problem. For example, Rutter, Tizard and Whitmore (1970) in a study of 10−11-year-old Isle of Wight children, found no cases of persistent school-refusal. While this finding is unusual, it is generally thought that school-refusers only form about 1–2 per cent of the child psychiatric population (Eisenberg, 1958). Mild object and situational fears are certainly common in young children (Shepherd, Oppenheim and Mitchell, 1971). However, most of these remit in early to middle childhood. Clinical samples of school-refusers vary according to the amount of psychopathology which they exhibit. At one extreme we find the child who presents with school-refusal as the only problem; at the other extreme there is the child in which the problem is just one symptom of more widespread personal and family difficulties. The cases at each extremity vary considerably in the aetiology, presentation, type of treatment required and prognosis. It is therefore convenient to categorise the school-refuser according to the classification suggested by Coolidge, Hahn and Peck (1957). These workers described two types of school-refuser:

Type 1. Normally young (of primary school age); the onset of school-refusal is acute; the child is referred during this first episode; the parents generally appear to be well adjusted. The anticipation of having to go to school frequently leads the child to complain of physical symptoms (which are usually of a psychosomatic origin), such as headache or stomach-ache. However, these physical complaints are common to both types of school-refuser.

Type 2. An older child (usually of secondary school age); the onset is incipient and the child has usually had several previous episodes of school-refusal. The families are typified by deviant patterns of interaction which will be outlined below.

AETIOLOGY

The school-refuser can be considered phobic. Perhaps he fears separation from his mother or else he is afraid to approach the school because it is associated with some unpleasant situation (for example, a punitive teacher, an academic subject which he finds difficult or the fact that he is bullied at school). Any behaviour that the child adopts which successfully avoids either of these two aversive situations (separation from mother or approach to school) is negatively reinforced. For example, he may avoid leaving home by complaining of stomach-ache, locking himself in his room or having a tantrum. The majority of children probably find separation or approach to school aversive at some time. However, avoidance of school is viewed by most parents as socially maladaptive, and this results in their firmly ensuring that the child does not stay home from school unnecessarily. Thus, any avoidance behaviours exhibited by the child are quickly extinguished. In the two types of school-refuser already mentioned, a number of factors may contribute to the parental failure to remediate the problem.

Type 1. It is probable in these simpler cases that the aetiology develops from situational factors which temporarily affect either the child or his parents. It is possible to postulate any number of temporary situations which may eventually lead to problems in school-refusal. For example, a recent child illness may have received increased maternal attention, but when the child returns to school the attention is reduced and this may lead to anxiety in the child and consequent refusal to separate. Similarly, recent maternal illness could result in the child developing morbid fears about the mother's future and reluctance to leave her side. When a child is starting school the parents may communicate to him their anxiety about his ability to function in the new situation. The birth of a sibling may lead to reduction in maternal attention, fear of rejection and eventual refusal to separate from the mother. Acute incidents at school may also be important precipitants. Obviously, in many instances the refusal results from an interplay of several factors.

Type 2. Over a number of years Berg (for example see Berg, Nichols and Pritchard 1969; Berg and McGuire, 1971; Berg and McGuire, 1974) has examined in detail an in-patient sample of adolescent school-refusers. He found that the mothers tended to be older than usual and the children to be the youngest in the family. In general this work demonstrates the mother's overprotectiveness and the child's dependency. The children are likely to rely on their mothers but also to have difficulty in communicating with them. Berg also noted that these children resemble other in-patient children with neurotic problems. The insidious onset of type 2 school-refusal in many cases reflects the discrepancy between what the child learns in his family and what is expected of him in the outside environment. In the latter situation the child is expected to exhibit more independence as he grows older, for example to take responsibility; to make decisions; to co-operate in peer activities; to cope with peer aggression. Typically, the family circumstances of these school-refusers seem to inhibit or retard the development of such skills. The mother's encouragement of dependency may be exhibited, for example by the way in which she carries out practical tasks for the child. For instance, she may make his bed, lay out his clothes or carry meals to him. She may encourage the child to stay at home immediately after school rather than play with 'rough' peers, and in the event of any peer difficulties she may intervene on behalf of her child. Often the child is pampered when he has minor illnesses and encouraged to stay off school. All these maternal behaviours will inhibit the development of effective reinforcers for the child, for example peer reinforcement, appropriate self-reinforcement for tasks completed on his own, etc. Interactional patterns within the type 2 refusers' families also tend to be deviant. Ferreira and Winter (1968) have noted that, in decision-making situations, neurotic families are less able to reach a decision and spend more time in silence and conflict than do 'normal' families. Their interactional problems often extend to other relationships which may include staff at the child's school and the therapist. The child in this situation is caught in a vicious circle. He is encouraged to be dependent on a poor family model. As he grows older his academic and social skills deficits become apparent and he experiences increasing difficulties in school and in interactional situations outside the home. In this way the child's fear of the school situation may become only too realistic.

TREATMENT

While both types of school-refuser may exhibit high levels of anxiety the treatment procedures which will be most effective in each case differ considerably. The type 1 refuser usually exhibits no other problems, whilst the type 2 refuser presents with many more difficulties which may serve to propagate high anxiety levels. The approach to each type differs in several ways:

Intensity and focus. Type 1 refusers respond rapidly to simple management programmes, whereas type 2 refusers require lengthy and extended intervention. The primary goal of treatment with any school-refuser is to return the child to school. Generally, this is a sufficient goal for the type 1 refuser. However, with the type 2 refuser, ideally this strategy should only be a precursor to further treatment. Due to his social deficits this child will continue to exhibit considerable anxiety, and therefore social skills training, in addition to family intervention, is usually required.

Method. The type 1 refuser responds to a firm and directive approach. Following preliminary assessment the child is simply taken to school. The type 2 refuser will often require a much more graduated approach (for example desensitisation, which is discussed below). In this section we have arbitrarily divided school-refusers into two categories. Obviously many cases fall between these extremes. Only the assessment, and perhaps subsequent treatment trials, will reveal which method is required to help the individual child. This highlights the importance of carefully assessing each environment (home and school) before beginning an intervention programme.

Rapid treatment method for the type 1 school-refuser
Once a child has been assessed as a type 1 refuser a number of steps are instigated:

(1) Any physical complaints in the child are investigated rapidly and with a minimum of fuss.

(2) The parents are instructed to inform the child that he will be going to school on the following day. They are to ignore any complaints or objections on his part.

(3) On the first new schoolday the child is sent to school or, if necessary, is accompanied by his parents.

(4) The therapist maintains his contact with the school and asks the staff to make arrangements for retaining the child in school once he has arrived.

The success of the programme depends upon the co-operation of the parents and the school. The method is usually effective within 3 days. Kennedy (1965) reported 100 per cent success with this strategy in a sample of 50 type 1 refusers. Imparting this sort of information to the parents may help in reassuring them about the success of the programme and the necessity for immediate and firm implementation. A large majority of type 1 refusers return to school on the first day of the programme. We hypothesise that the ease with which this is accomplished is due to the parents reaching a joint decision which they enact in an assertive manner. As we have already emphasised, changes in parental management style are of considerable importance in effecting change in a child's behaviour.

Treatment of the type 2 school-refuser
Intervention with these children can be divided into two stages. First, return to school and, secondly, management of other problems.

Type 2 refusers will rarely respond to the methods outlined above. In fact that kind of management may make matters worse and a more gradual approach is usually required. Nevertheless it is still important with these refusers to return them to school as rapidly as possible. Therapeutic indecision will simply reinforce those child and parental behaviours which have already contributed to the problem. Rodriguez, Rodriguez and Eisenberg (1959) stress that the parents should be warned of the legal consequences of school absence. In view of the parental handling difficulties the early stages of any gradual return to school should be managed by the therapist or alternative authority. As this succeeds the parents can then be introduced to the procedure. Several strategies of gradual return to school have been reported, two of which are outlined below:

(1) Desensitisation and extinction of anxiety in fantasy. This has been found successful in the management of phobias. In a relaxed state the child fantasises a gradual return to school. With older children, muscle relaxation may be taught (Wolpe and Lazarus, 1966). Following relaxation the child is asked to imagine situations associated with a gradual approach to school. The situations are usually graded into a hierarchical scale, and progression up the scale continues only as the child can imagine each stage without anxiety. The hierarchy might be as follows: (a) thinking about school on a Friday evening; (b) packing his school bag on Sunday evening; (c) waking up on Monday morning; (d) washing and dressing for school; (e) eating breakfast; (f) putting on his school coat; (g) leaving home to go to school, . . ., etc.

Such a procedure may prove difficult with a younger child and alternative methods may be required. For example, relaxation can be created in a play situation in which the therapist encourages the child to act out his refusal through a favoured toy such as a teddy bear or a toy soldier. Using suggestion in a narrative fashion the therapist gradually guides the child in returning the emotive character to school. As each successive step in a return to school is verbalised by the child, the therapist reinforces him with social or material reinforcers. An excellent example of this procedure is described by Patterson and Brodsky (1966).

In fantasy, treatments do not necessarily generalise to real-life situations, and therefore they should be followed up with practice in the real situation. Generally the authors favour a direct *in vivo* approach to the school, such as is described below.

(2) *In vivo* desensitisation. This simply involves a gradual real-life return to the school. A hierarchy of increasingly anxiety-provoking situations is drawn up, and the therapist guides the child through each of these until anxiety is minimal. Such a hierarchy might be as follows: (a) passing the school at the weekend; (b) going into the school grounds at the weekend; (c) approaching the school gates during a

weekday; (*d*) being in the empty school building, . . ., etc.

Hierarchies, whether they are to be used *in vivo* or in fantasy, should be constructed in consultation with the child. It is important that the therapist develops good rapport with the child and that he reinforces him as he successfully practises each stage of the hierarchy. Following initial success the parents are instructed in the gradual approach and they are asked to continue with the programme. Particular emphasis is placed on the parents not passing comment on the child's difficulties or anxiety but, rather, reinforcing him for progress towards return to school. Once parents become more active in the management it is extremely important that close supervision is maintained by the therapist, in order to deal with any crisis which may arise. A points system can be introduced to encourage the child's continued return to school, and the school authorities are also used to reinforce child and parent behaviours.

In the early stages of an *in vivo* programme, in order to facilitate rapid progress it is often expedient to use a small dose of a tranquilliser. As progress continues, the dosage is first reduced and then withdrawn. A more elaborate desensitisation procedure using tranquillisers has been successfully used with adult phobias. This procedure is called Declining Drug Dose Desensitisation (D.D.D.D.)—McCormick and O'Gorman (1971). On the first day the subject is introduced into the most anxiety-provoking situation, aided by a previously calculated heavy dose of tranquilliser, which should be just enough to cause the subject to feel drowsy. On successive days the drug dose is reduced, with the subject remaining in the most phobic situation. To the authors' knowledge this approach has not yet been tried with school-refusers. Its major disadvantage is that it requires medical supervision.

Ideally, following return to school the other problems which are commonly associated with type 2 refusers should be tackled. The authors have found little mention of such strategies in the behavioural literature. Lazarus, Davison and Polejka (1965) report the use of simple counselling techniques to handle parent difficulties following the child's return to school. This involved their defining the problems and suggesting methods by which they could be handled. They reported that the father's harsh management tendencies and the mother's inconsistencies were corrected by these counselling techniques. However, in severe cases more active management will be required. Following an assessment of the problems which remain in each family, an intervention programme, such as has been described in preceding chapters, may be implemented. For example, problem-solving behaviours between the parents may be improved by introducing the use of bargaining and contracting.

Peer relations may also be deficient in the child who presents with school-refusal or other anxiety problems. Within the confines of a routine out-patient commitment we have been unable to conduct work in this area. It is difficult to shape up appropriate social skills when a peer group is unavailable to the therapist. However, if groups of children are available (for example in residential care or in schools) then some general guidelines on training children in peer interactional skills may be useful.

Rose (1972) suggests teaching the following components: (a) greeting behaviours; (b) conversational behaviours; (c) initiating activity behaviours; (d) co-operation and play skills; for example, how to win, lose, share, and take turns; (e) coping with peer-initiated aggression; (f) reducing elicitors for aggression.

Within the group setting the children discuss the most appropriate aspects of each behaviour, including verbal and non-verbal components. Each behaviour is then modelled and practised. Group work of this kind, conducted at a clinic level, can be particularly useful as the group of children is used to define and set goals for what are, or are not, appropriate peer behaviours. Experienced members of the group may help new members by quickly recognising, reinforcing and shaping appropriate behaviours.

In a case study reported by Patterson and Brodsky (1966) a graduated approach to improving poor peer relations was implemented in a school setting. The steps were similar to steps (a) – (d) mentioned above. In this programme, however, the child's success at each stage resulted in material reinforcement not only for him but also for his peers. This technique was useful in that it motivated the peers to respond to the child's success with encouragement. In addition to peer problems, children with high anxiety may also have difficulties or deficits in interacting with adults. Again, these situations can be modelled and practised with adults, according to the outline suggested for peer interaction.

PROGNOSIS

Kennedy (1965) reported 100 per cent success with his type 1 refusers. This success was maintained at a 2-year follow-up of those children who could still be contacted. However, Kennedy is careful to point out that the follow-up referred only to the problem symptom. Rodriguez, Rodriguez and Eisenberg (1959) reported that success in school-refusers under the age of 11 was 89 per cent—the shortest follow-up being 15 months after intervention. Only 36 per cent of the children over the age of 11 were able to return to school. The same study indicated that poor communication between the clinic and school contributed to the failure of some cases. The group of children who failed to return to school apparently exhibited other features in common, such as multiple family problems and severe interactional difficulties.

Case Example of Management of a School-Refuser using a Desensitisation Approach

Thomas, a 12-year-old, was referred to the clinic by his school medical officer because of persistent complaints of loss of appetite, nausea, headaches, poor sleep and persistent crying. These had all been associated with frequent school absenteeism over the past year. Initially he had missed school 6–7 days per month, and more recently he had been completely absent from school except for 1–2 days each month. The physical complaints were most frequent in the morning before he was due to leave for school. On other occasions Thomas would complain on arriving at school and, because there was no sick bay, he was usually sent home. When Thomas attended school he was described as sullen and non-compliant. He had few friends and did not mix in peer activities. During the past year he had been attending the school counsellor. A psychological assessment revealed that he was of average ability but was approximately 2 years behind on reading and arithmetic attainments. When at home, Thomas was described as a shy, sensitive child who disliked separating from his mother.

Thomas lived at home with his 2 brothers, aged 5 and 10 years, and his parents. His brothers had not presented any problems. The father drank heavily and had been admitted to a psychiatric hospital on several occasions. He did not involve himself in either child or home management. Thomas's mother was a tense woman who had few friends or social outlets. She worried excessively about her children. For instance, they were discouraged from playing outside with peers, or from joining neighbourhood boys' clubs, or from going shopping on their own. On several occasions she had been in hospital with gynaecological complaints and on each occasion had discharged herself because of anxiety over how the family were managing, in spite of the fact that she had made adequate arrangements for their well-being.

Prior to the development of the school-refusal Thomas had not exhibited any serious behavioural problem. At the age of 5 he had refused school for a period of about 2 weeks. However, the mother said that following a firm approach by herself he returned easily. His developmental history was unremarkable.

Planning and intervention

The planning and treatment were conducted by a nurse therapist, with the aid of the school counsellor. Management was planned in two stages. First, Thomas's return to school and, secondly, management in regard to his mother and peer relationships.

Stage 1

Following discussions with Thomas, the school counsellor and the mother, the following intervention programme for reintroduction to school was designed.

(*a*) Anxiety was to be reduced first by using a small dose of valium, which was to be taken each morning prior to leaving for school and, secondly, with the aid of muscular relaxation, which was to be conducted in the school counsellor's room prior to entry into the classroom.

(*b*) Reintroduction into the class situation was to proceed in the following steps:

Step (*i*). After relaxation, Thomas would go to one class of his choosing. Following this, he would return to meet the therapist in the counsellor's room.

Step (*ii*). Relaxation—class of preference plus additional class—meet therapist at the end.

Step (*iii*). Relaxation—two classes—then home.

Step (*iv*). Relaxation—one morning's classes—then to meet therapist at home.

Step (*v*). One morning's classes—meet therapist at home.

Step (*vi*). A whole day in school—meet therapist at home.

Step (*vii*). Reduction in relaxing drug.

(*c*) At home, physical symptoms were to be ignored when Thomas did not obviously appear physically ill. If he then complained of physical symptoms in school he was, if necessary, to be relaxed by the school counsellor and returned to class.

(*d*) Both the mother and the school counsellor were to discuss and praise the successful completion of each step with Thomas.

(*e*) If Thomas refused to go to school, mother was to contact the therapist who would then go and collect him.

On the initial day of treatment, Thomas went to school and was relaxed by the therapist as planned but he then left the first class almost immediately. He was relaxed again and returned to class, where he remained until the end of the session. Progress from then on was uneventful. The mother was delighted and clearly reinforced Thomas. On a few early occasions Thomas had complained of headaches but these situations were effectively managed by his mother. She firmly told him to go to school and discuss the matter with the school counsellor. Towards the end of term, when Thomas was going regularly to school, the therapist reduced home visits to twice weekly. Figure 13.1 is a graph of the treatment progress—each of the steps (*i*)—(*vii*) are marked.

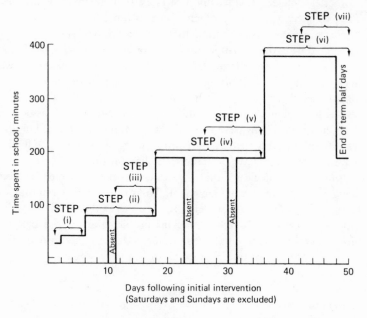

Figure 13.1   Graph depicting the progress of the desensitisation programme used to treat Thomas

Stage 2

Since at half-way through the school term the programme was

183

progressing satisfactorily, work then focused on the parent – child and child – peer relationship. This simply involved encouraging the mother to increase Thomas's independence. She persuaded him to join the neighbouring boys' club. During the summer holidays she encouraged Thomas to bring friends from this club to his home. His interaction with these peers increased. Mother encouraged Thomas when he suggested taking on a paper-round in the evening over the summer holidays. Progress continued over the next term. Thomas remained at school and was more actively involved in outdoor activities. However 1 month before Christmas, two events occurred which resulted in a deterioration. First, the maternal grandmother died and, secondly, Thomas's father's drinking increased and resulted in his admission to psychiatric hospital. At this stage the mother, who had been very attached to her own mother (they lived close and visited each other daily), became depressed. Thomas stopped going to school and his mother no longer provided the necessary reinforcement or firmness. This worsening of the problem demonstrated the importance of mother's previous contribution to the programme's success. Unfortunately during the Christmas holidays, for various reasons, the family had to move a considerable distance from the clinic and it was impossible for the therapist to continue working on the case.

Although therapy stopped when the problem was again at its worst, it was clearly demonstrated that the school-refusal and associated dependency problems were amenable to therapy and that the mother was capable of implementing the contingencies. We suggest that further management might have been successful had the therapist been able to continue. You will notice that the father has not been mentioned as being involved in the management. Unfortunately, after initial interviews it was felt that he was simply not motivated enough to provide support. Ideally, at a later stage, his problems and those between himself and his wife should have been tackled. In total, approximately 24 hours of therapist time was involved in this case.

Enuresis

BACKGROUND

Nocturnal enuresis (or bedwetting) is perhaps more common than has been recognised. Oppel, Harper and Rowland (1968) suggest that 20 per cent of 6-year-olds have this problem. The disorder is most common in boys, in lower socio-economic classes, neurologically handicapped children, children with bladder abnormalities and children from disturbed family backgrounds. Generally, it is not now regarded, *per se*, as a psychiatric symptom although there are a disproportionate number of enuretic children within the child psychiatric population. Most enuretics eventually remit, and probably only a very small number of enuretic children remain enuretic adolescents.

The aetiology of enuresis is unclear, although it seems that the disorder is probably related to a relative immaturity in the autonomic or vegetative nervous system (Broughton, 1968). Explanations in terms of faulty learning have been hypothesised; however, few of these hold much credibility. In a few cases, persistent bladder infections or bladder abnormalities may be causal.

MANAGEMENT

The majority of parents cope on their own with the problem. Many employ a simple regime in which fluids are restricted in the evening and the child is lifted before the parents retire at night. This regime is continued until the child remits. For those parents who do seek guidance a number of techniques have been used.

CONTROL OF NOCTURNAL ENURESIS BY OPERANT CONDITIONING

Samaan (1972) reported a technique which is similar to the home regime mentioned above (assuming that parents have applied their regime consistently). Briefly, the child is woken several times each evening and guided to the toilet. Following urination, a reinforcer is given. Once the procedure is established the parents are asked to fade out the wakening, the prompting and the reinforcer. Verbal reinforcement is given in the morning for dry nights. Should the child fail to use the toilet as necessary during the night, the prompting is recommenced. This approach was reported as successful with a child who had failed to respond to the conventional alarm bell treatment (as described later). However, the authors do not know how successful this approach might be when compared in larger numbers with the other techniques which we shall now discuss.

DRUG USE

Both amphetamines and antidepressants have been used with some degree of success. The amphetamines are thought to lighten sleep sufficiently to allow the occurrence of aroused bladder distension cues, which will waken the child. The antidepressants are thought to cause relative inhibition of bladder sphincter relaxation and thus inhibition of urination. It is generally accepted that the antidepressants are the most successful of the drug treatments, although this success is more often one of improvement rather than 'cure'. When therapists are hard pressed for time it would seem that antidepressant management warrants a trial.

ALARM BELL

Of all methods used in the treatment of enuresis most success has been reported with the alarm bell. The first systematic trials were carried out by Mowrer and Mowrer (1938) and, since that time, levels of success have been claimed which vary between 20 and 80 per cent. These figures vary according to the type of family treated and their motivation, the standard of instructions given, the criteria for success (for example, dry 7 nights per week or just 6 nights per week) and, most importantly, the length of the follow-up.

The alarm bell works on the principle that urine will act as a conductor between two points and will complete a circuit and thus activate a bell (figure 13.2). The bell is activated immediately the first drops of urine make electrical contact between the wire mesh. The bell continues to ring until the alarm is switched off. The system is reset by changing the sheets covering and separating one wire mesh from the other. The sudden ringing of the alarm usually wakens the child. This wakening is concurrently associated with bladder sphincter contraction

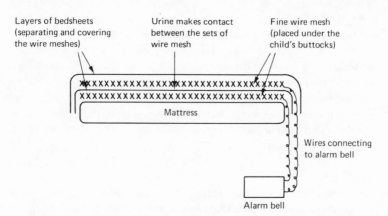

Figure 13.2 The alarm bell system for treatment of enuresis

and thus inhibition of urination. The child then gets up, switches off the system and completes urination at the toilet. The system is then reset and switched on again. In employing this method there are several practical points of importance.

(1) If the parents are supervising the child it must be remembered that they may have to get up once or twice each night to ensure that the procedure is followed, and that the alarm is reset. Having to get up at night will require a sufficient level of motivation for success.

(2) The therapist should ensure that the parents and child know how the system operates. It would be unusual to employ this method with a child under the age of 6. In addition to verbal instruction we try to observe the family using the system. The child should be acquainted with the bell so that it will not frighten him when it first rings in the night.

(3) The child must have his own bed. The authors conducted a small survey of 50 children treated with alarm bells and found that there was complete failure in the cases of 20 children who had to share beds.

(4) Follow-up visits should follow closely on receipt of the bell to ensure that it is working. One problem which parents often report is that the children fail to waken when the bell rings. There are several methods of dealing with this. First, we can employ a louder alarm. Secondly, in some cases the child can be taught to waken. When the child is asleep in bed the parents can, on two or three occasions each night, set off the alarm and then waken the child while the bell is ringing. After several days we have usually found that the child will then waken on his own when the bell rings. Thirdly, drugs may be used as an adjunct to lighten sleep. Research has demonstrated that the use of drugs speeds up the process of nocturnal continence (Young and Turner, 1965). Once continence has been reached stably for a period of 2 weeks, the alarm and the drugs can be withdrawn. However, this process should be gradual, as sudden withdrawal is associated with a fairly high rate of relapse. Initially the alarm can be faded to use on alternate nights and, if success continues, the period between usage gradually extended over a total period of 4−6 weeks. When the alarm has been ineffective and we are fairly sure that it is being correctly used, we would not persevere with it for more than 4 weeks.

BLADDER TRAINING REGIME (KIMMEL AND KIMMEL TECHNIQUE)
Enuretic children tend to have small bladder capacities and to use the toilet more often than other children. Kimmel and Kimmel (1970)

suggest that this is due to the children's response to weak bladder distension cues. On the basis of this hypothesis they suggest a method for indirectly managing enuresis. The method focuses on teaching the child only to respond to gradually stronger and stronger bladder distension cues. With younger children the procedure can be carried out with the aid of one of the parents. Older children and adolescents can (if sufficiently motivated) implement the procedure themselves. We will describe the procedure as it is applied to younger children. It is carried out in two steps.

(1) Pretreatment (baseline). The child is asked to inform the parent when he urinates, and is then asked to identify distension cues at this time (such as abdominal discomfort, feeling of pressure, need to urinate) and to describe whether they were weak, intermediate or strong. Co-operation is reinforced by material or social reward, or points given towards obtaining a privilege.

(2) Intervention. After 5 or 6 days of baseline recordings the child is asked to inform the parent each time he wishes to urinate. He is asked to describe the bladder cues and then to attempt to delay urination for 20–30 minutes—of course, this may need to be varied according to the child. During this waiting period some predetermined activity should be carried out. Before going to the toilet a further description of distension cues should be recorded and suitable rewards again applied. Over a period of a few weeks the frequency of toilet use should reduce. Generally we have found that enuresis only improves after several weeks of this treatment. Recordings should be carried on for 4–6 weeks after success. If the daytime programme is stopped abruptly this may result in relapse and increases in daily toilet use.

Bladder sphincter exercises

This technique may usefully and easily be combined with the Kimmel and Kimmel regime. The exercises are based on the fact that increased tone in the sphincter muscles may aid bladder control. When the child needs to go to the toilet the parent accompanies him and asks him to start and stop the process of urination several times during the whole act of urination. Young children may find this process of tightening the pelvic muscles difficult and therefore, when the child is not in the act of urination, practice with the help of a hand on the perineal region may be required.

These daytime regimes have a number of advantages: they avoid treatment at night, they can be implemented without alarms or drugs and they can be used in situations in which the alarm bell is not feasible (for example, when the child shares a bed). However, we have not been as successful with these methods as with the alarm bell system. This comparison is based on a small number of cases treated by the author using the Kimmel and Kimmel method (10 cases, of which only 2 were successful). The general effectiveness of the Kimmel and Kimmel method has yet to be assessed. The authors do not know of any trials which have compared it with the more traditional methods of treating enuresis.

Encopresis

Encopresis (or rectal incontinence) occurs in approximately 3 per cent of 7–8-year-old children (Bellman, 1966), and 1.6 per cent of 10–11-year-old children (Rutter, Tizard and Whitmore, 1970). The disorder is extremely infrequent in adolescence. Boys present with encopresis twice as commonly as girls. There is a relationship between the occurrence of encopresis and enuresis. Rutter, Tizard and Whitmore (1970) found, in the Isle of Wight study, that approximately 40 per cent of encopretic children were also enuretic. Two patterns of encopresis can be described. First, there is the child whose soiling consists of the passage of normal motions and, secondly, the child whose soiling resembles diarrhoea. In this latter type the rectum is often found to contain hard impacted faeces and the encopresis results from fluid overflow around this impacted mass. It has been argued that the former type of encopresis is associated with more psychopathology but there is no conclusive evidence of the truth of this assertion. Bellman (1966) found that clinic encopretics differed from matched normal controls in that they were more anxious, had less peer contact and came from more highly coercive backgrounds. However, he was unable to distinguish whether these factors were the cause, or the effect, of the encopresis. Some authorities suggest the importance of distinguishing between primary encopretics (those who have always soiled)and secondary encopretics (those who had been clean for some length of time before the encopresis emerged). However, Bellman (1966) was unable to find any significant differences between these two groups.

AETIOLOGY
In the infant, bowel emptying is reflexive. Usually it occurs after meals.

Stomach fulness is associated with reflexive contractions of the lower bowel. In the process of toilet training, the child learns to discriminate cues of bowel fulness and thus act appropriately, that is to defecate in the toilet. Eventually the toilet becomes a cue to elicit reflexive contractions in the lower bowel. Repeated sight of the toilet and its association with successful defecation after meals will eventually assume greater control of the reflex in the lower bowel. Unsuccessful development of toilet habits can be the result of several causes:

(1) Physical abnormalities. Sluggish bowel contractions may result in constipation and thus painful evacuations. Lesions of the anal sphincter (for example anal fissure) may result in painful evacuation which, in turn, results in constipation and later bowel overflow incontinence.

(2) Dietary abnormalities. Diets high in protein and low in carbohydrates and roughages may lead to constipation and painful evacuation.

(3) Lack of toilet training. Failure in toilet training may result in encopresis. Generally we have found that such cases occur in families which have multiple problems.

(4) Faulty toilet training. Highly punitive toilet training may result in the toilet becoming aversive to the child (for example, if he is forced to sit on the toilet for a long time following a soiling). Severe punishments for soiling may result in anxiety which generalises to all acts of defecation. Such a situation may lead to constipation and overflow encopresis.

(5) Inadequate training in the setting of widespread coercive behaviour. Normal toilet training may fail in situations where there are more widespread child oppositional behaviours, for example non-compliance, tantrums or aggression. The relevance of this category is that any treatment attempts will first have to focus on the more general problem of non-compliance.

TREATMENT AND MANAGEMENT

The routine history should give some indication of the aetiological factors in the encopresis, for example whether toileting skills have ever been established. The consistency of motions will suggest whether or not constipation is a problem. If motions are passed regularly and are of soft consistency, then it would seem appropriate to initiate an intervention programme. In cases of chronic or long-standing constipation, with overflow encopresis it is advisable to seek a medical opinion. Before an intervention programme is implemented these children should be assessed for bowel abnormalities, and they may require an enema to remove impacted faeces.

Several encopretic children treated by the authors have fallen between the above two groups. In this event we have proceeded with a short therapeutic trial, in order to avoid enemas and physical examination which may cause the child further anxiety. Fortunately, all 8 cases in this category, which we have treated in the past year, have succeeded without physical intervention.

The focus of intervention is on establishing regular toileting habits. The therapist should avoid focusing the contingencies of reward and punishment on the soiling as this may only serve to intensify the problem—in an effort to remain clean the child may attempt to retain faeces. Thus baseline recordings should focus on keeping records of the toileting habits of the child in addition to records of the soiling. If the child is secretive or attempts to hide soiled pants, the recording can be facilitated by keeping track of the pants which the child is wearing and by checking regularly, for example 4 times per day, on whether soiling has occurred. During the baseline we ask the parents to remove all punitive or rewarding contingencies previously used in dealing with the soiling. While this instruction affects the reliability of the baseline recordings it has the advantage of dissipating anxieties associated with soiling and toilet use.

Prior to intervention, several points should be considered in all cases. (a) Reinforcers to be used should be listed. (b) The child's normal diet must contain foods which will increase the bulk and softness of the motions. Foods should consist of reasonable amounts of carbohydrates and roughages. Diets consisting exclusively or mainly of protein are to be avoided as they exacerbate constipation. In some cases a mild laxative which adds bulk to the motions may be prescribed. (c) The toileting regime should occur after meals—in this way we make maximum use of the bowel reflex mentioned earlier.

The authors have used 3 types of intervention programme in the treatment of encopresis. A brief case example is given to elucidate each approach.

(1) Teaching the child normal components of toileting
Winifred, a 5-year-old girl, had always soiled. Baseline recordings demonstrated that soiling occurred on the average 3 times per day and that although Winifred used the toilet for urination she never used it

191

for defecation. Her motions were soft and well formed. Initially, a regime was set up in which she was to be reinforced (with sweets, pocket money, praise, etc.) for bowel motions in the toilet. Her mother took her to the toilet regularly after each meal but 10 days later there was no change. It appeared that the girl was making no effort to defecate while she was at the toilet and so an extra dimension was added to the programme. When Winifred went to the toilet after meals her mother accompanied her and first modelled, and then reinforced, elimination efforts (expiring against a closed glottis, tightening stomach muscles and pushing down). For example, mother might say: 'Watch me close my mouth trying to push air out; see how my face goes red; feel my flat tummy. Now you try'. After 3 days the girl began to have success, and after 1 week soiling had reduced to occasional staining. At this stage, reinforcement was given only for successful elimination rather than for elimination efforts. Over a further period of 10 days all programmed reinforcement was faded out, and 5 weeks after intervention the mother encouraged Winifred to go to the toilet on her own. Following a slight relapse (3 episodes of soiling) the mother recommenced accompanying Winifred to the toilet after each evening meal and praising her for successful elimination.

Maintained in this way, soiling had not recurred 6 months after intervention. Approximately 5 hours' therapist time was spent on this case but more accurate initial assessment would have shortened the time. This case demostrates the importance of ensuring that the child has acquired the necessary toileting skills. Often, with younger children, training in these skills has to be incorporated into the programme.

(2) Anxiety in the toileting situation
Simon, a 7-year-old child, was referred to the clinic with a 3-year history of soiling. He had been admitted to a paediatric ward on 3 occasions for establishment of toileting, but this relapsed following each discharge. His parents described Simon as anxious, and for a short time previously he had been school-phobic. He had few friends and disliked entering new situations. No other problems were presented. Simon hated the bathroom and frequently wept when his parents attempted to take him there. Recently his parents had become angry about his soiling and resorted to smacking him or forcing him to sit on the toilet after soiling episodes.

Baseline recordings revealed that soiling occurred on the average once in every 2 days. The motions were firm. It was hypothesised that Simon found the bathroom anxiety-provoking. As such anxiety will inhibit successful toilet use we planned a graduated programme which would first extinguish Simon's anxiety of the bathroom and later his anxiety of the toilet. The stages were as follows:

(a) All other activities in the bathroom were reinforced, for example washing face, brushing teeth, bathing. As we assessed that Simon was responsive to social reinforcers, these were used. The praise and approval were, as far as possible, to be conducted in the bathroom.

(b) Simon was to be reinforced for sitting on the toilet. Initially a few seconds would earn a reinforcer (for example parent approval, a story, a sweet). These sessions were to be conducted 3 times a day after meals. The length of time required on the toilet to earn the reinforcer was to be gradually extended to 5–10 minutes. During these longer periods Simon was allowed to have a comic or sweet while he sat on the toilet. It was explained to him that he was not required to defecate.

(c) Elimination efforts were now required in order to earn the reinforcers. These were to be conducted in the presence of the parents. Again, no stress was placed on successful elimination.

(d) Finally, successful elimination was required in order to earn the reinforcers.

Following 6 days' baseline data, Simon was put on a mild laxative and the roughages in his diet were increased. Stage (a) passed successfully and on the fifth day the parents proceeded to (b) after a further 5 days, stage (c) was introduced and the following day Simon used the toilet appropriately. The parents then moved on to (d) and within the next few days the soiling ceased altogether. At a 6-month follow-up there had been no recurrence. This total programme involved about 3 hours of therapeutic time. Much of the contact with the parents was maintained by telephone.

(3) Re-establishing toileting in situations in which anxiety is not of importance
The success of the above approach will largely depend on the child's co-operation. If the child, in addition, presents problems of non-compliance, then this type of programme may not work. We adopted the same approach with a child who presented in a rather similar way to Simon. However, the parents had considerable difficulty when they reached stage (b) of the approach outlined in (2) above. Two home visits were then made to discuss the programme and we realised that the child presented a more general management problem, although the

parents originally denied such difficulties. However, they agreed to place the child in time-out for refusal to co-operate. Three days after the application of time-out, the child was successfully using the toilet. The majority of encopretic cases managed by the authors have fallen into this group. Following baseline recordings and case assessment the programme consists of removing the focus from soiling to toileting, adjusting the diet, regularising the toileting (after meals), the provision of reinforcers, first for effort and then for success, and the application of time-out (if necessary) for refusal to sit on the toilet.

A final point worthy of mention is that encopretic children are often reported to have poor peer relations. This may, in part, result from the smell due to soiling and also rejection of the child for his inappropriate toileting behaviour. In many cases, reversal of the soiling may have a direct effect on peer relations.

Two major informational sources which have been found useful in our work with encopretic children are Neale (1963) and Young (1973).

14

Failure: Some Theoretical and Practical Considerations

The past decade has witnessed the enthusiastic development of behavioural methodology. Numerous new journals have emerged (for example *Behavior Therapy*, *Behaviour Research and Therapy*, *Journal of Applied Behaviour Analysis*, *Journal of Behaviour Therapy* and *Experimental Psychiatry*); multitudes of successful single-case studies have been reported; new and large organisations have developed (for example Association for Advancement of Behavior Therapy and European Association for Behaviour Therapy); and many behaviour therapy handbooks have appeared on the American market. However, recent reports suggest that any representation of a high success rate is misleading when the behavioural method is applied routinely in the field (Patterson, 1975; Wahler, Berland and Leske, 1975; Jayaratne, Stuart and Tripodi, 1974; Weathers and Liberman, 1975).

Our own clinical experience in managing child behavioural problems supports these studies. We find that our overall success rate within this group is no greater than 25 per cent. By success we imply: (*a*) an observed and substantial reduction in the targeted behaviours, over an extended period; (*b*) that the parents continue to use the techniques which they have learned in dealing with the target behaviours and they adapt these techniques to cope with other child behaviours—in other words they show that they have generalised their handling skills; (*c*) positive attitudinal change between parents and child. Our own low success rate with child behavioural problems has been substantiated by the findings of other, much more experienced authors. In a recent 2-year follow-up study of aggressive children, Patterson (1975) reported that in approximately one-third of these cases direct management of the targeted behaviours was successful; a further third required more widespread management programmes which also aimed at correcting family interaction (the outcome in this group was far from satisfactory); and finally the remaining third were resistant to all attempts to modify family behaviour.

Such a low success rate may at first appear startling. Frequently studies have suggested that between 35 and 75 per cent of child psychiatric problems spontaneously remit or improve without treatment. However, Subotnik (1972), in an extensive review of psychotherapeutic studies, suggests that the occurrence of spontaneous remission has never been established. Certainly the variability of figures derived from the many studies indicates a lack of agreement. Subotnik has outlined the weaknesses in research design and methodology of many of these studies, such as the use of waiting list control groups and the failure to account for the fact that psychological disorders fluctuate in the degree of pathology which they exhibit at any one moment in time, and that follow-up may occur when the symptoms are minimal. The spontaneous remission rate will depend considerably on the quality of the assessment and reassessment techniques employed. For example at the simplest level, telephone follow-up is likely to reveal a high rate of spontaneous remission, while detailed observational methods conducted in all of the child's environments are likely to reveal a much lower rate. Long term follow-up studies in children are perhaps particularly difficult because symptoms may change and present in new forms as the child matures.

This text has outlined in detail methods for managing child behavioural problems which are mainly confined to the interaction between the target child and his parents. In our experience these methods are most likely to succeed with families where the origin of the problem lies in some feature peculiar to the individual child. Often the parents of these children already possess adequate handling techniques, as evidenced by their handling of other children in the family; however, the idiosyncrasy of the referred child may have resulted in the parents failing to apply their skills. Intervention programmes within this group are effective in 1–2 weeks. Characteristics often found in the histories of such families are as follows:

(1) The child is hyperactive (that is, he is overactive and has difficulty maintaining attention). Hyperactivity can be upsetting to parents as it draws their continual attention. Under such circumstances, aversive situations multiply and the parents may become inconsistent. In our experience, hyperactive children seem to require

greater management consistency than one would normally expect.

(2) Temperamental clashes between a parent and child may result in later behavioural problems. A mother may find difficulty with her child because he does not conform to her concept of how her child should behave, for example he may not feed at 'ideal times', he may not be responsive to cuddling, or perhaps he cries frequently. Such a situation can trigger off annoyance and anxiety in the mother and result in inappropriate handling.

(3) Some aspect of the child's health or status may result in faulty parent handling. For example, the parents of an epileptic child may believe that he should never be 'frustrated'. We have encountered several cases in which outside advice of this nature, concerning children who are physically or mentally handicapped, has resulted in the parents submitting to the child's every whim, simply to avoid tantrums.

So much for the families with whom we are most likely to succeed; but what about the large group of families with whom we, and other authors, have met with most difficulty and failure? Generally, these families exhibit the following broad characteristics:

(a) Widespread interactional difficulties which are typified by frequent use of aversive stimuli and infrequent use of positive reinforcers (both of which are often inconsistently or non-contingently applied).

(b) Low motivation or inability to seek or implement change in their life-styles. This is evidenced by the fact that they request help only when their child's behaviour results in considerable social difficulty, for example when persistent truancy results in legal pressures. Once contact with helping agencies has been established these families often fail to complete any therapeutic programme which has been offered. Typically they will have had contact with many social agencies.

In attempting to conceptualise and understand these difficulties, which undoubtedly contribute to failure, we may employ two social interactional models based on learning or reinforcement theory—the reciprocity and coercion model and the learned helplessness model. These models suggest directions in which we might move in an attempt to help some of these families.

The Reciprocity and Coercion Model

Over the past 7–8 years, Patterson and his colleagues at the Oregon Research Institute have been conducting research aimed at understanding the development of social behaviour in normal and behaviourally disordered children. The model described below is the result of some of this work (Patterson and Reid, 1970).

In the statistically normal family, pleasantness is reciprocated or returned. Aversive methods of control are used infrequently and only when positive methods fail. Deviant families tend to be characterised by a lack of reciprocity and a frequent use of aversive or coercive methods of control. Reciprocity centres on the dispensing and receiving of positive reinforcements. The system depends upon the stable delivery and return of such positives in any ongoing interaction. Coercion centres on the dispensing of aversive stimuli in order to achieve either positive reinforcement or the withdrawal of a negative stimulus. The individual applies the noxious stimuli in order to force the other person to capitulate. In interactional situations, where reciprocal skills are low and in which two persons are evenly matched in coercive skills, it is probable that the coercive interactions will escalate in intensity, until one party concedes. For example, a child screams because he is not given sweets, the mother shouts at the child to stop, the child screams louder, the mother smacks him, he continues to scream, the mother smacks him harder, etc. This pattern is often observed between deviant children and their parents. Such families can, in time, gradually shape up aggression in each other to a highly skilled level. It is probable that some non-accidental injuries to children result in this fashion.

Reciprocity can be viewed as a socially created phenomenon, whereas coercion appears to have some innate survival value. For example, when a baby is hungry he will usually cry or scream until fed. Patterson (1975) suggests that coercive skills are an important aspect of children's behaviour. Such skills are at their most sophisticated around the age of 3. It is at this time that most parents gradually begin to extinguish coercive behaviours in the child (such as tantrums or non-compliance) and in their place establish prosocial skills and reciprocity. If the parents' own reciprocal skills are poor or their tracking inconsistent, if they attempt to reduce coercive behaviours at too early an age, or if they become involved in highly coercive interactions with the child, then it is probable that the child will continue to use coercion as a major interactional method. In other words the coercive behaviours which we often observe in older deviant children are usually those behaviours which most normal children exhibit at a very young age. It has been suggested by Robins (1972) that deviant behaviours in children under the age of 6 or 7 have little predictive value in terms of the child's future adjustment. With the younger child the parents' behaviour is probably of more predictive value.

The child or the family who habitually interact coercively will differ from the normal family in the way in which they discriminate social cues, the manner in which they respond in social situations and by their relatively poor self-control.

INADEQUATE DISCRIMINATION OF SOCIAL CUES

Some recent research findings indirectly suggest that highly coercive children may fail to discriminate social cues for appropriate behaviour, from other individuals in their environment. The findings which point in this direction are as follows:

(1) Coercive children are more stereotyped (limited) in their responses than normal children who habitually use reciprocity. This means that in social situations the latter child has a greater range of response choices. Moore (1975) observed normal and deviant children in both home and school settings; the observational system employed was developed by Wahler, Berland and Leske (1975). This system contains 19 response categories and 6 stimulus categories. The categories can broadly be grouped into behaviours which are: oppositional; self-stimulatory; sustained work; and interactional. A cluster analysis of all the observed behaviours revealed that the normal children's behaviour in the class setting fell into 3 separate clusters (one contained aversive, interactional and oppositional behaviours, another was composed of non-aversive adult attentional behaviours, and the third contained child-to-child social and sustained play behaviours). In the deviant children, only one large cluster emerged, which contained a wide range of related and diverse behaviours. The clustering of the normal children's behaviour perhaps suggests that they are beginning to discriminate when certain behaviours are appropriate or inappropriate. The results for the deviant children suggest the opposite.

Anecdotally, a recent classroom modification programme conducted by the first author suggests that deviant children's behaviours tended to continue at a steady level regardless of the regular classroom teacher, while the normal children's behaviours tended to fluctuate depending on which teacher was present. For instance, in the presence of the regular class teacher the normal children's oppositional behaviours were infrequent; however, in the presence of a different teacher these increased dramatically, often to levels much higher than the deviant children. One could suggest that the normals were more able to discriminate cues indicating a teacher's ability to manage the class than were the deviant children.

(2) Taplin (1974) suggests that in managing deviant behaviour problems the intervention contingencies should be contrasted or intensified. The consequences for appropriate or deviant behaviour should be clearly specified to the child, intense punishments and rewards should be employed, and prosocial behaviours should be rehearsed following infringements. In this way we may aid the deviant child in learning to rapidly discriminate social cues.

(3) Generalisation of new behaviours across settings, or between individuals (for example parents, teachers, peers), does not seem to occur following successful modification of a deviant child's behaviour. Most behaviour modification programmes focus primarily on changing the deviant responses, and whilst they may examine the stimuli associated with the onset of deviant behaviours there is rarely any attempt to focus systematically on teaching children how to respond to adult and situational cues. At the simplest level this would include teaching the child to assess what behaviours different adults will expect of him. For example, Werner et al. (1974) examined how police expect adolescents to behave when being interviewed. They found that some of the behaviours important in such a situation were: 'facial orientation, politeness, understanding, co-operation and a verbal expression of reform'. At a finer level, non-verbal and verbal behaviours may provide important discriminative cues, for example parental stance and posture, facial expression, verbal tone and content. Clearly we lack knowledge of such components and further collaboration with ethologists in this area would seem to be a progressive step. In the meantime we must continue to make treatment plans which take into account the phenomenon of non-generalisation, rather than just hoping that generalisation will occur.

The question of discrimination is complex. In order that the coercive child continues to succeed he must be able to discriminate his success in the environment. For example it is observed that often these children will escalate their coercion in efforts to thwart outside control. However, in this situation the discrimination is one which provides feedback on the child's status as an environmental controller. Whether or not these informational cues are similar to those which the normal child will utilise in gaining information about socially appropriate behaviour, is open to further research.

Coercive children may not be responsive to 'normal' social reinforcers. This is easily understood, since their needs from the environment are more often demanded than depended upon. If coercion has been successful there is little need for social responsiveness. In the reciprocal interaction each member is providing reinforcers to the other, whereas in the coercive interchange the reinforcement results from submission of one party. In the former interchange the reinforcement value of one party to the other is probably high, whereas in the latter interchange the reinforcement value of the coerced person to the coercer is probably low. We are more likely to pay attention to, and discriminate social cues from, highly reinforcing persons. The propensity to imitate and model parent prosocial skills is of obvious importance. Wahler and Nordquist (1973) demonstrated that imitation of parent behaviours was low in coercive children and that modification of the children's oppositional behaviours (usually the first aim of any intervention programme) enhanced the children's imitation of their parents. Obviously this research has important practical implications for therapy.

Highly coercive children receive from their parents relatively more positive and negative social consequences for their behaviour than do other members of the family (Patterson and Reid, 1970). In the second case study in chapter 9, the deviant child received about 90 per cent of parent attention in several situations in which two older siblings were also present. In these situations the parental behaviours observed were: look at, talk to, command, praise, scold and physically punish.

Observations of the parents of coercive children frequently reveal that punishment only follows after several coercive attempts by the child, and that attention or positive social consequences are frequently used in an effort to reduce the deviant behaviours. Thus, often the attention is non-contingent and inappropriately applied. On the basis of such observations one might suppose that the application of differential attention (that is, ignore inappropriate behaviour and attend to appropriate behaviour) would eliminate the behaviour problem. While this is often the case with preschool children (see Wagner and Ora, 1970), it may prove ineffective with deviant children of primary school age and above. The behaviour of these children may not change when appropriate social reinforcers are applied. In such cases social reinforcers may only become effective after they have been paired with intense rewards and punishments (for example material rewards and time-out).

In a review of differential adult attention procedures, Sajwaj and Dillon (1976) noted that while in some cases the technique is simply ineffective, in others paradoxical effects may occur. Herbert *et al.* (1973) quoted several cases in which the differential attention resulted in sustained increases in the deviant behaviours. Sajwaj and Hedges (1971) outlined one case in which several months' trial of differential attention failed in its effectiveness and the deviant behaviour only started to drop when the father ignored compliance and praised disruptions. It would seem in this case that praise was functioning as a punisher, that is it resulted in suppression of behaviour. Thus, sometimes appropriately applied differential attention may not only prove to be ineffective, it may also result in an enhancement of the problems.

Clearly, as Sajwaj and Dillon (1976) suggest, responsiveness to adult social behaviours is a complex area which merits further research. From a therapeutic point of view, if we are to employ differential attention techniques it is important that the case progress is carefully recorded and stronger procedures (such as time-out) implemented if side effects occur. The side effects (or increases in deviance) should not, of course, be mistaken for the transient rises in deviant behaviour which often occur in the early stages of a treatment programme.

SELF-CONTROL IN COERCIVE CHILDREN
Our level of self-control is demonstrated when we make some decision about now versus later. For example, the decision to study now may relate to the probability of passing an examination later. Rachlin (1974) indicates that the central issue in self-control is a temporal one. Very few people, in choosing between a pleasant and unpleasant option at one moment in time, would select the latter course unless some future consequence were involved. For example by having a tooth filled now we avoid the unpleasant consequences of prolonged pain in the future.

Coercive children and many of their families lack self-control skills. Immediate environmental stimuli tend to control their behaviour. For example the coercive child may demand another child's toy, the parents may spend money impulsively, or leave jobs because of a row with the boss, drive their cars without insurance, etc. Although we all at times lack self-control, in the problem family lack of self-control tends to be a pattern which goes beyond their cultural norm. They are orientated towards immediate reinforcement and will frequently apply coercive methods when this is denied. Perhaps one of the most important reasons why many parents fail to keep observational records or to maintain change in their children lies in the fact that they do not foresee, or are not motivated by, the long term consequences. In addition the coercive child's environment will not encourage the development of self-control, as feedback to him tends to focus not on any prosocial skills but on his disruptive behaviour. Neither will the child's self-evaluation, which is probably either low or distorted, encourage him to develop self-control. Further, the high levels of adult attention mentioned above are not conducive to the fostering of independence.

Simple examples of the way in which children are taught self-control are as follows: the parent reinforces the child for waiting until he arrives home before going to the toilet, or encourages the child to save money or not to eat all his sweets at once. More generally, simple contingency rules such as, 'You can have your sweets after you have tidied away your toys', demonstrate the beginnings of reward following a specified behavioural interval. In most simple contingency management procedures some aspect of self-control is stressed. As a result of the application of such external contingencies and of modelling, it is hoped that the child will eventually develop more control over his own behaviour. Perhaps most important is the development of self-evaluative behaviour. Thus, in a situation in which self-control is required, the individual's problem-solving behaviour will be influenced by internal cues (both cognitive and emotional) in addition to external environmental cues. As already noted in the section on delinquency in chapter 12, psychopaths often fail to exhibit physiological or emotional arousal (which would probably act as an internal cue for self-control) at times of transgression.

The development of techniques for strengthening self-control has mainly been restricted to managing adult problems, for example in treating obesity (Ferster, Nurnberger and Levitt, 1962). Experimental analyses of the eating behaviours of obese persons tend to show that the behaviours of these people are controlled by the immediate external cues (the presence and sight of food), rather than self-evaluative cues about place, time (appropriate time to eat) or physiological state (whether the stomach is empty or full). In teaching self-control skills the focus has been on reliable and valid self-evaluation, for example teaching obese persons to observe all the circumstances under which they eat. Such a simple monitoring procedure may have a dramatic effect when the problem is straightforward. For example, a colleague of ours observed and recorded her own eating behaviour. She discovered, to her amazement, that while she was in the kitchen each day, either working or cleaning, she was consuming approximately 600 extra calories. Once a true evaluation of the situation has been reached then change through the application of contingencies or self-imposed rules with consequences is made easier (for example all food must be eaten while sitting at the meal table).

The use and development of self-control procedures has been neglected in the area of child problems. Two recent studies demonstrated that children in a classroom situation could accurately monitor their own behaviours each day, even though such recordings contained negative as well as positive self-evaluation (Turkewitz, O'Leary and Ironsmith, 1975; Bolstad and Johnson, 1972). Commonly, deviant classroom behaviour has been managed using external contingencies such as time-out, points loss and gain, praise, etc. The importance of the above studies is their focus on teaching the children observational and self-evaluative skills, which foster the growth of self-control. Ideally, if further research into self-evaluation and self-control in children is conducted, effective techniques may be developed which will be used not only to influence the child's behaviour but also to aid in reducing the problem of non-generalisation across settings. If the child is able to play a larger part in managing his own behaviour, he will carry such control from setting to setting. If, during a treatment programme, parents fail to exhibit changes in their consequating behaviours, it may be that one of the only ways of effecting change in the child's deviant behaviours is to focus on his self-control skills. Treatment of this order will probably only be possible outside the home setting, for example in the classroom or residential setting, where it can be successfully managed.

In summary, the coercive child presents a number of peculiar difficulties: he is a poor discriminator of cues for appropriate social behaviour; he is unresponsive to normal social reinforcers; and he lacks self-control skills. At the current stage of knowledge, treatment techniques tend to be response and consequence orientated. Our examination of the coercive model emphasises the importance of stimuli preceding the response—that is, discriminative stimuli which may be external or internal cues. Until we reach a further understanding of such aspects we are bound to fail with a substantial number of cases.

The Learned Helplessness Model

Of all aspects of parenting, which may include dimensions such as love – hate, warmth – coldness, Hetherington and Martin (1972) suggest that perhaps the most important dimension is consistency – inconsistency. If there is a serious lack of consistency, the shaping of prosocial skills will probably not occur, regardless of the warmth or coldness of the parent – child relationship. The importance of consistency has already been stressed in the assessment and treatment sections of this text.

Inconsistency in management may result from some idiosyncrasy of the parent – child relationship, parental conflict over ways of handling the child, or lack of parenting skills. Many parents of deviant children present themselves at the clinic saying, 'I've rewarded him and punished him, when he is good or bad, but it just hasn't worked'. While in some cases this may be viewed as a rationalisation (for example, 'there must be some innate cause for his behaviour'), in others it may be a statement of helplessness. Often, following observation (which may demonstrate parental inconsistency), we have had difficulty in persuading parents to now reapply techniques which they have already used—such as praise or an isolation procedure. In these cases we must somehow demonstrate that inconsistency is the problem, rather than the use of faulty techniques. If a child is punished (or rewarded) in a random, non-contingent and inconsistent manner, it is possible that he will fail to relate social consequences to the behaviours he adopts. In his experience, reward is not linked to good behaviour, nor punishment to bad behaviour. His environment is unpredictable and he learns that he has no control over the consequences of his behaviour in interactional situations. In such cases it may take some time to establish the concept of behavioural consequences in the child's mind.

The fact that helplessness can be learned has been demonstrated by some recent experiments. Maier, Seligman and Solomon (1969) reported experiments which demonstrated that approximately 80 per cent of a sample of experimental dogs, exposed to several trials of non-contingent and unavoidable shock, failed to learn how to avoid shock in future avoidance-learning experiments. In contrast, control dogs (that is those not pretreated with non-contingent and unavoidable shocks) rapidly developed avoidance behaviours in similar avoidance-learning experiments. The authors, in attempting to explain the behaviours of the former dogs, examined several hypotheses. The most valid explanation seemed to be that those dogs had learned that shock was unavoidable and that it was pointless to respond when future shocks were presented. In order to successfully reverse the learned helplessness the above authors found it necessary to apply many trials in which the animal was physically forced to exhibit avoidance behaviours. Learned helplessness has also been demonstrated experimentally in human subjects (Seligman, 1975). Wolpe (1971) suggests that the model may help to explain many of the behaviours in neurotic depression. More recently, Seligman (1975) has summarised the experimental evidence and applied some of the findings to the understanding and management of human behaviour problems.

In an attempt to illustrate the model, we present three hypothetical examples in which learned helplessness plays some part:

(1) Sandy, who is 8 years old, has a reading problem. He is far behind his classmates in reading skills. The teacher ignores Sandy because she has a large class and she has not the time to give him the intensity of individual instruction required. There is no remedial reading class in the school. In reading class, Sandy sits at the back and does nothing. On some occasions he tries really hard, but because of his difficulty makes only a little progress, which goes unnoticed. Eventually he gives up and says, 'I'm never going to be able to read so what's the point in trying'—learned helplessness.

(2) Jack and Ruth, who have been married 5 years, are having frequent quarrels. They now rarely have pleasant times together. Ruth, anxious that her marriage should not break up, has attempted on many occasions to initiate pleasant interchanges with Jack. From past quarrelling experience Jack is suspicious of any interaction and thus rarely responds in a positive manner to Ruth's advances. Ruth, in discussing her marital problems with her general practitioner (who has suggested referral to Marriage Guidance), states that counselling or therapy will not help. She says, 'I know I have been unpleasant to Jack, but I have also tried very hard to be pleasant and to make up. However, it makes little difference what I do, Jack just continues to either ignore me or shout at me'—again, learned helplessness.

(3) Bob, a 12 year old, whose main problems were stealing and fire-setting, was brought to a child psychiatric clinic by his mother. Following an initial visit they failed to attend for further appointments. Eventually a social worker visited the home. The mother stated that she had not returned because she did not think that child psychiatry could help. She described how in the past a social worker, the general

practitioner and a priest had all tried to give advice about Bob's problems. Everything has failed: 'It's a waste of time, nothing will help him'—yet again, learned helplessness.

The model of learned helplessness would seem to partially explain some of the behaviours of many difficult or problem families whom we see. These families repeatedly appear to fail at things at which others succeed. Despite initial good intentions (for example to pay the rent arrears) they cannot continue to meet society's expectations and they inevitably suffer negative consequences such as social isolation, eviction, etc. (Tonge, James and Hillam, 1975). They are often 'written off' and it is the enormous task of Social Services Departments to carry and 'prop up' such families. Sometimes the statutory services propagate the helplessness. For example the supply of supplementary benefits or of home helps to problem families may reinforce their helplessness. Non-contingent positive consequences can be as harmful as non-contingent negative consequences. For example the mother of the overprotected child does everything for him unconditionally. There is thus no need for him to learn social behaviours and he may simply continue to exhibit infantile social skills (which, as we pointed out earlier, are largely coercive in nature).

High motivation has traditionally been stressed as one of the most important variables which determine a successful outcome in therapy. What, if anything, can be done to break the vicious circle of those families who persistently fail? They usually exhibit low motivation and tend to see their environment as unhelpful or unpredictable. In attempting to help the helpless family we can visualise two general tactical approaches—the direct and the indirect approach.

DIRECT APPROACH
Results of the early animal experiments on helplessness tend to suggest that force must be applied in order to reverse the failure to learn or to problem-solve. Paradoxically these results suggest that we should apply methods (that is force or coercion) which we are attempting to teach families to reduce. In practical terms this means regularly visiting the families in their own homes (thus reducing the early tendency to opt out of attending the clinic) and gradually and persistently setting up a programme which is the result of parental decisions drawn judiciously out of interactions with the family. As far as possible it is important to avoid adopting an authoritarian attitude, since problem families are likely to have had many negative experiences with authorities in the

past. It is our practice to conduct therapeutic efforts in the home setting, and we assess that over the past 4 years this strategy has succeeded with several families who definitely would have failed if therapy had been conducted in a clinic setting.

In addition, attempts should be made to motivate these families in therapy. Ideally reinforcement should be provided for performance. Obviously in most cases we do this verbally. However, social approval is not enough with the difficult or problem family. As has already been mentioned these families may not be responsive to social reinforcers, but may require more powerful reinforcers. In chapter 11 we suggested that continuing therapy made contingent on family progress (in terms of carrying out tasks, etc.) may not be reinforcing, and that monetary rewards might provide an alternative source of reinforcement. State expenditure on these families is already very high, but as pointed out it is usually contingent on failure rather than success. In some recent pilot investigations, Wahler (1975c) has employed monetary rewards for parent group attendance. Although in this case the small group of parents continued to meet regularly each week, it is difficult at this stage to say how much the monetary contract contributed to both initial and continued attendance. Ideally with each helpless family we should sample any reinforcers which we might usefully employ in their management, and put these into operation in order to enhance the likelihood of successful therapy.

INDIRECT APPROACH

In his book on learned helplessness, Seligman (1975) anecdotally discusses a programme set up to cope with a child who was having reading difficulty. After a number of weeks the programme was not progressing. At this stage (perhaps out of curiosity) the child was introduced to learning a foreign language. On a similar treatment regime the child made enormous learning leaps with the new language. Seligman hypothesised that the child had become helpless in learning to read English. However, when introduced to a new language with which he had not previously experienced failure, he succeeded. Although the anecdote does not report follow-up, we could hypothesise that having thus increased the child's self-esteem, a gradual and successful return to learning English might have been made.

This case perhaps suggests that we may indirectly be able to aid families with learned helplessness. First, in managing a child's problem the use of novel punishments and rewards may avoid the argument, 'I have tried that many times and it does not work'. If new techniques succeed then the increase in parent self-esteem and confidence in relation to the child may generalise to the use of older, tried out techniques. In addition the parents may begin to recognise the importance of consistency. Secondly, a focus on other areas which are less problematic (or are assessed as having less learned helplessness associated with them) may be another way of demonstrating to families that they can be effective and that we, as therapists, may be able to aid them. These procedures can involve simple practical steps such as helping the mother to obtain a part-time job, or setting up a group which focuses on teaching household skills and communication skills. When teaching any of these parents a new skill it is highly important that every small step of progress is enthusiastically reinforced. The weekly groups run by Wahler, which we referred to above, in part fulfil some of these latter requirements. Initially parents come together and begin to communicate in depersonalised exercises. The group leaders perform the function of encouraging the interaction and providing performance feedback to the parents. Gradually the communication is led to more personal aspects. Having been a participant in the groups it was the first author's experience that each week the parents showed increasing confidence in verbalising and attempting to solve problem situations of a more and more personal nature. If such groups are to be established then parents or participants must be selected (people who volunteer rarely suffer from learned helplessness) and attendance facilitated by the provision of transport to and from the group, with concurrent child care facilities. Rose (1972) has discussed the uses of groups with delinquent children. These groups progress along similar lines. However, other than the descriptive work, we are unfamiliar with any follow-up data. Learned helplessness is a relatively new and probably important model in behavioural therapy. Its relative importance and the techniques for dealing with it are still to be developed and evaluated.

New Directions in Behaviour Therapy

The discussion in this chapter has so far centred on understanding failure within the framework of learning theory. Many believe that this theory has wide and potent applications, for example changing and shaping cultures and societies. Such an ideal is discussed in Skinner's

(1948) utopian novel *Walden Two*. The belief in such power has given rise to many legal and ethical issues concerning behavioural application—see for example the series of papers by Lucero *et al.*, Miron, Cahoon, etc., which have been reissued by Ulrich, Stachnik and Mabry (1970). The development of an effective technology of behaviour certainly requires the resolution of ethical issues in order to guard against malpractice. However, in the author's opinion, learning theory has not reached such an effective or influential stage. A casual perusal of any of the behavioural journals mentioned at the beginning of this chapter quickly reveals that many behaviourists apply their treatments and studies on an extremely narrow base. For example we are often left with the impression that assessments focus exclusively on target behaviours without reference to the subject's total interactional situation. As Willems (1973) so cogently emphasises, whilst we may be successful in managing target behaviours—for example in reducing a child's tantrums—on a broader base we may be failing, for example if the child's mother becomes depressed following reduction of his tantrums. It is now time for behaviourists to give attention to the wider implications of their treatment procedures. In discussing current thinking in these areas we will attend first to the possible effects in the individual and secondly to those effects which might occur in his environment.

BEHAVIOURAL CHANGE IN THE INDIVIDUAL SUBJECT
Changing an individual's behaviour may have effects which can be observed in the short term or in the long term.

(1) The short term effects. In chapter 8 we referred to the fact that behaviours which covary stably with each other, whether reciprocally or inversely, can be referred to as members of a response class (for example, obedience and co-operative behaviours will probably vary reciprocally). While in many instances the behaviours in a response class can be understood because (as in the above example) they are closely related in social form and consequences, some recent researchers have been finding stable covariations in behaviours for which these explanations are untenable. Wahler *et al.* (1970) noted that a child's stuttering decreased dramatically following a programme designed to reduce his non-verbal problem behaviours. Sajwaj, Twardoz and Burke (1972) report that, following the successful targeted reduction of a child's adult attention-seeking behaviours, they found that the child's peer interactions increased, his play with girls' toys decreased and his

behaviour in group settings became more disruptive and oppositional. Even more perplexing is the report by Wahler (1975a) which, over long term assessments, showed stable behavioural covariations across settings. For instance, with one subject treated in a classroom setting for behaviour problems, his classroom schoolwork and home self-stimulatory behaviour covaried stably over 2-year period. In a second subject, as oppositional behaviours decreased at home, his peer interactions and oppositional behaviour increased in the school setting. These covariations continued over a reversal and reapplication of home treatment for his opposition (that is, the treatment was stopped and later reapplied). In these reports the assessments were carried out using wide stimulus and response category observational systems. Detailed analysis revealed no causes for the observed effects (in terms of changes in social contingencies, etc.). One could, of course, argue that the assessments and searches for stimulus control in the above reports were not fine enough to pick up controlling stimuli relevant to the response class. However, they do at least once again highlight the complexity of behaviour.

(2) The long term effects. So far we have focused on covariations which occur on a more or less direct temporal basis. However, changes in an individual's behaviour at one moment in time may result in long term and far reaching consequences. Breland and Breland (1966) noted that, some time after successful training and many highly skilled performances, some of their circus animals stopped performing or responding to the contingencies of reinforcement. The authors do not know of any experimental evidence of similar long term changes or effects of behaviour modification programmes on humans. However, before we can be sure of the utility of behaviour modification, the possibility of long term side effects require to be examined.

In applying behavioural treatment procedures we can try to utilise the beneficial effects of the response class phenomena, for example possibly in the management of low rate delinquent behaviours. Hopefully, longer and wider assessments may reveal any detrimental side effects and contribute to further intervention tactics which avoid these effects.

THE ENVIRONMENTAL EFFECTS OF BEHAVIOUR CHANGE

In discussing behaviour from an ecological perspective, Willems (1973) indicates the possible environmental problems which may occur when advances in scientific technology are applied enthusiastically, narrowly and without forethought. Behaviour modifiers can frequently be accused of such narrow enthusiasm. Too often it is assumed that good behaviour will be maintained or reinforced by the environment. However, we must clearly remember that attitudes may not change as rapidly as behaviour (see chapter 3 for the report on Wahler and Leske's (1973) study). In a more recent study, Wahler, Berland and Leske (1975) found that the successful establishment of prosocial skills in adolescent offenders was not maintained at 1-year follow-up. Forty-five per cent of this sample had re-presented at the courts and a further 35 per cent were considered to be in need of further intervention. The parent, peer and authority attitudes had probably remained unchanged. (For example, the police may have continued to view the adolescent as deviant, and thus failed to recognise or reinforce his 'good' behaviour.) Ideally, attempts should be made to integrate and systematically analyse the total community's effect on and response to deviant behaviour. At a practical level, continued community and group work with deviant individuals may help to establish more stably functioning subcultures, in which feedback is more accurate than that provided by the outside community.

Even if we are able to change a child's deviant behaviours and shape them in a more socially appropriate manner, we cannot assume that the changes in his behaviour will be found reinforcing to other persons in his environment. We stated earlier in the text that changes in a positive direction should ideally provide parents with the motivation to continue utilising their 'new' skills. That this does not always occur is evidenced by the high relapse rates following initial successful intervention (Patterson, 1975). Apart from the fact that we may have to supply continued and long term follow-up for such cases, we must also carefully consider what components make up the parents' attitude to the child. Wahler, Berland and Leske (1976) recently demonstrated that while one mother's attitude to her child was partially determined by behaviours which she recognised and recorded, other child behaviours were observed which she had not identified or recorded, and these also correlated highly with her daily attitudinal ratings of the child. These latter behaviours included episodes of approaching other children and non-interaction. The recognition of such factors may be important in determining success or failure in therapy.

While in many cases narrow application may simply lead to failure, in other cases it is possible that we do damage. Willems (1973) quotes two cases to illustrate this point: one, in which a mother, following some success in managing her child, became anxious, over-ate and eventually abandoned the child; the second, a successful programme to reduce petty vandalism in a neighbourhood. Following this, there was a rise in more serious delinquent offences in the same neighbourhood.

Questioning the Theory

It may eventually be found that reinforcement theory is not enough. While reinforcement works, its overall importance is still questionable. Willems (1973) illustrates this point in the following analogy. While aspirin relieves a headache, we know that the absence of aspirin does not cause a headache. Similarly, while reinforcers modify social behaviours, can we say that deviant or deficient social behaviours are solely the result of 'abnormal' reinforcement contingencies? The whole question of the sufficiency of the theory and its methods is posed by Wahler (1975b). He stresses that many behaviourists are moving into and exploring the fields of attitudinal and cognitive psychology, ecology, ethology, etc. At all costs we must avoid the circular argument that unexplained behaviour changes occur solely as a result of faulty behavioural procedures. For example, findings such as those reported by Breland and Breland (1966), see above, may stimulate rigid learning theorists to reject the reports on the grounds that there must have been some fault in the application of the principles. These arguments, although they may be valid in some cases are nevertheless counter-productive to theoretical advancement. Such findings deserve closer examination. Despite these discouraging views about the absolute value of theory the authors believe that the discipline has clearly established one firm and unassailable principle—that of empirical assessment. In the final analysis we shall only be able to gain knowledge and use it practically by gathering data in a scientific and objective manner. Without this it is impossible to assess the effectiveness of any technological development.

Appendix A:
Selected Textbooks

Selecting behaviour therapy textbooks is difficult, since the large majority originate in the USA. Below we provide a reference list of those books which we have personally found useful either as reference source books or as practical handbooks. This is not intended to imply that alternative texts are necessarily inferior.

(1) SOURCE TEXTBOOKS

(a) General theory and practice
> Bandura, A. (1969). *Principles of Behavior Modification*. New York: Holt, Rinehart and Winston
> Kanfer, F. and Phillips, J. (1970). *Learning Foundations of Behaviour Therapy*. New York: Wiley
> Rimm, D. C. and Masters, J. C. (1974). *Behavior Therapy: Techniques and Empirical Findings*. New York: Academic Press
> Wolpe, J. (1973). *The Practice of Behavior Therapy*. New York: Pergamon

The Rimm and Masters (1974) book is an excellent text for both beginner and experienced behaviour therapist. These authors present theory and practice in a well integrated and readable form.

(b) General theory and practice of behaviour therapy with children
> Blackham, G. J. and Silberman, A. (1975). *Modification of Child and Adolescent Behavior*. Belmont, California: Wadsworth
> Gelfand, D. M. and Hartman, D. (1975). *Child Behaviour: Analysis and Therapy*. New York: Pergamon

The first of these texts is useful in that it contains chapters which discuss a vast range of specific behaviour problems under separate headings. Unfortunately it is becoming somewhat outdated. Gelfand and Hartman's book provides an excellent and critical account of assessment, treatment and follow-up procedures. However, parts of the text (for example the discussion on reliability and experimental design) are perhaps of more interest to the research-oriented therapist.

(c) Edited collections of papers and chapters pertaining to child behaviour therapy
    Ashem, B. A. and Poser, E. G. (1973). *Adaptive Learning: Behavior Modification with Children.* New York: Pergamon
    Grazianio, A. M. (1971). *Behavior Therapy with Children.* Chicago, Illinois: Aldine-Atherton

Both books contain a wide variety of useful papers relating to the management of problems specific to retarded, psychotic and behaviourally disordered children.

(2) TEXTBOOKS AND MANUALS WHICH FOCUS ON THE CLINICAL APPLICATION OF BEHAVIOUR THERAPY WITH CHILDREN

(a) Assessment of child behaviour
    Hutt, S. J. and Hutt, C. (1970). *Direct Observation and Measurement of Behavior.* Springfield, Illinois: Thomas
    Wahler, R. G., House, A. E. and Stambaugh, E. E (1976). *Ecological Assessment of Child Problem Behavior: A Clinical Package for Home, School and Institutional Settings.* New York: Pergamon

Both texts focus on observational assessment of child behaviour.

(b) Management of child behaviour in the home setting
    Becker, W. C. (1971). *Parents are Teachers.* Champaign, Illinois: Research Press
    Madsen, C. K. and Madsen, C. H. (1972). *Parents—Children—Discipline: A Positive Approach.* Boston: Allyn and Bacon
    Patterson, G. R. (1971). *Families: Application of Social Learning to Family Life.* Champaign, Illinois: Research Press
    Patterson, G. R. and Gullion, M. E. (1971). *Living with Children: New Methods for Parents and Teachers.* Champaign, Illinois: Research Press
    Peine, H. A. and Howarth, R. (1975). *Children and Parents.*Harmondsworth, Middlesex: Penguin Books
    Phillips, E. L., Phillips, E. A., Fixsen, D. L. and Wolf, M. M. (1974). *The Teaching Family Handbook.* University of Kansas, Lawrence, Kansas (obtainable from Bureau of Child Research, University of Kansas)
    Watson, L. (1973). *Child Behavior Modification.* New York: Pergamon

All these books are prepared in manual form and except for the one by

Madsen and Madsen are designed to be used by parents as well as therapists. They all provide an easy introduction to the basic techniques common to child behaviour modification. Madsen and Madsen provide a wide range of simple techniques for dealing with behaviour problems. Watson's text is perhaps aimed more at the management of retarded and autistic children, since many of the techniques outlined relate to the training of simple social skills, for example dressing, eating and toileting. The handbook by Phillips *et al.* contains a 'goldmine' of information about methods and techniques for teaching delinquent offenders appropriate social skills.

(c) Management of child behaviour using group therapy
>   Rose, S. D. (1972). *Treating Children in Groups: A Behavioral Approach.* San Francisco, California: Jossey-Bass

This text is perhaps specially useful to professionals working within residential settings. The author clearly describes the techniques used in initiating, maintaining and reaching behavioural goals, and finally terminating child groups.

(d) Management of child behaviour in the classroom
>   Homme, L. (1970). *How to Use Contingency Contracting in the Classroom.* Champaign, Illinois: Research Press
>   MacDonald, W. S. (1971). *Battle in the Classroom.* Scranton, Pennsylvania: In Text Educational Publishers

MacDonald realistically discusses the application and effects of a variety of techniques for dealing with deviant children of various age ranges. The procedures outlined by Homme are equally useful in the home setting.

(e) Modification of adolescent and adult behaviours
>   Knox, D. (1971). *Marriage Happiness: A Behavioral Approach to Counseling* Champaign, Illinois: Research Press
>   Liberman, R. P., King, L. W., DeRisi, W. J. and McCann, M. (1975). *Personal Effectiveness.* Champaign, Illinois: Research Press
>   Watson, D. L. and Tharp, R. G. (1972). *Self-Directed Behavior: Self-Modification for Personal Adjustment.* Monterey, California: Brooks-Cole

Though we have not covered the areas presented in these texts, a knowledge of the techniques used in marital work, social skills training and self-control is crucial when working with families of disturbed children. Many of the therapeutic strategies outlined in these books can easily be adapted for use with children.

Appendix B:
Selected Journal Articles

Over the past few years we have collected a series of journal articles which have proved useful in our clinical practice. The list below (which includes some of these) is neither exclusive nor totally comprehensive, but it may offer the reader new roads into behaviour therapy.

(1) APPETITE DISORDERS

Aragona, J., Cassady, J. and Drabman, R. S. (1975). Treating overweight children through parental training and contingency contracting. *Journal of Applied Behavior Analysis*, **8**, 269–278

Azerrad, J. and Stafford, R. L. (1969). Restoration of eating behavior in Anorexia Nervosa through operant conditioning and environmental manipulation. *Behavior Research and Therapy*, **7**, 165–171

Ferster, C. B., Nurnberger, J. I. and Levitt, E. B. (1962). The control of eating. *Journal of Mathetics*, **1**, 87–109

Hall, S. M. (1972). Self-control and therapist control in the behavioral treatment of overweight women. *Behavior Research and Therapy*, **10**, 59–68

Hallsten, E. A. (1965). Adolescent Anorexia Nervosa treated by desensitisation. *Behavior Research and Therapy*, **3**, 87–91

Kohlenberg, R. J. (1970). The punishment of persistent vomiting: a case study. *Journal of Applied Behavior Analysis*, **3**, 241–245

Stuart, R. B. (1967). Behavioral control of over-eating. *Behavior Research and Therapy*, **5**, 357–367

Stunkard, A. (1972). New therapies for eating disorders: behavior modification of obesity and Anorexia Nervosa. *Archives of General Psychiatry*, **26**, 391–398

(2) ASSESSMENT AND METHOD

Bijou, S. W., Peterson, R. F., Harris, F. R., Allen, E. and Johnston, M. S. (1969). Methodology for experimental studies of young children in natural settings. *The Psychological Record*, **19**, 177–210

Kazdin, A. E. (1973). Methodological and assessment considerations in evaluating reinforcement programs in applied settings. *Journal of Applied Behavior Analysis*, **6**, 517–531

Lazarus, A. A. (1973). The basic id: multimodel assessment in behavior therapy. *Journal of Nervous and Mental Diesease*, **156**, 404–411

McNamara, J. R. and MacDonough, T. S. (1972). Some methodological considerations in the design and implementation of behavior therapy research. *Behavior Therapy*, **3**, 361–379

Wahler, R. G. and Leske, M. S. (1973). Accurate and inaccurate observer summary reports. *Journal of Nervous and Mental Disease*, **156**, 386–394

(3) BEHAVIOURAL MANAGEMENT OF DISRUPTIVE PROBLEMS: CRYING, FIRE-SETTING, OPPOSITIONAL, STEALING AND DELINQUENT BEHAVIOURS

Bernal, M. E., Duryee, J. S., Pruett, H. L. and Burns, B. J. (1968). Behavior modification and the 'brat syndrome'. *Journal of Consulting and Clinical Psychology*, **52**, 447–455

Braukmann, C. J. and Fixsen, D. L. (1975). Behavior modification with delinquents. In: M. Hersen, R. M. Eisler and P. M. Miller (Eds.), *Progress in Behavior Modification*. New York: Academic Press

Etzel, B. C. and Gerwitz, J. L. (1967). Experimental modification of caretaker-maintained high-rate operant crying in a 6 and 20-week-old infant; extinction of crying with reinforcement of eye contact and smiling. *Journal of Experimental Child Psychology*, **5**, 303–317

Hart, B. M., Allen, K. E., Buell, J. S., Harris, F. R. and Wolf, M. M. (1964). Effects of social reinforcement on operant crying. *Journal of Experimental Child Psychology*, **1**, 145–153

Holland, C. J. (1969). Elimination by the parents of fire-setting in a seven year old boy. *Behaviour Research and Therapy*, **7**, 135–137

Patterson, G. R. and Brodsky, G. (1966). A behavior modification programme for a child with multiple problem behaviors. *Journal of Child Psychology and Psychiatry*, **7**, 277–295

Patterson, G. R., Cobb, J. A. and Ray, R. A. (1973). A social engineering technology for retraining the families of aggressive boys. In: H. E. Adams and I. P. Unikel (Eds.), *Issues and Trends in Behavior Therapy*. Springfield, Illinois: Charles C. Thomas

Patterson, G. R., McNeal, S., Hawkins, N. and Phelps, R. (1967). Reprogramming the social environment. *Journal of Child Psychology and Psychiatry*, **8**, 181–195

Wetzel, R. (1966). Use of behavioral techniques in a case of compulsive stealing. *Journal of Consulting Psychology*, **30**, 367–374

(4) CLASSROOM MANAGEMENT

Bailey, J. S., Wolf, M. M. and Phillips, E. L. (1970). Home-based reinforcement and the modification of pre-delinquents' classroom behavior. *Journal of Applied Behaviour Analysis*, **3**, 223–233

McAllister, L. W., Stachowiak, J. G., Baer, D. M. and Conderman (1969). The application of operant conditioning techniques in a secondary school classroom. *Journal of Applied Behavior Analysis*, **2**, 277–285

Madsen, C. H., Becker, W. C. and Thomas, D. R. (1968). Rules, praise and ignoring: elements of elementary classroom control. *Journal of Applied Behavior Analysis*, **1**, 139–150

Sulzbacher, S. I. and Houser, J. E. (1970). A tactic to eliminate disruptive behaviors in the classroom: group contingent consequences. In: R. Ulrich, T.

Stachnik and J. Mabry (Eds.), *Control of Human Behavior*, vol. 2. Oakland, New Jersey: Scott, Foresman and Company

Thomas, D. R., Becker, W. C. and Armstrong, M. (1968). Production and elimination of disruptive classroom behavior by systematically varying teacher's behaviour. *Journal of Applied Behavior Analysis*, **1**, 35–45

Winnett, R. A. and Winkler, R. C. (1972). Current behavior modification in the classroom: be still, be quiet, be docile. *Journal of Applied Behavior Analysis*, **5**, 499–504

(5) CONTRACTING AND NEGOTIATING

Kifer, R. E., Lewis, M. A., Green, D. R. and Phillips, E. L. (1974). Training pre-delinquent youths and their parents to negotiate conflict situations. *Journal of Applied Behavior Analysis*, **7**, 357–364

Stuart, R. B. (1971) Behavioral contracting within the families of delinquents. *Journal of Behavior Therapy and Experimental Psychiatry*, **2**, 1–11

Weathers, L. and Liberman, R. P. (1975). The family contracting exercise. *Journal of Behavior Therapy and Experimental Psychiatry*, **6**, 208–214

Weathers, L. and Liberman, R. P. (1975). Contingency contracting with familes of delinquent adolescents. *Behavior Therapy*, **6**, 356–366

(6) ENCOPRESIS

Neale, D. H. (1963). Behavior therapy and encopresis in children. *Behaviour Research and Therapy*, **1**, 139–143

Young, G. C. (1973). The treatment of childhood encopresis by conditioned gastro-ileal reflex training. *Behaviour Research and Therapy*, **11**, 499–504

(7) ENURESIS

Kimmel, H. D. and Kimmel, E. (1970). An instrumental conditioning method for the treatment of enuresis. *Journal of Behavior Therapy and Experimental Psychiatry*, **1**, 121–123

Turner, R. K., Young, G. C. and Rackman, S. (1970). Treatment of nocturnal enuresis by conditioning techniques. *Behaviour Research and Therapy*, **8**, 367–381

(8) MARITAL AND SEXUAL PROBLEMS

Azrin, N. H., Naster, B. J. and Jones, R. (1973). Reciprocity counseling: a rapid learning-based procedure for marital counseling. *Behaviour Research and Therapy*, **11**, 365–382

Patterson, G. R. and Hops, H. (1973). Coercion, a game for two: intervention techniques for marital conflict. In: R. E. Ulrich and P. Mountjoy (Eds.), *The Experimental Analysis of Social Behavior*. New York: Appleton-Century-Crofts

Pines, M. (1968). 'Human sexual response'—A discussion of the work of Masters and Johnson. *Journal of Psychosomatic Research*, **12**, 39–49

Stuart, R. B. (1969). Operant-interpersonal treatment for marital discord. *Journal of Consulting and Clinical Psychology*, **33**, 675–682

(9) PARENTS AS THERAPISTS

Berkowitz, B. P. and Graziano, A. M. (1972). Training parents as behaviour therapists: A review. *Behaviour Research and Therapy*, **10**, 297–318

Johnson, C. A. and Katz, R. C. (1973). Using parents as change agents for their children: A review. *Journal of Child Psychology and Psychiatry*, **14**, 181–200

Johnson, S. M. and Brown, R. A. (1969). Producing behavior change in parents of disturbed children. *Journal of Child Psychology and Psychiatry*, **10**, 107–121

Rose, S. D. (1974). Training parents in groups as behavior modifiers of their mentally retarded children. *Journal of Behavior Therapy and Experimental Psychiatry*, **5**, 135–141

Wahler, R. G., Winkel, G. H., Peterson, R. F. and Morrison, D. C. (1965). Mothers as behavior therapists for their own children. *Behaviour Research and Therapy*, **3**, 113–124

Zeilberger, J., Sampen, S. and Sloane, H. (1968). Modification of a child's problem behaviors in the home with the mother as therapist. *Journal of Applied Behavior Analysis*, **1**, 47–53

(10) POINTS SYSTEMS

Christopherson, E. R., Arnold, C. M., Hill, D. W. and Quilitch, H. R. (1972). The home points system: token reinforcement procedures for application by parents of children with behavior problems. *Journal of Applied Behavior Analysis*, **5**, 485–497

Phillips, E. L. (1968). Achievement Place: token reinforcement procedures in a home-style rehabilitation setting for 'pre-delinquent' boys. *Journal of Applied Behavior Analysis*, **1**, 213–224

(11) SCHOOL-REFUSAL AND SEPARATION ANXIETY

Kennedy, W. A. (1965). School phobia: rapid treatment of fifty cases. *Journal of Abnormal Psychology*, **70**, 285–289

Lazarus, A. A., Davison, G. C. and Polejka, D. A. (1965). Classical and operant factors in the treatment of a school phobia. *Journal of Abnormal Psychology*, **70**, 3, 225–229

Montenegro, H. (1968). Severe separation anxiety in two preschool children: successfully treated by reciprocal inhibition. *Journal of Child Psychology and Psychiatry*, **9**, 93–103

Patterson, G. R. (1966). A learning theory approach to the treatment of a school phobic child. In: L. P. Ullman and L. Krasner (Eds.), *Case Studies in Behavior Modification*. New York: Holt, Rinehart and Winston

(12) SELF-CONTROL IN CHILDREN

Bolstad, O. D. and Johnson, S. M. (1972). Self-regulation in the modification of disruptive classroom behavior. *Journal of Applied Behavior Analysis*, **5**, 443–454

Kaufman, K. F. and O'Leary, K. D. (1972). Reward, cost and self-evaluation procedures for disruptive adolescents in a psychiatric hospital school. *Journal of Applied Behavior Analysis*, **5**, 293–310

Kropp, H., Calhoon, B. and Verner, R. (1971). Modification of the self-concept of emotionally disturbed children by covert reinforcement. *Behavior Therapy*, **2**, 201–204

Glossary of Selected
Behavioural Terms

Terms commonly used in behaviour modification are often difficult to define because of their frequent loose clinical usage. The definitions provided below represent the authors' understanding of the theoretical meaning of these terms.

ANTECEDENTS

See *Stimulus*.

AVERSIVE

Unpleasant or noxious.

BASELINE

A record of behaviours, usually carried out prior to treatment.

BEHAVIOUR MODIFICATION

A therapeutic methodology for changing behaviour which has been developed from reinforcement theory. Behaviour is changed by altering stimuli, responses and/or consequences.

COERCION

The dispensing of aversive stimuli in order to achieve either positive reinforcement or the withdrawal of a negative stimulus.

CONSEQUATE

To implement the contingencies of punishment and reward.

CONTINGENCY

A term commonly used when describing the relationship that certain consequences (of either reward or punishment) have to a designated behaviour.

CONTINGENT

Reward or punishment are contingent when they consistently follow specified behaviours.

DEFICIT

Deficiencies in emotional and/or social skill behaviours are referred to as behavioural 'deficits'. In assessment these should be carefully pinpointed and defined.

DESENSITISATION

A technique employed to extinguish fears or phobias, whereby the patient is relaxed and then gradually exposed to the feared stimulus.

DIFFERENTIAL ATTENTION

A therapeutic technique which entails the parent or therapist in socially reinforcing appropriate child behaviours and ignoring inappropriate child behaviours.

EVENT RECORDING

Descriptive accounts or records of each incident of a target behaviour.

EXTINCTION

When the reinforcers for a behaviour are removed, that behaviour will eventually disappear. We can then say that extinction has occurred.

FREQUENCY COUNT

A record of the rate of a behaviour as it occurs over a period of time.

GENERALISATION

If we change a behaviour and we note, (a) that this behavioural change transfers to other settings, or (b) that related behaviours exhibit similar change, then we can state that generalisation has occurred.

HIGH RATE BEHAVIOUR

Frequent daily occurring behaviour.

INCOMPATIBLE BEHAVIOURS

Two behaviours which by their very nature cannot be exhibited simultaneously by one person, for example obedience and disobedience.

INTERMITTENT REINFORCEMENT

Occasional reward. A reinforcement schedule stipulates the frequency of reward for appropriate behaviour. For example one reward for every three occurrences of the behaviour.

LEARNING THEORY

Focuses on discrimination. It is based on the observation that organisms will discriminate and learn (either consciously or unconsciously), from the relationships between their own behaviours and the antecedents and consequences thereof.

See also *Reinforcement theory* and *Operant theory*.

LOW RATE BEHAVIOUR

Infrequently occurring behaviour, for example once or twice a week.

MODELLING

The demonstration of behaviours. In therapy we act or model target behaviours for clients.

OBSERVATION

Looking at and recording behaviour.

OPERANT THEORY

Focuses on responses. It is based on the observation that the behaviours of organisms are instrumental in gaining their own reinforcement. The organism operates to gain 'pleasure' and avoid pain.

See also *Reinforcement theory* and *Learning theory*.

OVERT BEHAVIOURS

Observable behaviours.

POINTS SYSTEM

An intervention technique whereby the child earns points when he exhibits previously defined behaviours. Later these points are exchanged for previously defined rewards.

PROSOCIAL SKILLS

Socially appropriate behaviours.

PUNISHMENT

Any stimulus or event which will result in the suppression of a behaviour when it is made consequent on that behaviour, is known as a 'punisher'.

RECIPROCITY

Centres on the dispensing and receiving of positive reinforcements. It depends upon the stable delivery and return of such positives, in any ongoing interaction.

REINFORCEMENT

(*a*) A positive reinforcer (synonymously referred to as a reward) is any stimulus which increases the probability that the child's preceding behaviour will recur; (*b*) a negative reinforcer is any stimulus (usually aversive) which increases the probability that the behaviour which resulted in its removal or termination will recur.

REINFORCEMENT THEORY

Focuses on consequences. It is based on the observation that certain events (see *Reinforcement* and *Extinction*) are significant in the establishment, maintenance or disappearance of behaviour.

See also *Operant theory* and *Learning theory*.

RESPONSE CLASS

Behaviours which covary stably in relationship to each other (either reciprocally or inversely) can be said to belong to a common response class.

RESPONSE COST

A punishment technique which involves the loss of points or privileges.

REWARD

See *Reinforcement*.

SCAN

To observe the occurrence of target behaviours, a certain number of times, over a specified period, for example 3 times every half-hour.

SHAPE UP

To progressively reinforce increased approximations to a designated behaviour.

SIMPLE CONTINGENCY MANAGEMENT

An intervention approach, typified by the use of rewards and punishments, which are both immediate and simple. The rewards are either social or material and the punishment is either the withdrawal of attention or the application of time-out.

SPECIMEN RECORDING

A description of all interactions which have occurred during the observational period.

STIMULUS

An event (situational, emotional, cognitive, perceptual, etc.) which acts as a cue for behaviour.

SUPPRESS

See *Punishment*.

THREE-STEP CONTINGENCY PROCEDURE

A three-stage procedure for the implementation of time-out.

TIME-OUT

A punishment technique whereby, consequent on deviant behaviour, the child is removed or isolated for a short time from any reinforcers. It is an abbreviation of the phrase 'time-out from reinforcement'.

TIME SAMPLING

A sample of behaviour, recorded during specified time intervals.

TRACK

To accurately follow behaviour in terms of its antecedents and consequences.

References

Allyon, T. and Azrin, N. H. (1968). *The Token Economy: A Motivational System for Therapy and Rehabilitation.* New York: Appleton-Century-Crofts

Allyon, T. and Kelly, K. (1972). Effects of reinforcement on standardised test performance. *Journal of Applied Behaviour Analysis,* **5,** 477–484

Azrin, N. H. and Holz, W. C. (1966). Punishment. In: W. K. Honig (Ed.), *Operant Behavior: Areas of Research and Application.* New York: Appleton-Century-Crofts

Azrin, N. H., Naster, B. J. and Jones, R. (1973). Reciprocity counseling: A rapid learning based procedure for marital counseling. *Behaviour Research and Therapy,* **11,** 365–382

Bandura, A. (1969). *Principles of Behavior Modification.* New York: Holt, Rinehart and Winston

Bellman, M. (1966). Studies on encopresis. *Acta Pediatrica Scandinavia,* **170** (Suppl.)

Berg, I. and McGuire, R. (1971). Are school phobic adolescents over-dependent? *British Journal of Psychiatry,* **119,** 167–168

Berg, I. and McGuire, R. (1974). Are mothers of school phobic adolescents overprotective? *British Journal of Psychiatry,* **124,** 10–13

Berg, I., Nichols, K. and Pritchard, C. (1969). School phobia—its classification and relationship to dependency. *Journal of Child Psychology and Psychiatry,* **10,** 123–141

Bolstad, O. D. and Johnson, M. (1972). Self-regulation in the modification of disruptive classroom behavior. *Journal of Applied Behavior Analysis,* **5,** 443–454

Borkovec, T. D. (1970). Autonomic reactivity to sensory stimulation in psychopathic, neurotic and normal juvenile delinquents. *Journal of Consulting and Clinical Psychology,* **35,** 217–222

Breland, K. and Breland, M. (1966). *Animal Behavior.* New York: MacMillan

Broughton, R. J. (1968). Sleep disorders: disorders of arousal? *Science,* **159,** 1070–1078

Carter, R. D. and Levy, R. L. (1972). Interim report on interaction research. Unpublished manuscript, Family and School Consultation Project, Ann Arbor, Michigan

Chess, S., Thomas, A. and Birch, H. G. (1968). Behavior problems revisited. In: S. Chess and T. Birch (Eds), *Annual Progress in Child Psychiatry and Child Development.* New York: Brunner Mazel

Christopherson, E. R., Arnold, C. M., Hill, D. W. and Quilitch, H. R. (1972). The home point system: token reinforcement procedures for application by parents of children with behavior problems. *Journal of Applied Behavior Analysis*, **5**, 485—497

Church, R. M. (1969). Response suppression. In: B. A. Church and R. M. Church (Eds.), *Punishment and Aversive Behavior*. New York: Appleton-Century-Crofts

Coolidge, J. C., Hahn, P. B. and Peck, A. L. (1957). School phobia: neurotic crisis or way of life. *American Journal of Orthopsychiatry*, **27**, 296—306

Craig, M. M. and Glick, S. J. (1965). *A Manual of Procedures for Application of Glueck Prediction Table*. University of London Press

Eisenberg, L. (1958). School phobia: a study in the communication of anxiety. *American Journal of Psychiatry*, **114**, 712—718

Eyberg, S. M. and Johnson, S. M. (1974). Multiple assessment of behavior modification with families: effects of contingency contracting and order of treated problems. *Journal of Consulting and Clinical Psychology*, **42**, 594—606

Eysenck, H. J. (1957). *The Dynamics of Anxiety and Hysteria*. New York: Prager

Ferreira, A. J. and Winter, W. D. (1968). Information exchange and silence in normal and abnormal families. *Family Process*, **7**, 251—276

Ferster, C. B., Nurnberger, J. I. and Levitt, E. G. (1962). The control of eating. *Journal of Mathetics*, **1**, 87—109

Gardner, J. M. (1972). Teaching behavior modification to non-professionals. *Journal of Applied Behavior Analysis*, **5**, 517—521

Goldberg, E. M. (1976). Towards accountability in social work: a case review system for social workers. *British Journal of Social Work*, **6**, 3—22

Hathaway, S. R. (1965). Personality inventories. In: B. B. Wolman (Ed.), *Handbook of Clinical Psychology*. New York: McGraw-Hill

Herbert, E. W., Pinkston, E. M., Hayden, M. L., Sajwaj, T. E., Pinkston, S., Cordua, G. and Jackson, C. (1973). Adverse effects of differential parental attention. *Journal of Applied Behavior Analysis*, **6**, 15—30

Hetherington, M. E. and Martin, B. (1972). Family interaction and psychopathology in children. In: H. C. Quay and J. S. Werry (Eds.), *Psychopathological Disorders of Childhood*. New York: Wiley

Jayaratne, S., Stuart, R. B. and Tripodi, T. (1974). Methodological issues and problems in evaluating treatment outcomes in the Family and School Consultation Project, 1970—1973. In: P. O. Davidson, F. W. Clark and L. A. Hamerlynck (Eds.), *Evaluations of Behavioral Programs in Community Residential and School Settings*. Champaign, Illinois: Research Press

Jephcott, A. P. and Carter, M. P. (1955). The social background of delinquency. University of Nottingham. Cited in Wilson, H. (1962). *Delinquency and Child Neglect*. Allen and Unwin

Johnson, S. M. and Bolstad, O. D. (1973). Methodological issues in naturalistic observation: some problems and solutions for field research. In: L. A. Hamerlynck, L. C. Hardy and E. J. Mash (Eds.), *Behavior Change: Methodology, Concepts, and Change*. Champaign, Illinois: Research Press

Kanfer, F. H. and Phillips, J. S. (1970). *Learning Foundations of Behavior Therapy*. New York: Wiley

Kara, A. (1975). The operant conditioning model in relation to response class phenomena. Unpublished Dissertation, University of Tennessee, Knoxville

Kazdin, A. E. (1972). Response cost: the removal of conditioned reinforcers for therapeutic change. *Behavior Therapy*, **3**, 533–546

Kennedy, W. A. (1965). School phobia: rapid treatment of 50 cases. *Journal of Abnormal Psychology*, **70**, 285–289

Kent, R. (1976). A methodological critique for boys with conduct problems. *Journal of Consulting and Clinical Psychology*, **44**, 297–302

Kimmel, H. D. and Kimmel, E. (1970). An instrumental conditioning method for the treatment of enuresis. *Journal of Behavior Therapy and Experimental Psychiatry*, **1**, 121–123

Knox, D. (1971). *Marriage Happiness: A Behavioral Approach to Counseling*. Champaign, Illinois: Research Press

Lazarus, A. A. (1973). The basic id: multimodel behavior therapy. *Journal of Nervous and Mental Disease*, **156**, 404–411

Lazarus, A. A., Davison, G. C. and Polejka, D. A. (1965). Classical operant factors in the treatment of a school phobia. *Journal of Abnormal Psychology*, **70** (3), 225–229

Lindsley, O. R. (1968). A reliable wrist counter for recording behavior rates. *Journal of Applied Behavior Analysis*, **1**, 77–78

Lobitz, G. K. and Johnson, S. M. (1974). Normal versus deviant children: a multimethod comparison. Paper presented at the Sixth Annual Banff International Conference on Behaviour Modification

Lovaas, O. I., Schaeffer, B. and Simmons, J. Q. (1965). Building social behavior in autistic children by use of electric shock. *Journal of Experimental Research in Personality*, **1**, 99–109

Luborsky, L., Chandler, M., Auerbach, A. H., Cohen, J. and Bachrach, H. M. (1971). Factors influencing the outcome of psychotherapy: a review of quantitative research. *Psychological Bulletin*, **75**, 145–185

McCord, W., McCord, J. and Zola, I. (1959). *Origins of Crime*. New York: University of Columbia

McCormick, W. O. and O'Gorman, E. C. (1971). Declining-dose-drug-desensitisation for phobias. *Psychological Medicine*, **1**, 339–342

Maier, S. F., Seligman, M. E. P. and Solomon, R. L. (1969). Pavlovian fear conditioning and Learned Helplessness: effects on escape and avoidance behavior of (a) the CS – US contingency and (b) the independence of the US and voluntary responding. In: B. A. Campbell and R. M. Church (Eds.), *Punishment and Aversive Behavior*. New York: Appleton-Century-Crofts

Maloney, D. M., Maloney, K. B. and Timbers, G. D. (1975). Improvement school grades and reduced truancy. *West Carolina Center Papers and Reports*, **5**, 2

Mattos, R. L. (1968). A manual counter for recording multiple behaviors. *Journal of Applied Behavior Analysis*, **1**, 130

Moore, D. R. (1975). Determinants of deviancy: a behavioral comparison of normal and deviant children in multiple settings. Unpublished doctoral thesis, University of Tennessee, Knoxville

Mowrer, O. and Mowrer, W. (1938). Enuresis: a method for its study and treatment. *Americal Journal of Orthopsychiatry*, **8**, 436–447

Nay, W. R. (1975). A systematic comparison of instructional techniques for parents. *Behavior Therapy*, **6**, 14–21

Neale, D. H. (1963). Behavior therapy and encopresis in children. *Behaviour Research and Therapy*, **1**, 139–149

Oppel, W., Harper, P. and Rowland, V. (1968). The age of attaining bladder control. *Journal of Paediatrics*, **42**, 614–626

Parke, R. D. (1972). Some effects of punishment on children's behavior. In: U. Bronfenbrenner and B. A. Mahoney (Eds.), *Influences on Human Development*. Hinsdale, Illinois: The Dryden Press

Patterson, G. R. (1973). Changes in status of family members as controlling stimuli: a basis for describing the treatment process. In: L. A. Hamerlynck, L. C. Handy and E. Mash (Eds.), *Behavior Change: Methodology, Concepts and Practice*. Champaign, Illinois: Research Press

Patterson, G. R. (1975). The aggressive child: victim and architect of coercive system. In: L. A. Hamerlynck, E. J. Mash and L. C. Handy (Eds.), *Behavior Modification and Families—I. Theory and Research, II. Applications and Developments*. New York: Brunner and Mazel

Patterson, G. R. and Brodsky, G. (1966). A behavior modification programme for a child with multiple problem behaviors. *Journal of Child Psychology and Psychiatry*, **7**, 277–295

Patterson, G. R., Cobb, J. A. and Ray, R.R. (1973). A social engineering technology for retraining the families of aggressive boys. In: H. E. Adams and I. P. Unikel (Eds.), *Issues and Trends in Behavior Therapy*. Illinois: Charles C. Thomas

Patterson, G. R. and Reid, J. B. (1970). Reciprocity and coercion: two facets of social systems. In: C. Neuringer and J. L. Michael (Eds.), *Behavior Modification in Clinical Psychology*. New York: Appleton-Century-Crofts

Phillips, E. L., Phillips, E. A., Fixsen, D. L. and Wolf, M. M. (1971). Achievement Place: Modification of the behaviors of pre-delinquent boys within a token economy. *Journal of Applied Behavior Analysis*, **4**, 45–59

Quay, H. C. (1972). Patterns of aggression, withdrawal and immaturity. In: H. C. Quay and J. S. Werry (Eds.), *Psychopathological Disorders in Childhood*. New York: Wiley

Quay, H. C. and Werry, J. S. (Eds.) (1972). *Psychopathological Disorders in Childhood*. New York: Wiley

Rachlin, H. (1974). Self-control. *Behaviorism*, **2**, 94–107

Rimm, D. C. and Masters, J. C. (1974). *Behavior Therapy: Techniques and Empirical Findings*. New York: Academic Press

Risley, T. R. (1968). The effects and side effects of punishing the autistic behaviors of a deviant child. *Journal of Applied Behavior Analysis*, **1**, 21–34

Robins, L. N. (1966). *Deviant Children Grown Up*. Baltimore: Williams and Wilkins

Robins, L. N. (1972). Follow-up studies of behavior disorders in children. In: H. C. Quay and J. S. Werry (Ed.), *Psychopathological Disorders in Childhood*. New York: Wiley

Rodriquez, A., Rodriquez, M. and Eisenberg, L. (1959). The outcome of school phobia: a follow-up study based on 41 cases. *American Journal of Psychiatry*, **116**, 540–544

Rose, S. D. (1972). *Treating Children in Groups*. San Francisco, California: Jossey-Bass

Rutter, M. (1966). *Children of Sick Parents: An Environmental and Psychiatric Study*. Maudsley Monograph, No. 16, Oxford University Press

Rutter, M. (1972). *Maternal Deprivation Reassessed*. Harmondsworth, Middlesex: Penguin

Rutter, M. (1975). *Helping Troubled Children*, Harmondsworth, Middlesex: Penguin

Rutter, M. and Graham, P. (1968). The reliability and validity of the psychiatric assessment of the child: I. Interview with the child. *British Journal of Psychiatry*, **114**, 563–579

Rutter, M., Tizard, J. and Whitmore, K. (1970). *Education, Health, and Behaviour*. London: Longman

Sajwaj, T. (1973). Difficulty in the use of behavioral techniques found by parents in changing child behavior: guides to success. *Journal of Nervous and Mental Diseases*, **156** (6), 399–403

Sajwaj, T. and Dillon, A. (1976). Complexities of an 'elementary' behavior modification procedure: differential adult attention used for children's behavior disorders. In: B. Etzel, J. LeBlanc and D. Baer (Eds.), *New Developments in Behavioral Research: Theory, Methods and Application*. Hillsdale, New Jersey: Lawrence Erlbaum

Sajwaj, T. and Hedges, D. (1971). Functions of parental attention in an oppositional, retarded boy. Proceedings of the 79th Annual Convention of the American Psychological Association

Sajwaj, T., Twardoz, S. and Burke, M. (1972). Side-effects of extinction procedures in a remedial preschool. *Journal of Applied Behavior Analysis*, **5**, 163–175

Samaan, N. (1972). The control of nocturnal enuresis by operant conditioning. *Journal of Behavior Therapy and Experimental Psychiatry*, **3**, 103–105

Seligman, M. E. P. (1975). *Helplessness: On Depression, Development and Death*. San Francisco, California: W. H. Freeman

Shepherd, M., Oppenheim, A. N. and Mitchell, S. (1971). *Childhood Behaviour and Mental Health*. University of London Press

Skinner, B. F. (1948). *Walden Two*. New York: MacMillan

Smith, S. M., and Hanson, R. (1975). Interpersonal relationships and child-rearing practices in 214 parents of battered children. *British Journal of Psychiatry*, **127**, 513–525

Subotnik, L. (1972). Spontaneous remissions: fact or artifact? *Psychological Bulletin*, **77**, 32–48

Taplin, P. (1974). Changes in parental consequation as a function of intervention. Unpublished doctoral thesis, University of Wisconsin

Thomas, A., Chess, S. and Birch, H. G. (1968). *Temperament and Behavior Disorders in Children*. New York: University Press

Tonge, W. L., James, D. S. and Hillam, S. M. (1975). Families without hope: a controlled study of 33 problem families. *British Journal of Psychiatry Special Publication*, No. 11. Ashford, Kent: Headley Brothers

Turkewitz, H., O'Leary, K. D. and Ironsmith, M. (1975). Generalization and maintenance of appropriate behavior through self-control. *Journal of Consulting and Clinical Psychology*, **43**, 577–583

Ullman, L. P. and Krasner, L. (1969). *A Psychological Approach to Abnormal*

Behavior. Englewood Cliffs, New Jersey: Prentice-Hall

Ulrich, R., Stachnik, T. and Mabry, J. (1970). *Control of Human Behavior*. Glenview, Illinois: Scott, Foresman and Company

Wagner, L. I. and Ora, J. P. (1970). Parental control of the very young severely oppositional child. Paper presented at the Southeastern Psychological Association's Annual Conference, Louisville, Kentucky

Wahler, R. G. (1969). Setting generality: some specific and general effects of child behavior therapy. *Journal of Applied Behavior Analysis*, **2**, 239–246

Wahler, R. G. (1974). Annual research report to the National Institute of Mental Health. Unpublished manuscript. University of Tennessee, Knoxville

Wahler, R. G. (1975*a*). Some structural aspects of deviant child behavior. *Journal of Applied Behavior Analysis*, **8**, 27–42

Wahler, R. G. (1975*b*). The decline and fall of the 'operant conditioning' therapies. Paper presented at the Southeastern Psychological Association's Annual Congress, Atlanta, Georgia

Wahler, R. G. (1975*c*). Annual research report to the National Institute of Mental Health. Unpublished manuscript. University of Tennessee, Knoxville

Wahler, R. G. (1976). Deviant child behavior within the family: developmental speculations and behavior change strategies. In: H. Leitenberg (Ed.), *Handbook of Behavior Modification*. New York: Appleton-Century-Crofts

Wahler, R. G., Berland, R. M. and Leske, G. (1975). Environmental boundaries in behavior modification. University of Tennessee, Knoxville (unpublished)

Wahler, R. G., Berland, R. M. and Leske, G. (1976). Phenomenological reports: an empirical model. In: B. Etsel, J. LeBlanc and D. Baer (Eds.), *New Developments in Behavioral Research: Theory, Methods and Application*. Hillsdale, New Jersey: Lawrence Erlbaum

Wahler, R. G. and Erikson, M. (1969). Child behavior therapy: a community programme in Appalachia. *Behaviour Research and Therapy*, **7**, 71–78

Wahler, R. G., House, A. E. and Stambaugh, E. E. (1976). *Ecological Assessment of Child Problem Behavior: A Clinical Package for Home, School and Institutional Settings*. New York: Pergamon

Wahler, R. G. and Leske, M. Ş. (1973). Accurate and inaccurate observer summary reports. *Journal of Nervous and Mental Disease*, **156**, 386–394

Wahler, R. G. and Nordquist, V. M. (1973). Adult discipline as a factor in childhood imitation. *Journal of Abnormal Child Psychology*, **1** (1), 40–56

Wahler, R. G., Sperling, K., Thomas, M., Teeter, N. and Lupar, H. (1970). The modification of childhood stuttering: some response-response relationships. *Journal of Experimental Child Psychology*, **9**, 411–428

Watson, D. L. and Tharp, R. G. (1972). *Self-Directed Behavior: Self-Modification for Personal Adjustment*. Monterey, California: Brooks-Cole

Watson, L. S. (1973). *Child Behavior Modification: A Manual for Teachers, Nurses and Parents*. New York: Pergamon

Weathers, L. and Liberman, R. P. (1975). Contingency contracting with families of delinquent adolescents. *Behavior Therapy*, **6**, 356–366

Weiss, R. L., Krasner, L. and Ullman, L. P. (1960). Responsivity to verbal conditioning as a function of emotional atmosphere and pattern of reinforcement. *Psychological Reports*, **6**, 415–426

Werner, J. S., Minkin, N., Minkin, B. L., Fixsen, D. L. and Wolf, M. M. (1974). What should kids say to the cops? An analysis of an 'intervention program'. Paper presented at the American Psychological Association Convention, New Orleans, Lousiana

White, G. D., Nielson, G. and Johnson, S. M. (1972). Time-out duration and the suppression of deviant behavior in children. *Journal of Applied Behavior Analysis*, **5**, 111–120

Willems, E. P. (1973). Go ye into the world and modify behavior: an ecologist's view. *Representative Research into Social Psychology*, **4**, 93–105

Wolpe, J. (1971). Neurotic depression: experimental analog, clinical syndromes and treatment. *American Journal of Psychotherapy*, **25**, 362–368

Wolpe, J. and Lazarus, A. A. (1966). *Behaviour Therapy Techniques*. Oxford: Pergamon

Wright, H. F. (1960). Observational child study. In: P. H. Mussen (Ed.), *Handbook of Research Methods in Child Development*. New York: Wiley

Yarrow, L. J. (1961). Maternal deprivation towards an empirical and conceptual re-evaluation. *Psychological Bulletin*, **58**, 459–490

Young, G. and Turner, R. (1965). CNS stimulant drugs and conditioning treatment of nocturnal enuresis. *Behaviour Research and Therapy*, **3**, 93–101

Young, G. C. (1973). The treatment of childhood encopresis by conditioned gastro-ileal reflex training. *Behaviour Research and Therapy*, **11**, 499–503

Index

237